THE

POPULAR RELIGION

AND

FOLK-LORE

OF

NORTHERN INDIA

THE POPULAR RELIGION AND FOLK-LORE OF NORTHERN INDIA

BY

W. CROOKE, B.A.

IN TWO VOLUMES
VOL. I.

GYAN

Published by

Gyan Publishing House
5, Ansari Road
Daryaganj, New Delhi-110002
Phone: 011-47034999, 9811692060
E-mail: books@gyanbooks.com

Distribution Network
gyanbooks.com
India, USA, Canada, UK, Australia

ISBN: 978-93-6280-113-5 (Set)
978-93-6280-243-9 (HB)
First Published, 1896

2nd Impression 2024

Printed at: Gyan Press, Delhi.

THE POPULAR RELIGION AND FOLK-LORE OF NORTHERN INDIA, (VOL. I.)
Author: W. CROOKE

FOLK-LORE OF NORTHERN INDIA

BATHING IN THE GANGES, HARDWÁR.

THE POPULAR RELIGION AND FOLK-LORE OF NORTHERN INDIA

BY

W. CROOKE, B.A.

BENGAL CIVIL SERVICE

IN TWO VOLUMES

VOL. I.

A NEW EDITION, REVISED AND ILLUSTRATED

WESTMINSTER

ARCHIBALD CONSTABLE & CO.

2, WHITEHALL GARDENS, S.W.

1896

PREFACE TO THE SECOND EDITION.

THE success of this book has been much beyond my expectations. That a considerable edition has been exhausted within a few months after publication proves that it meets a want.

I have now practically re-written the book, and have taken the opportunity of introducing a considerable amount of fresh information collected in the course of the Ethnographical Survey of the North-Western Provinces, the results of which will be separately published.

For the illustrations, which now appear for the first time, I am indebted to the photographic skill of Mr. J. O'Neal, of the Thomason Engineering College, Rurki. I could have wished that they could have been drawn from a wider area. But Hardwar and its shrines are very fairly representative of popular Hinduism in Northern India.

W. CROOKE.

SAHARANPUR,
February, 1895.

PREFACE TO THE FIRST EDITION.

MANY books have been written on Brâhmanism, or the official religion of the Hindu; but, as far as I am aware, this is the first attempt to bring together some of the information available on the popular beliefs of the races of Upper India.

My object in writing this book has been threefold. In the first place I desired to collect, for the use of all officers whose work lies among the rural classes, some information on the beliefs of the people which will enable them, in some degree, to understand the mysterious inner life of the races among whom their lot is cast; secondly, it may be hoped that this introductory sketch will stimulate inquiry, particularly among the educated races of the country, who have, as yet, done little to enable Europeans to gain a fuller and more sympathetic knowledge of their rural brethren; and lastly, while I have endeavoured more to collect facts than to theorize upon them, I hope that European scholars may find in these pages some fresh examples of familiar principles. My difficulty has arisen not so much from deficiency of material, as in the selection and arrangement of the mass of information, which lies scattered through a considerable literature, much of which is fugitive.

I believe that the more we explore these popular superstitions and usages, the nearer are we likely to attain to the discovery of the basis on which Hinduism has been founded. The official creed has always been characterized by extreme catholicism and receptivity, and many of its principles and legends have undoubtedly been derived from that stratum of the people which it is convenient to call non-Aryan or Drâvidian. The necessity, then, of investigating these beliefs before they become absorbed in Brâhminism, one of the most active missionary religions of the world, is obvious.

I may say that the materials of this book were practically complete before I was able to use Mr. J. S. Campbell's valuable collection of "Notes on the Spirit Basis of Belief and Custom;" but, in revising the manuscript, I have availed myself to some extent of this useful collection, and when I have done so, I have been careful to acknowledge my obligations to it. Even at the risk of overloading the notes with references, I have quoted the authorities which I have used, and I have added a Bibliography which may be of use to students to whom the subject is unfamiliar.

The only excuse I can plead for the obvious imperfections of this hasty survey of a very wide subject is that it has been written in the intervals of the scanty leisure of a District Officer's life in India, and often at a distance from works of reference and libraries.

W. CROOKE.

MIRZAPUR,
February, 1893.

CONTENTS.

FOLK-LORE

OF

NORTHERN INDIA.

CHAPTER I.

THE GODLINGS OF NATURE.

'Εν μὲν γαῖαν ἐτεύξ' ἐν δ' οὐρανὸν, ἐν δὲ θάλασσαν
ἠέλιόν τ' ἀκάμαντα σελήνην τε πλήθουσαν,
ἐν δὲ τὰ τείρεα πάντα, τά τ' οὐρανὸς ἐστεφάνωται
Πληϊάδας θ' Ὑάδας τε, τό τε σθένος 'Ωρίωνος
Ἄρκτον θ', ἣν καὶ ἄμαξαν ἐπίκλησιν καλέουσιν,
ἥτ αὐτοῦ στρέφεται καί τ' 'Ωρίωνα δοκεύει,
οἴη δ' ἄμμορος ἐστι λοετρῶν 'Ωκεανοῖο.

Iliad, xviii. 483-88.

AMONG all the great religions of the world there is none more catholic, more assimilative than the mass of beliefs which go to make up what is popularly known as Hinduism. To what was probably its original form—a nature worship in a large degree introduced by the Aryan missionaries—has been added an enormous amount of demonolatry, fetishism and kindred forms of primitive religion, much of which has been adopted from races which it is convenient to describe as aboriginal or autochthonous.

The same was the case in Western lands. As the Romans extended their Empire they brought with them and included in the national pantheon the deities of the conquered peoples. Greece and Syria, Egypt, Gallia and Germania were thus successively laid under contribution. This power of assimilation in the domain of religion had its advantages as well as its dangers. While on the one hand it tended to promote the unity of the empire, it degraded, on the other hand, the national character by the introduction of the impure cults which flourished along the eastern shores of the Mediterranean.[1]

But, besides these forms of religion which were directly imported from foreign lands, there remained a stratum of local beliefs which even after twenty centuries of Christianity still flourish, discredited though they may be by priests and placed under the ban of the official creed. Thus in Greece, while the high gods of the divine race of Achilles and Agamemnon are forgotten, the Nereids, the Cyclopes and the Lamia still live in the faith of the peasants of Thessaly.[2] So in modern Tuscany there is actually as much heathenism as catholicism, and they still believe in La Vecchia Religione—"the old religion;"—and while on great occasions they have recourse to the priests, they use magic and witchcraft for all ordinary purposes.[3]

It is part of the object of the following pages to show that in India the history of religious belief has been developed on similar lines. Everywhere we find that the great primal gods of Hinduism have suffered grievous degradation. Throughout the length and breadth of the Indian peninsula Brahma, the Creator, has hardly more than a couple of shrines specially dedicated to him.[4] Indra has, as we shall see, become a vague weather deity, who rules the choirs of fairies in his heaven Indra-loka: Varuna, as Barun, has also become a degraded weather godling, and sailors worship their boat as his fetish when they commence a voyage. The worship of Agni survives in the fire sacrifice which has been specialized by the Agnihotri Brâhmans. Of Pûshan and Ushas, Vâyu and the Maruts, hardly even the names survive, except among the small philosophical class of reformers who

[1] On the assimilation by Rome of Celtic faiths, see Rhys, "Origin and Growth of Religion as illustrated by Celtic Heathendom," 2 sq.

[2] Lang, "Custom and Myth," 178.

[3] Leland, "Etruscan Remains," 9.

[4] At Pushkar and Idar. Monier Williams, "Brâhmanism and Hinduism," 566 sqq.

aim at restoring Vedism, a faith which is as dead as Jupiter or Aphrodite.

THE DEVA.

The general term for these great gods of Hinduism is Deva, or "the shining ones." Of these even the survivors have in the course of the development of the religious belief of the people suffered serious change. Modern Vaishnavism has little left of the original conception of the solar deity who in the Rig Veda strides in three steps through the seven regions of the universe, and envelops all things in the dust of his beams. To his cult has, in modern times, been added the erotic cycle of myths which centre round Krishna and Râdhâ and Rukminî. The successive Avatâras or incarnations mark the progressive development of the cultus which has absorbed in succession the totemistic or fetish worship of the tortoise, the boar, the fish and the man-lion. In the same way Rudra-Siva has annexed various faiths, many of which are probably of local origin, such as the worship of the bull and the linga. Durgâ-Devî, again, most likely is indebted to the same sources for the blood sacrifices which she loves in her forms of Kâlî, Bhawânî, Chandikâ or Bhairavî. A still later development is that of the foul mysteries of the Tantra and the Sâktis.

THE DEOTÂ.

But in the present survey of the popular, as contrasted with the official faith, we have little concern with these supremely powerful deities. They are the gods of the richer or higher classes, and to the ordinary peasant of Northern India are now little more than a name. He will, it is true, occasionally bow at their shrines; he will pour some water or lay some flowers on the images or fetish stones which are the special resting-places of these divinities or represent the productive powers of nature. But from time immemorial, when Brâhmanism had as yet not succeeded in occupying the land, his allegiance was bestowed on a class of deities of a much lower and more primitive kind. Their inferiority to the greater gods is marked in their title: they are Devatâ or Deotâ, "godlings," not "gods." [1]

GODLINGS PURE AND IMPURE.

These godlings fall into two well marked classes—the "pure" and the "impure." The former are, as a rule, served by priests of the Brâhman castes or one of the ascetic orders: their offerings are such things as are pure food to the Hindu —cakes of wheaten flour, particularly those which have been still further purified by intermixture with clarified butter (*ghî*), the most valued product of the sacred cow, washed rice (*akshata*) and sweetmeats. They are very generally worshipped on a Sunday, and the officiating high-caste priest accepts the offerings. The offerings to the "impure" godlings contain articles such as pork and spirits, which are abomination to the orthodox Hindu. In the Central Indian hills their priest is the Baiga, who rules the ghosts and demons of the village and is always drawn from one of the Drâvidian tribes. In the plain country the priest is a non-Aryan Chamâr, Dusâdh, or even a sweeper or a Muhammadan Dafâli or drummer. No respectable Hindu will, it is needless to say, partake of a share of the food consecrated (*prasâd*) to a hedge deity of this class. Much of the worship consists in offering of blood. But the jungle man or the village menial of the plains can seldom, except in an hour of grievous need, afford an expensive animal victim, and it is only when the village shrine has come under the patronage of the official priests of the orthodox faith, that the altar of the goddess reeks with gore, like those of the Devîs of Bindhâchal or Devî Pâtan.

But as regards the acceptance of a share of the offering the line is often not very rigidly drawn. As Mr. Ibbetson writing of the Panjâb says: [2] "Of course, the line cannot always be

[1] Devatâ in Sanskrit properly means "the state or nature of a deity, divinity," without any very decided idea of inferiority. In modern usage it certainly has this implication.

[2] "Panjâb Ethnography," 113.

drawn with precision, and Brâhmans will often consent to be fed in the name of a deity, while they will not take offerings made at his shrine, or will allow their girls, but not their boys, to accept the offering, as, if the girls die in consequence, it does not much matter." In fact, as we shall see later on, the Baiga or devil priest of the aboriginal tribes, is gradually merging into the Ojha or meaner class of demon exorciser, who calls himself a Brâhman and performs the same functions for tribes of a somewhat higher social rank.

SÛRAJ NÂRÂYAN, THE SUN GODLING.

The first and greatest of the "pure" godlings is Sûrya or Sûraj Nârâyan, the Sun godling. He is thus regarded as Nârâyana or Vishnu occupying the sun. A curiously primitive legend represents his father-in-law, Viswakarma, as placing the deity on his lathe and trimming away one-eighth of his effulgence, leaving only his feet. Out of the blazing fragments he welded the weapons of the gods. Sûrya was one of the great deities of the Vedic pantheon: he is called Prajapati or "lord of creatures:" he was the son of Dyaus, or the bright sky. Ushas, the dawn, was his wife, and he moves through the sky drawn by seven ruddy mares. His worship was perhaps originally connected with that of fire, but it is easy to understand how, under a tropical sky, the Indian peasant came to look on him as the lord of life and death, the bringer of plenty or of famine. If one interpretation of the rite be correct, the Holî festival is intended as a means of propitiating sunshine. He is now, however, like Helios in the Homeric mythology, looked on as only a godling, not a god, and even as a hero who had once lived and reigned on earth.

As far as the village worship of Sûraj Nârâyan goes, the assertion, which has sometimes been made, that no shrine has been erected in his honour is correct enough; and there is no doubt that images of Sûrya and Aditya are comparatively rare in recent epochs. But there are many noted temples dedicated to him, such as those at Taxila, Gwâlior, Gaya, Multân, Jaypur, and in the North-Western Provinces at Indor, Hawalbâgh, Sûrya Bhîta and Lakhmipur.[1] His shrine at Kanârak in Orissa near that of Jagannâth, is described as one of the most exquisite memorials of Sun-worship in existence.[2] Mr. Bendall recently found in Nepâl an image dedicated to him as late as the eleventh century.[3] There is a small shrine in his honour close to the Anna-pûrna temple in Benares, where the god is represented seated in a chariot drawn by seven horses, and is worshipped with the fire sacrifice (*homa*) in a building detached from the temple.[4]

In the time of Sankara Achârya (A.D. 1000) there were six distinct sects of Sun-worshippers—one worshipping the rising sun as identified with Brahma; the second the meridian sun as Siva; the third the setting sun as Vishnu; the fourth worshippers of the sun in all the above phases as identified with the Trimurti; the fifth worshippers of the sun regarded as a material being in the form of a man with a golden beard and golden hair. Zealous members of this sect refused to eat anything in the morning till they had seen the sun rise. The last class worshipped an image of the sun formed in the mind. These spent all their time meditating on the sun, and were in the habit of branding circular representations of his disc on their foreheads, arms and breasts.[5]

The Saura sect worship Sûryapati as their special god. They wear a crystal necklace in his honour, abstain from eating salt on Sundays and on the days when the sun enters a sign of the zodiac. They make a frontal mark with red sandars, and nowadays have their headquarters in Oudh.[6]

Another sect of Vaishnavas, the Nîmbârak, worship the sun in a modified form. Their name means "the sun in a Nîm tree" (*Azidirachta Indica*). The story of the sect runs

[1] Cunningham, "Archæological Reports," ii. 114, 342, 353; iii. 110, 112; xiii. 63; "Râjputâna Gazetteer," ii. 160; Führer, "Monumental Antiquities," 6, 50, 145, 286.

[2] Hunter, "Orissa," i. 188; Jarrett, "Aîn-i-Akbari," ii. 128.

[3] "Asiatic Quarterly Review," ii. 236.

[4] Sherring, "Sacred City of the Hindus," 59, 157; Bholanâth Chandra, "Travels," ii. 384.

[5] Monier-Williams, "Brâhmanism and Hinduism," 342.

[6] Wilson, "Essays," ii. 384.

that their founder, an ascetic named Bhâskarâchârya, had invited a Bairâgi to dine with him, and had arranged everything for his reception, but unfortunately delayed to call his guest till after sunset. The holy man was forbidden by the rules of his order to eat except in the day-time, and was afraid that he would be compelled to practise an unwilling abstinence; but at the solicitation of his host, the Sun god, Sûraj Nârâyan, descended on the Nîm tree under which the feast was spread and continued beaming on them until dinner was over.[1] In this we observe an approximation to the Jaina rule by which it is forbidden to eat after sunset, lest insects may enter the mouth and be destroyed. This overstrained respect for animal life is one of the main features of the creed. As a curious parallel it may be noted that when an Australian black-fellow wishes to stay the sun from going down till he gets home, he places a sod in the fork of a tree exactly facing the setting sun; and an Indian of Yucatan, journeying westward, places a stone in a tree, or pulls out some of his eye-lashes and blows them towards the sun.[2]

The great Emperor Akbar endeavoured to introduce a special form of Sun-worship. He ordered that it was to be adored four times a day: in the morning, noon, evening, and midnight. "His majesty had also one thousand and one Sanskrit names of the sun collected, and read them daily, devoutly turning to the sun. He then used to get hold of both ears, and turning himself quickly round, used to strike the lower ends of his ears with his fists." He ordered his band to play at midnight, and used to be weighed against gold at his solar anniversary.[3]

VILLAGE WORSHIP OF SÛRAJ NÂRÂYAN.

The village worship of Sûraj Nârâyan is quite distinct from this. Many peasants in Upper India do not eat salt on Sundays, and do not set their milk for butter, but make

[1] Growse, "Mathura," 180. The story of Joshua (x. 12-14) is an obvious parallel.
[2] Frazer, "Golden Bough," i. 25.
[3] Blochmann, "Aîn-i-Akbari," i. 200-266.

rice-milk of it, and give a portion to Brâhmans. Brâhmans are sometimes fed in his honour at harvests, and the pious householder bows to him as he leaves his house in the morning. His more learned brethren repeat the Gâyatrî, that most ancient of Aryan prayers: "*Tat savitur varenyam bhargo devasya dhîmahi, Dhiyo yo nah prachodayât*" ("May we receive the glorious brightness of this, the generator, the God who shall prosper our works!"). In the chilly mornings of the cold weather you will hear the sleepy coolies as they wake, yawning and muttering *Sûraj Nârâyan*, as the yellow gleam of dawn spreads over the Eastern sky. In fact, even in Vedic times there seems to have been a local worship of Sûrya connected with some primitive folk-lore. Haradatta mentions as one of the customs not sanctioned in the Veda, that when the sun is in Aries the young girls would paint the sun with his retinue on the soil in coloured dust, and worship this in the morning and evening;[1] and in Central India the sun was in the Middle Ages worshipped under the local form of Bhâilla, or "Lord of Life," a term which appears to have been the origin of the name Bhilsa, known to more recent ages as a famous seat of Buddhism.[2]

At Udaypur in Râjputâna the sun has universal precedence. His portal (*Sûryapul*) is the chief entrance to the city; his name gives dignity to the chief apartment or hall (*Sûryamahal*) of the palace, and from the balcony of the sun (*Sûrya-gokhru*), the descendant of Râma shows himself in the dark monsoon as the sun's representative. A large painted sun of gypsum in high relief with gilded rays adorns the hall of audience, and in front of it is the throne. The sacred standard bears his image, as does the disc (*changî*) of black felt or ostrich feathers with a plate of gold in its centre to represent the sun, borne aloft on a pole. The royal parasol is called Kiraniya, in allusion to its shape, like a ray (*kiran*) of the orb.[3]

[1] Max Müller, "Ancient Sanskrit Literature," 53, note.
[2] Hall, "Vishnu Purâna," ii. 150; "Journal Asiatic Society, Bengal," 1862, p. 112.
[3] Tod, "Annals," i. 597.

Another famous centre of Sun-worship was Multân, where, as we have seen, a temple dedicated to him has been discovered, and where the tribes of the Bâlas and Kâthis were devoted to him. The worship continued till the idol was destroyed by orders of Aurangzeb.

SUN-WORSHIP AMONG THE NON-ARYAN RACES.

The Aheriyas, a tribe of jungle-livers and thieves in the Central Duâb of the Ganges and Jumna, have adopted as their mythical ancestor Priyavrata, who being dissatisfied that only half the earth was at one time illuminated by the rays of the sun, followed him seven times round the earth in his flaming car, resolved to turn night into day. But he was stopped by Brahma, and the wheels of his chariot formed the seven oceans which divide the seven continents of the world.

In the lower ranges of the Himâlaya Sun-worship is conducted in the months of December and January and when eclipses occur. The principal observances are the eating of a meal without salt at each passage of the sun into a new sign of zodiac, and eating meals on other days only when the sun has risen.

Among the Drâvidian races, along the Central Indian hills, Sun-worship is widely prevalent. When in great affliction the Kharwârs appeal to the sun. Any open space in which he shines may be his altar. The Kisâns offer a white cock to him when a sacrifice is needed. He is worshipped by the Bhuiyas and Orâons as Borâm or Dharm Devatâ, "the godling of pity," and is propitiated at the sowing season by the sacrifice of a white cock. The Korwas worship him as Bhagwân, or "the only God," in an open space with an ant-hill as an altar. The Khariyas adore him under the name of Bero. "Every head of a family should during his lifetime make not less than five sacrifices to this deity—the first of fowls, the second of a pig, the third of a white goat, the fourth of a ram, and the fifth of a buffalo. He is then considered sufficiently propitiated for that generation, and regarded as an ungrateful god if he does not behave handsomely to his votary." He is addressed as Parameswar, or "great god," and his sacrifices are always made in front of an ant-hill which is regarded as his altar. The Kols worship Sing Bonga, the creator and preserver, as the sun. Prayer and sacrifice are made to him, as to a beneficent deity, who has no pleasure in the destruction of any of his subjects, though, as a father, he chastises his erring children, who owe him gratitude for all the blessings they enjoy. He is said to have married Chando Omal, the moon. She deceived him on one occasion, and he cut her in two; but repenting of his anger, he restores her to her original shape once a month, when she shines in her full beauty. The Orâons address the sun as Dharmi, or "the holy one," and do not regard him as the author of sickness or calamity; but he may be invoked to avert it, and this appeal is often made when the sacrifices to minor deities have been unproductive. He is the tribal god of the Korkus of Hoshangâbâd; they do not, however, offer libations to him, as Hindus do; but once in three years the head of each family, on some Sunday in April or May, offers outside the village a white she-goat and a white fowl, turning his face to the East during the sacrifice. Similarly the Kûrs of the Central Provinces carve rude representations of the sun and moon on wooden pillars, which they worship, near their villages.[1]

SUN-WORSHIP IN THE DOMESTIC RITUAL.

It is needless to say that the custom of walking round any sacred object in the course of the sun prevails widely. Thus in Ireland, when in a graveyard, it is customary to walk as much as possible "with the sun," with the right hand towards the centre of the circle.[2] Even to this day in the Hebrides animals are led round a sick person, following the

[1] Dalton, "Descriptive Ethnology," 130, 132, 133, 141, 157, 159, 186, 223; Elliott, "Hoshangâbâd Settlement Report," 255; Hislop, "Papers," 26.

[2] "Folk-lore," iv. 358.

sun; and in the Highlands it is the custom to make the "deazil" or walk three times in the sun's course round those whom they wish well. When a Highlander goes to bathe or to drink water out of a consecrated spring, he must always approach by going round the place from east to west on the south side, in imitation of the daily motion of the sun.[1] We follow the same rule when we pass the decanters round our dinner tables. In the same way in India the bride and bridegroom are made to revolve round the sacred fire or the central pole of the marriage-shed in the course of the sun; the pilgrim makes his solemn perambulation (*parikrama*) round a temple or shrine in the same way; in this direction the cattle move as they tread out the grain.

One special part of the purificatory rite following childbirth is to bring the mother out and expose her to the rays of the sun. All through the range of popular belief and folk-lore appears the idea that girls may be impregnated by the sun.[2] Hence they are not allowed to expose themselves to his rays at the menstrual period. For the same reason the bride is brought out to salute the rising sun on the morning after she begins to live with her husband. A survival of the same belief may be traced in the English belief that happy is the bride on whom the sun shines. The same belief in the power of the sun is shown in the principle so common in folk-lore that to show a certain thing to it (in a Kashmîr tale it is a tuft of the hair of the kindly tigress) will be sufficient to summon an absent friend.[3]

The mystical emblem of the Swâstika, which appears to represent the sun in his journey through the heavens, is of constant occurrence. The trader paints it on the fly-leaf of

[1] Gordon Cumming, "From the Hebrides to the Himâlayas," ii. 164; Brand, "Observations," 126; Henderson, "Folk-lore of the Northern Counties," 61; Tawney, "Katha Sarit Sâgara," i. 98, 573.

[2] Frazer, "Golden Bough," ii. 234; Grimm, "Household Tales," ii. 493, 524; Leland, "Etruscan Roman Remains," 160; Hartland, "Legend of Perseus," i. 99, 139, 170.

[3] Knowles, "Kashmîr Folk-tales," 3; fire is used in the same way; Temple, "Wideawake Stories," 32, 271; "Legends of the Panjâb," i. 42; "Folk-lore Journal," ii. 104.

his ledger; the man who has young children or animals liable to the Evil Eye makes a representation of it on the wall beside his door-post; it holds the first place among the lucky marks of the Jainas; it is drawn on the shaven heads of children on the marriage-day in Gujarât; a red circle with a Swâstika in the centre is depicted on the place where the gods are kept.[1] In those parts of the country where Bhûmiya is worshipped as a village guardian deity his votary constructs a rude model of it on the shrine by fixing up two crossed straws with a daub of plaster. It often occurs in folk-lore. In the drama of the "Toy Cart" the thief hesitates whether he shall make the hole in the wall of Charudatta's house in the likeness of a Swâstika or of a water jar. A hymn of the Rigveda[2] speaks of the all-seeing eye of the sun whose beams reveal his presence, gleaming like brilliant flames to nation after nation. This same conception of the sun as an eye is common in the folk-lore of the West.[3]

MOON-WORSHIP.

The fate of Chandra or Soma, the Moon godling, is very similar. The name Soma, originally applied to the plant the juice of which was used as a religious intoxicant, came to be used in connection with the moon in the post-Vedic mythology. There are many legends to account for the waning of the moon and the spots on his surface, for the moon, like the sun, is always treated as a male godling. One of the legends current to explain the phases of the moon has been already referred to. According to another story the moon married the twenty-seven asterisms, the daughters of the Rishi Daksha, who is the hero of the curious tale of the sacrifice now located at Kankhal, a suburb of Hardwâr. Umâ or Pârvatî, the spouse of Siva, was also a daughter of Daksha, and when he, offended with his son-in-law Siva, did not invite him to the great sacrifice, Uma became Satî, and in his rage Siva created Vîrabhadra, who killed the

[1] Campbell, "Notes," 70. [2] i. 50.
[3] Grimm, "Household Tales," ii. 415.

sage. Soma after marrying the asterisms devoted himself to one of them, Rohinî, which aroused the jealousy of the others. They complained to their father Daksha, who cursed the moon with childlessness and consumption. His wives, in pity, interceded for him, but the curse of the angry sage could not be wholly removed: all that was possible was to modify it so that it should be periodical, not permanent. In an earlier legend, of which there is a trace in the Rig Veda,[1] the gods, by drinking up the nectar, caused the waning of the moon. Another curious explanation is current in Bombay. One evening Ganesa fell off his steed, the rat, and the moon could not help laughing at his misfortune. To punish him the angry god vowed that no one should ever see the moon again. The moon prayed for forgiveness, and Ganesa agreed that the moon should be disgraced only on his birthday, the Ganesa Chaturthî. On this night the wild hogs hide themselves that they may not see the moon, and the Kunbis hunt them down and kill them.[2]

There are also many explanations to account for the spots in the moon. In Western lands the moon is inhabited by a man with a bundle of sticks on his back; but it is not clear of what offence this was the punishment. Dante says he is Cain; Chaucer says he was a thief, and gives him a thorn-bush to carry; Shakespeare gives him thorns to carry, but provides him with a dog as a companion. In Ireland children are taught that he picked faggots on a Sunday and is punished as a Sabbath-breaker. In India the creature in the moon is usually a hare, and hence the moon is called Sasadhara, "he that is marked like a hare." According to one legend the moon became enamoured of Ahalyâ, the wife of the Rishi Gautama, and visited her in the absence of her husband. He returned, and finding the guilty pair together, cursed his wife, who was turned into a stone; then he threw his shoe at the moon, which left a black mark, and this remains to this day. The scene of this event has been

[1] x. 85, 5.

[2] "Bombay Gazetteer," xiii. 93.

localized at Gondar in the Karnâl District. By another variant of the legend it was Vrihaspati, the Guru or religious adviser of the gods, who found the moon with his wife. The holy man was just returning from his bath in the Ganges, and he threw his dripping loin-cloth at the moon, which produced the spots. In Upper India, again, little children are taught to call the moon Mâmû or "maternal uncle," and the dark spots are said to represent an old woman who sits there working her spinning-wheel.

The moon has one special function in connection with disease. One of his titles is Oshadhipati or "lord of the medicinal plants." Hence comes the idea that roots and simples, and in particular those that are to be used for any magical or mystic purpose, should be collected by moonlight. Thus in Shakespeare Jessica says,—

> "In such a night Medea gathered the enchanted herbs
> That did renew old Aeson."

And Laertes speaks of the poison "collected from all simples that have virtue under the moon."[1] Hence the belief that the moon has a sympathetic influence over vegetation. Tusser[2] advised the peasant,—

> "Sow peason and beans, in the wane of the moon.
> Who soweth them sooner, he soweth too soon;
> That they with the planet may rest and arise,
> And flourish, with bearing most plentiful wise."

The same rule applies all over Northern India, and the phases of the moon exercise an important influence on all agricultural operations.

Based on the same principle is the custom of drinking the moon. Among Muhammadans in Oudh, "a silver basin being filled with water, is held in such a situation that the full moon may be reflected in it. The person to be benefited by the draught is required to look steadfastly on the moon in the basin, then shut his eyes and quaff the liquid at a draught. This remedy is advised by medical professors in

[1] "Merchant of Venice," v. 1; "Hamlet," iv. 7.
[2] "Five Hundred Points of Good Husbandry, February;" see other references collected by Frazer, "Golden Bough," i. 318.

nervous cases, and also for palpitation of the heart."[1] Somewhat similar customs prevail among Hindus in Northern India. At the full moon of the month Kuâr (September-October) people lay out food on the house-tops, and when it has absorbed the rays of the moon they distribute it among their relations; this is supposed to lengthen life. On the same night girls pour out water in the moonlight, and say that they are pouring out the cold weather, which was hidden in the water jar. The habit of making patients look at the moon in ghi, oil, or milk is common, and is said to be specially efficacious for leprosy and similar diseases.

There is now little special worship of Soma or Chandra, and when an image is erected to him it is generally associated with that of Sûrya. In the old ritual Anumati or the moon just short of full was specially worshipped in connection with the Manes. The full-moon day was provided with a special goddess, Râkâ. Nowadays the phases largely influence the domestic ritual. All over the world we find the idea that anything done or suffered by man on a waxing moon tends to develop, whereas anything done or suffered on a waning moon tends to diminish. Thus a popular trick charm for warts is to look at the new moon, lift some dust from under the left foot, rub the wart with it, and as the moon wanes the wart dies.[2] It is on the days of the new and full moon that spirits are most numerous and active. The Code of Manu directs that ceremonies are to be performed at the conjunction and opposition of the moon.[3] Among the Jews it would seem that the full moon was prescribed for national celebrations, while those of a domestic character took place at the new moon; there is some evidence to show that this may be connected with the habit of pastoral nations performing journeys in the cool moonlight nights.[4]

[1] Mrs. Mîr Hasan 'Ali, "Manners and Customs of the Muhammadans of India," i. 275.
[2] "Folk-lore," ii. 222; iv. 355.
[3] "Institutes," vi. 9; Wilson, "Vishnu Purâna," 145, 275 note.
[4] Ewald, "Antiquities of Israel," 349 sq.; Goldziher, "Mythology among the Hebrews," 63.

Horace speaks of rustic Phidyle,—

> "Coelo supinas si tuleris manus,
> Nascente Lunâ rustica Phidyle,"[1]

and Aubrey of the Yorkshire maids who "doe worship the new moon on their bare knees, kneeling upon an earth-fast stone." Irish girls on first seeing the moon when new fall on their knees and address her with a loud voice in the prayer—"O Moon! Leave us as well as you found us!"[2] It is a common practice in Europe to turn a piece of silver, which being white is the lunar metal, when the new moon is first seen. So Hindus at the first sight of the new moon hold one end of their turbans in their hands, take from it seven threads, present them to the moon with a prayer, and then exchange the compliments of the season. In Bombay[3] on all new moon days Brâhmans offer oblations of water and sesamum seed to their ancestors, and those who are Agnihotris and do the fire sacrifice kindle the sacred fire on all new and full moon days. Musalmâns on the new moon which comes after the new year sprinkle the blood of a goat beside the house door. In Bombay a young Musalmân girl will not go out at the new moon or on a Thursday, apparently because this is the time that evil spirits roam abroad. In Upper India the houses of the pious are freely plastered with a mixture of earth and cow-dung, and no animal is yoked.

A curious idea applies to the new moon of Bhâdon (August). Whoever looks at the moon on this day will be the victim of false accusations during the following year. The only way to avoid this is to perform a sort of penance by getting someone to shy brickbats at your house, which at other times is regarded as an extreme form of insult and degradation. There is a regular festival held for this purpose at Benares on the fourth day of Bhâdon (August), which is known as the Dhela Chauth Mela, or "the clod festival of the

[1] "Odes," iii. 23, 1, 2, and compare Job xxxi. 26, 27; Psalm lxxxi. 3.
[2] Lady Wilde, "Legends," 205 sq.
[3] Campbell, "Notes," 187.

fourth."[1] We shall come across later on other examples of the principle that to court abuse under certain circumstances is a means of propitiating the spirits of evil and avoiding danger from them. This is probably the origin of the practice in Orissa—"On the Khurda estate the peasants give a curious reason for the absence of garden cultivation and fruit trees, which form a salient feature in that part of the country. In our own districts every homestead has its little ring of vegetable ground. But in Khurda one seldom meets with these green spots except in Brâhman villages. The common cultivators say that from time immemorial they considered it lucky at a certain festival for a man to be annoyed and abused by his neighbours. With a view to giving ample cause of offence they mutilate the fruit trees and trample the gardens of their neighbours, and so court fortune by bringing down the wrath of the injured owner."[2] We shall see that this is one probable explanation of the indecency which prevails at the Holî festival.

Moon-worship appears to be more popular in Bihâr and Bengal than in the North-West Provinces or the Panjâb.[3] The fourth day of the waxing moon in the month of Bhâdon is sacred to the moon and known as Chauk Chanda. It is very unlucky to look at the moon on that day, as whoever does so will make his name infamous. The story runs that Takshaka, the king of the snakes, stole the ear-rings of King Aditi, who, being unable to discover the thief, laid it to the charge of Krishna, whose thefts of milk and cream from the Gopis had made him sufficiently notorious. Krishna, mortified at this false accusation, recovered and restored the ear-ring, and as this was the day on which Krishna was wrongfully disgraced, the moon of that night is invested with associations of special sinfulness. Some people fast and in the evening eat only rice and curds. Brâhmans worship the moon with offerings of flowers and sweetmeats, and people

[1] Sherring, "Sacred City," 221; "Panjâb Notes and Queries," ii. 42.
[2] Hunter, "Orissa," ii. 140.
[3] Sarat Chandra Mitra, "Vestiges of Moon-worship in Bihâr and Bengal," in the "Journal Anthropological Society of Bombay," 1893.

get stones thrown at their houses, as further west on the day of the Dhela Chauth. On this day schoolboys visit their friends and make a peculiar noise by knocking together two coloured sticks, like castanets.

One idea lying at the base of much of the respect paid to the moon is that it is the abode of the Pitri or sainted dead. This is a theory which is the common property of many primitive races.[1] The explanation probably is that the soul of the dead man rises with the smoke of the funeral pyre, and hence the realm of Yama would naturally be fixed in the moon. This seems to be the reason why the early Indian Buddhists worshipped the moon. At the new moon the monks bathed and shaved each other; and at a special service the duties of a monk were recited. On full moon days they dined at the houses of laymen. On that night a platform was raised in the preaching hall. The superior brethren chanted the law, and the people greeted the name of Buddha with shouts of "Sâdhu" or "the holy one."[2]

ECLIPSES AND THE FIRE SACRIFICE.

Hindus, like other primitive races, have their eclipse demons. "When once the practice of bringing down the moon had become familiar to the primitive Greek, who saw it done at sacred marriages and other rites, he was provided with an explanation of lunar eclipses; some other fellow was bringing down the moon for his private ends. And at the present day in Greece the proper way to stop a lunar eclipse is to call out 'I see you!' and thus make the worker of this deed of darkness desist. So completely did this theory, which we must regard as peculiarly Greek, establish itself in ancient Greece, that strange to say, not a trace of the earlier primitive theory, according to which some monster swallows the eclipsed moon, is to be found in classical Greek

[1] "Folk-lore," ii. 221; Monier Williams, "Brâhmanism and Hinduism," 343.

[2] Hardy, "Eastern Monachism," 149.

literature, unless the beating of metal instruments to frighten away the monster be a survival of the primitive practice."[1]

In India, however, this earlier explanation of the phenomena of eclipses flourishes in full vigour. The eclipse demon, Râhu, whose name means "the looser" or "the seizer," was one of the Asuras or demons. When the gods produced the Amrita, or nectar, from the churned ocean, he disguised himself like one of them and drank a portion of it. The sun and moon detected his fraud and informed Vishnu, who severed the head and two of the arms of Râhu from the trunk. The portion of nectar which he had drunk secured his immortality; the head and tail were transferred to the solar sphere, the head wreaking its vengeance on the sun and moon by occasionally swallowing them, while the tail, under the name of Ketu, gave birth to a numerous progeny of comets and fiery meteors. By another legend Ketu was turned into the demon Sainhikeya and the Arunah Ketavah or "Red apparitions," which often appear in the older folk-lore.

Ketu nowadays is only a vague demon of disease, and Râhu too has suffered a grievous degradation. He is now the special godling of the Dusâdhs and Dhângars, two menial tribes found in the Eastern districts of the North-Western Provinces. His worship is a kind of fire sacrifice. A ditch seven cubits long and one and a quarter cubits broad (both numbers of mystical significance) is dug and filled with burning faggots, which are allowed to smoulder into cinders. One of the tribal priests in a state of religious afflatus walks through the fire, into which some oil or butter is poured to make a sudden blaze. It is said that the sacred fire is harmless; but some admit that a certain preservative ointment is used by the performers. The worshippers insist on the priest coming in actual contact with the flames, and a case occurred some years ago in Gorakhpur when one of the priests was degraded on account of his perfunctory discharge of this sacred duty. The same rule applies to the priest who performs the rites at the lighting of the Holî fire. It is needless

[1] "Folk-lore," ii. 228.

to say that similar rites prevail elsewhere, chiefly in Southern India.[1]

In connection with this rite of fire-walking they have another function in which a ladder is made of wooden sword-blades, up which the priest is compelled to climb, resting the soles of his feet on the edges of the weapons. When he reaches the top he decapitates a white cock which is tied to the summit of the ladder. This kind of victim is, as we have already seen, appropriate to propitiate the Sun godling, and there can be little doubt that the main object of this form of symbolical magic is to appease the deities which control the rain and harvests.

Brâhmans so far join in this low-caste worship as to perform the fire sacrifice (*homa*) near the trench where the ceremony is being performed. In Mirzapur one of the songs recited on this occasion runs: "O devotee! How many cubits long is the trench which thou hast dug? How many maunds of butter hast thou poured upon it that the fire billows rise in the air? Seven cubits long is the trench; seven maunds of firewood hast thou placed within it. One and a quarter maunds of firewood hast thou placed within it. One and a quarter maunds of butter hast thou poured into the trench that the fire billows rise to the sky." All this is based on the idea that fire is a scarer of demons, a theory which widely prevails. The Romans made their flocks and herds pass through fire, over which they leaped themselves. In Ireland, when the St. John's Eve fire has burnt low, "the young men strip to the waist and leap over or through the flames, and he who braves the greatest blaze is considered the victor over the powers of evil."[2]

By a curious process of anthropomorphism, another legend makes Râh or Râhu, the Dusâdh godling, to have been not an eclipse demon, but the ghost of an ancient

[1] Oppert, "Original Inhabitants of Bharatavarsa," 97, 98, 40.

[2] Ovid, "Fasti," iv. 728; Lady Wilde, "Legends," 113; "Folk-lore," ii. 128; Dalton, "Descriptive Ethnology," 326; "Indian Antiquary," ii. 90; iii. 68; vii. 126 sqq.; Wilson, "Essays," s.v. "Holî;" Leviticus xviii. 21; 2 Kings xxiii. 10; Herklot, "Qânûn-i-Islâm," s.v. "Muharram."

leader of the tribe who was killed in battle.[1] A still grosser theory of eclipses is found in the belief held by the Ghasiyas of Mirzapur that the sun and moon once borrowed money from some of the Dom tribe and did not pay it back. Now in revenge a Dom occasionally devours them and vomits them up again when the eclipse is over.

ECLIPSE OBSERVANCES.

Eclipses are of evil omen. Gloucester sums up the matter :[2] "These late eclipses in the sun and moon portend no good to us; though the wisdom of nature can reason it thus and thus, yet nature finds itself scourged by the sequent effects; love cools, friendship falls off, brothers divide; in cities mutinies; in countries discord; in palaces treason; and the bond cracked 'twixt son and father." The Hindu authority[3] writes much to the same effect. "Eclipses usually portend or cause grief; but if rain without unusual symptoms fall within a week of the eclipse, all baneful influences come to nought."

Among high-caste Hindus no food which has remained in the house during an eclipse of the sun or moon can be eaten; it must be given away, and all earthen vessels in use in the house at the time must be broken. Mr. Conway[4] takes this to mean that "the eclipse was to have his attention called by outcries and prayers to the fact that if it was fire he needed there was plenty on earth; and if food, he might have all in the house, provided he would consent to satisfy his appetite with articles of food less important than the luminaries of heaven." The observance is more probably based on the idea of ceremonial pollution caused by the actual working of demoniacal agency.

Food is particularly liable to this form of pollution. The wise housewife, when an eclipse is announced, takes a leaf of the Tulasî or sacred basil, and sprinkling Ganges water on

[1] Cunningham, "Archæological Reports," xvi. 28. [2] "Lear," i. 2.
[3] "Brihat Sanhita." Manning, "Ancient India," i. 371.
[4] "Demonology," i. 45.

it, puts the leaf in the jars containing the drinking water for the use of the family and the cooked food, and thus keeps them pure while the eclipse is going on. Confectioners, who are obliged to keep large quantities of cooked food ready, relieve themselves and their customers from the taboo by keeping some of the sacred Kusa or Dûb grass in their vessels when an eclipse is expected. A pregnant woman will do no work during an eclipse, as otherwise she believes that her child would be deformed, and the deformity is supposed to bear some relation to the work which is being done by her at the time. Thus, if she were to sew anything, the baby would have a hole in its flesh, generally near the ear; if she cut anything, the child would have a hare-lip. On the same principle the horns of pregnant cattle are smeared with red paint during an eclipse, because red is a colour abhorred by demons. While the eclipse is going on, drinking water, eating food, and all household business, as well as the worship of the gods, are all prohibited. No respectable Hindu will at such a time sleep on a bedstead or lie down to rest, and he will give alms in barley or copper coins to relieve the pain of the suffering luminaries.

So among Muhammadans,[1] a bride-elect sends offerings of intercession (*sadqa*) to her intended husband, accompanied by a goat or kid, which must be tied to his bedstead during the continuance of the eclipse. These offerings are afterwards distributed in charity. Women expecting to be mothers are carefully kept awake, as they believe that the security of the coming infant depends on the mother being kept from sleep. They are not allowed to use a needle, scissors, knife, or any other instrument for fear of drawing blood, which at that time would be injurious to both mother and child.

But among Hindus the most effectual means of scaring the demon and releasing the afflicted planet is to bathe in some sacred stream. At this time a Brâhman should stand in the water beside the worshipper and recite the Gâyatrî. At an eclipse of the moon it is advisable to bathe at Benares, and when the sun is eclipsed at Kurukshetra. Bernier[2]

[1] Mrs. Mîr Hasan 'Ali, "Observations," i. 297 sq. [2] "Travels," 301.

gives a very curious account of the bathing which he witnessed at Delhi during the great eclipse of 1666. In the lower Himâlayas the current ritual prescribes an elaborate ceremony, when numerous articles are placed in the sacred water jar; the image of the snake god, stamped in silver, is worshipped, and the usual gifts are made.[1]

In Ladâkh ram horns are fixed on the stems of fruit trees as a propitiatory offering at the time of an eclipse, and trees thus honoured are believed to bear an unfailing crop of the choicest fruit.[2]

Another effectual means of scaring the demon is by music and noise, of which we shall find instances later on. "The Irish and Welsh, during eclipses, run about beating kettles and pans, thinking their clamour and vexations available to the assistance of the higher orbs."[3] So in India, women go about with brass pans and beat them to drive Râhu from his prey.

Of course, the time of an eclipse is most inauspicious for the commencement of any important business. Here again the learned Aubrey confirms the current Hindu belief. "According to the rules of astrology," he says, "it is not good to undertake any business of importance in the new moon or at an eclipse."

STAR-WORSHIP.

The worship of the other constellations is much less important than those of the greater luminaries which we have been discussing. The Hindu names nine constellations, known as Nava-graha, "the nine seizers," specially in reference to Râhu, which grips the sun and moon in eclipses, and more generally in the astrological sense of influencing the destinies of men. These nine stars are the sun (Sûrya), the moon (Soma, Chandra), the ascending and descending nodes (Râhu, Ketu), and the five planets—Mercury (Budha), Venus (Sukra), Mars (Mangala, Angâraka), Jupiter (Vrihas-

[1] Atkinson, "Himâlayan Gazetteer," ii. 913 sq.
[2] "North Indian Notes and Queries," i. 38.
[3] Brand, "Observations," 665; Aubrey, "Remaines," 37, 85.

pati), and Saturn (Sani). This group of nine stars is worshipped at marriages and other important religious rites. Of the signs of the Zodiac (*râsi-chakra*) the rural Hindu knows little more than the names—Mesha (Aries), Vrisha (Taurus), Mithuna (Gemini), Karka (Cancer), Sinha (Leo), Kanya (Virgo), Tula (Libra), Vrischika (Scorpio), Dhanu (Sagittarius), Makara (Capricornus), Kumbha (Aquarius), and Mîna (Pisces). Practically the only direct influence they exercise over his life is that from the opening Râsi or sign in which he is born the first letter of the secret name which he bears is selected. Still less concern has he with the asterisms or Nakshatra, a word which has been variously interpreted to mean "coming or ascending," "night guardians," or "undecaying." As already stated, they are said to have been the twenty-seven daughters of the Rishi Daksha, and wives of Soma or the moon. The usual enumeration gives twenty-eight, and they are vaguely supposed to represent certain stars or constellations, but the identification of these is very uncertain. One list, with some of the corresponding stars, gives Sravishthâ or Dhanishthâ (Delphinus), Sata-bhishaj (Aquarius), Pûrva Bhâdrapadâ, Uttara Bhâdrapadâ, Revatî, Asvinî (Aries), Bharanî (Musca), Krittikâ (the Pleiades), Rohinî (Aldebaran), Mriga-siras (Orion), Ârdrâ, Punarvasû, Pushya, Âsleshâ, Maghâ (Leo), Pûrvâ-Phalgunî, Uttara Phalgunî, Hasta (Corvus), Chitrâ (Spica Virginis), Svâtî (Arcturus), Visâkha (Libra), Anurâdhâ, Jyeshthâ, Mûla, Pûrva Âshâdhâ, Uttara Âshâdhâ, Abhijit (Lyra), and Sravana. These are used only in calculating the marriage horoscope, and the only one of them with which the fairly well-to-do rustic has much concern is with the unlucky Mûla. Should by an evil chance his son be born in this asterism, he has to undergo a most elaborate rite of purification.

Others stars have their legends. The Riksha or constellation of the Great Bear represents the seven deified Rishis —Gautama, Bhâradwaja, Viswamitra, Jamadagni, Vashishtha, Kasyapa and Atri. Dhruva, the Pole Star, was the grandson of Manu Swayambhuva, and was driven from his home by his step-mother. He, though a Kshatriya, joined the company of the Rishis and was finally raised to the skies as Grahadhâra, "the pivot of the plants." So Canopus is the Rishi Agastya who was perhaps one of the early Aryan missionaries to Southern India and won a place in heaven by his piety. Orion is Mrigasiras, the head of Brahma in the form of a stag which was struck off by Siva when the deity attempted violence to his own daughter Sandhyâ, the twilight. Krittikâ or the Pleiades represent the six nurses of Kârttikeya, the god of war.

Part of the purificatory rite for a woman after her delivery is to bring her out at night and let her look at the stars, while her husband stands over her with a bludgeon to guard her from the assaults of demons. One interesting survival of the old mythology is that in Upper India women are fond of teaching their children that the stars are kine and the moon their shepherd, an idea which has formed the basis of much of the speculations of a school of comparative mythology now almost completely discredited.

THE RAINBOW.

There is much curious folk-lore about the rainbow. By most Hindus it is called the Dhanus or bow of Râma Chandra, and by Muhammadans the bow of Bâbâ Âdam or father Adam. In the Panjâb it is often known as the swing of Bîbî Bâî, the wife of the Saint Sakhi Sarwar. The Persians call it the bow of Rustam or of Shaitân or Satan, or Shamsher-i-'Ali—"the sword of 'Ali." In Sanskrit it is Rohitam, the invisible bow of Indra. In the hills it is called Panihârin or the female water-bearer.

THE MILKY WAY.

So with the Milky Way, of which an early name is Nâgavithi or the path of the snake. The Persians call it Kahkashân, the dragging of a bundle of straw through the sky. The Hindu calls it Akâsh Gangâ or the heavenly Ganges, Bhagwân kî kachahrî or the Court of God,

Swarga-duâri or the door of Paradise; while to the Panjâbi it is known as Bera dâ ghâs or the path of Noah's Ark. In Celtic legend it is the road along which Gwydion pursued his erring wife.

EARTH-WORSHIP.

Next in order of reverence to the heavenly bodies comes the Earth goddess, Dharitrî or Dhartî Mâtâ or Dhartî Mâî, a name which means "the upholder" or "supporter." She is distinguished from Bhûmi, "the soil," which, as we shall see, has a god of its own, and from Prithivî, "the wide extended world," which in the Vedas is personified as the mother of all things, an idea common to all folk-lore. The myth of Dyaus, the sky, and Prithivî, the earth, once joined and now separated, is the basis of a great chapter in mythology, such as the mutilation of Uranus by Cronus and other tales of a most distinctively savage type.[1] We meet the same idea in the case of Demeter, "the fruitful soil," as contrasted with Gaea, the earlier, Titanic, formless earth; unless, indeed, we are to accept Mr. Frazer's identification of Demeter with the Corn Mother.[2]

WORSHIP OF MOTHER EARTH.

The worship of Mother Earth assumes many varied forms. The pious Hindu does reverence to her as he rises from his bed in the morning; and even the indifferent follows his example when he begins to plough and sow. In the Panjâb,[3] "when a cow or buffalo is first bought, or when she first gives milk after calving, the first five streams of milk drawn from her are allowed to fall on the ground in honour of the goddess, and every time of milking the first stream is so treated. So, when medicine is taken, a little is sprinkled in

[1] The Celtic form of the myth is given by Rhys, "Lectures," 140 sq.; the Indian legend in Muir, "Ancient Sanskrit Texts," ii. 23.

[2] "Golden Bough," i. 331 sq.; and see Lang, "Custom and Myth," ii. 262.

[3] Ibbetson, "Panjâb Ethnology," 114.

her honour." On the same principle the great Kublai Khân used to sprinkle the milk of his mares on the ground. "This is done," says Marco Polo,[1] "on the injunction of the idolaters and idol priests, who say that it is an excellent thing to sprinkle milk on the ground every 28th of August, so that the earth and the air and the false gods shall have their share of it, and the spirits likewise that inhabit the air and the earth, and those beings will protect and bless the Kaan and his children, and his wives, and his folk and his gear, and his cattle and his horses, and all that is his."

The same feeling is also shown in the primitive taboo, which forbids that any holy thing, such as the blood of a tribesman, should fall upon the ground. Thus we are told that Kublai Khân ordered his captive Nayan "to be wrapped in a carpet and tossed to and fro so mercilessly that he died, and the Kaan caused him to be put to death in this way, because he would not have the blood of his Line Imperial spilt upon the ground, and exposed to the eye of heaven and before the sun." Even some savages when they are obliged to shed the blood of a member of the tribe, as at the rite of circumcision, receive it upon their own bodies. The soul, in fact, is supposed to be in the blood, and any ground on which the blood falls becomes taboo or accursed.[2]

Throughout Northern India the belief in the sanctity of the earth is universal. The dying man is laid on the earth at the moment of dissolution, and so is the mother at the time of parturition. In the case of the dying there is perhaps another influence at work in this precaution, the idea that the soul must not be barred by roof or wall, and allowed to wing its course unimpeded to the place reserved for it.

In the eastern districts of the North-Western Provinces there is a regular rite common to all the inferior castes that a few days before a wedding the women go in procession to the village clay-pit and fetch from there the sacred earth (*matmangara*), which is used in making the marriage altar and the fireplace on which the wedding feast is cooked.

[1] Yule, "Marco Polo," i. 291, with note ii. 543.
[2] For instances, see Frazer, "Golden Bough," i. 179.

There are various elements in the ritual which point to a very primitive origin. Thus, one part of the proceedings is that a Chamâr, one of the non-Aryan castes, leads the procession, beating his drum the whole time to scare demons. When the earth has been collected the drum is worshipped and smeared with red lead. There can be little doubt that the drum was one of the very primitive fetishes of the aboriginal races. One, and perhaps about the most primitive, form of it is the Damaru or drum shaped like an hour-glass which accompanies Siva, and next to this comes the Mândar, the sides of which are formed out of earthenware, and which is the first stage in the development of a musical instrument from a vessel covered with some substance which resounds when beaten. This latter form of drum is the national musical instrument of the Central Indian Gonds and their brethren. The Chamâr, again, digs the earth with an affectation of secrecy, which, as we shall see, is indispensable in rites of this class. The mother of the bride or bridegroom veils herself with her sheet, and the digger passes the earth over his left shoulder to a virgin who stands behind him and receives it in a corner of her robe.

Dust, again, which has been trodden on has mystic powers. In the villages you may see little children after an elephant has passed patting the marks of his feet in the dust and singing a song. Among the Kunbis of Kolâba, when the women neighbours come to inspect a newly-born child, they touch the soles of the mother's feet, as if picking some dust off them, wave it over the child, and blow the dust particularly into the air and partly over the baby.[1] In Thâna, when a mother goes out with a young child on her hip, if she cannot get lamp-black to rub between its eyes, she takes dust off her left foot and rubs it on the child's forehead.[2] So we read of the Isle of Man—"If a person endowed with the Evil Eye has just passed by a farmer's herd of cattle, and a calf has suddenly been seized with a serious illness, the farmer hurries after the man with the Evil Eye to get the dust from under his feet. If he objects, he may, as has sometimes been very

[1] "Bombay Gazetteer," xi. 55.

[2] Campbell, "Notes," 79.

unceremoniously done, throw him down by force, take off his shoes and scrape off the dust adhering to their soles, and carry it back to throw over the calf. Even that is not always necessary, as it appears to be quite enough if he takes up dust where he of the Evil Eye has just trod."[1]

Earth, again, is regarded as a remedy for disease. I have seen people in Ireland take a pinch of earth from the grave of a priest noted for his piety, and drink it dissolved in water. People suffering from a certain class of disease come to the tomb of the Saint Kadri at Yemnur in Dharwâr and smear their bodies with mud that they may be cured of the disease.[2] There are numerous instances of the use of earth as a poultice and an application for the cure of wounds and sores among the savage tribes of Africa and elsewhere.

It is on much the same principle that among some tribes in India Mother Earth is worshipped as a Kuladevatâ or household goddess and appealed to in times of danger. The Hindu troopers at the battle of Kâmpti, at the crisis of the engagement, took dust from their grooms and threw it over their heads. At Sûrat in 1640, in fear of drought, Brâhmans went about carrying a board with earth on it on their heads.[3] So wrestlers, when they are about to engage in a contest, rub earth on their arms and legs and roll on the ground. As in the classical legend of Antaeus, they believe that they derive strength from the touch of Mother Earth.

The same principle, also, appears to be at the bottom of many similiar practices. Thus the Hindu always uses earth to purify his cooking vessels, which he regards with peculiar respect. Mourners of the Jaina creed on going home after a funeral rub their hands with earth and water to remove the death impurity. In his daily bath the pious Hindu rubs a little Ganges mud on his body. The Pârsis cover the parings of their hair and nails with a little earth so that demons may not enter into them. The Muhammadan uses earth for the purpose of purification when water is not procurable. For the same reason the ascetic rubs his body with

1 "Folk-lore," ii. 298.
2 "Bombay Gazetteer," xxii. 790.
3 Fryer, "Travels," 418; Campbell, "Notes," 81.

dust and ashes, which, as we shall see, is a potent scarer of demons. Though here there is possibly another theory at work at the same time. The practice was common to the Greek as well as to the barbarian mysteries, and according to Mr. Lang, "the idea clearly was that by cleaning away the filth plastered over the body was symbolized the pure and free condition of the initiate." [1]

Lastly, it is perhaps on the same principle that many universal burial customs have originated. The Muhammadan phrase for burial is *mattî-denâ*, "to give earth." The unburied mariner asks Horace for the gift of a little earth. We ourselves consider it a pious duty to throw a little earth on the coffin of a departed friend. The same custom prevails among many Hindu tribes. The Chambhârs of Pûna throw handfuls of earth over the corpse; so do the Halâlkhors; the Lingâyats of Dharwâr follow the same practice. The Bani Isrâils at a funeral stuff a handful of earth into a pillow which is put under the head of the corpse.[2] The same conception was probably the basis of the universal custom of funeral oblations. Even nowadays in Scotland all the milk in the house is poured on the ground at a death, and the same custom is familiar through many Hebrew and Homeric instances. The same idea appears in the custom prevalent in the Middle Ages in Germany, that when a nun renounced the world and became civilly dead her relations threw dust on her arms.[3]

EARTH-WORSHIP AMONG THE DRÂVIDIANS.

Among the Drâvidian races of Central India earth-worship prevails widely. In Chota Nâgpur the Orâons celebrate in spring the marriage of the earth. The Dryad of the Sâl tree (*Shorea robusta*), who controls the rain, is propitiated with a sacrifice of fowls. Flowers of the Sâl tree are taken to the village and carried round from house to house in a

[1] "Custom and Myth," i. 285; ii. 229, note.
[2] Campbell, "Notes," 78 sqq.
[3] Gregor, "Folk-lore of North-East Scotland," 206; Aubrey, "Remaines," 37; Ewald, "Antiquities of Israel," 34; Spencer, "Principles of Sociology," i. 259, 314; Grimm, "Teutonic Mythology," ii. 643.

basket. The women wash the feet of the priest and do obeisance to him. He dances with them and puts some flowers upon them and upon the house. They first douse him with water as a means of bringing the rain, and then refresh him with beer.[1]

In Hoshangâbâd, when the sowing is over, its completion is celebrated by the Machandrî Pûjâ, or worship of Mother Earth, a ceremony intended to invoke fertility. "Every cultivator does the worship himself, with his family, servants, etc.; no Brâhman need join in it. At the edge of one of his fields intended for the spring harvest, he puts up a little semicircle or three-sided wall of clods about a foot high, meant to represent a hut. This is covered over with green Kâns grass (*Imperata spontanea*) to represent thatch. At the two ends of the hut two posts of Palâsa wood (*Butea frondosa*) are erected, with leaves round the head like those which are put up at marriage. They are tied to the thatch with red thread. In the centre of this little house, which is the temple of Machandrî, or Mother Earth, a little fire is made, and milk placed on it to boil in a tiny earthen pot. It is allowed to boil over as a sign of abundance. While this is going on, the ploughmen, who are all collected in a field, drive their bullocks at a trot, striking them wildly; it is the end of the year's labour for the cattle. The cultivator meanwhile offers a little rice, molasses, and saffron to Machandrî, and then makes two tiny holes in the ground to represent granaries; he drops a few grains in and covers them over; this is a symbol of prayer, that his granary may be filled from the produce of the land." Similar instances of symbolical magic will constantly occur in connection with similar rites. Then he puts a little saffron on the foreheads of the ploughman and the bullocks, and ties a red thread round the horns of the cattle. The animals are then let go, and the ploughmen run off at full speed across country, scattering wheat boiled whole as a sign of abundance. This concludes the rite, and every one returns home.[2]

[1] Dalton, "Descriptive Ethnology," 261.
[2] Elliott, "Settlement Report," 125.

Many similar usages prevail among the jungle tribes of South Mirzapur. The Korwas consider Dhartî Mâtâ one of their chief godlings. She lives in the village in the Deohâr or general village shrine under a Sâl tree. In the month of Aghan (November-December) she is worshipped with flowers and the offering of a goat. When she is duly worshipped the crops prosper and there are no epidemics. The Patâris and Majhwârs also recognize her as a goddess, and worship her in the month of Sâwan (August). The local devil priest or Baiga offers to her a goat, cock, and rich cakes (*pûri*). She is also worshipped in the cold weather before the grain and barley are sown, and again on the threshing-floor before the winnowing begins. The flesh of the animals is consumed by the males and unmarried girls; no grown-up girl or married woman is allowed to touch the flesh. The Ghasiyas also believe in Dhartî Mâtâ. She is their village goddess, and is presented with a ram or a goat or cakes. The offering is made by the Baiga, for whom the materials are provided by a general contribution in the village. The Kharwârs worship her at the village shrine before wood-cutting and ploughing begin. In the month of Sâwan (August) they do a special service in her honour, known as the Hariyârî Pûjâ, or "worship of greenery," at the time of transplanting the rice. In Aghan (November) they do the Khar Pûjâ, when they begin cutting thatching-grass (*khar*). A cock, some Mahua (*Bassia latifolia*) and parched grain are offered to her. All this is done by the Baiga, who receives the offerings, and none but males are allowed to attend. Similarly the Pankas worship her before sowing and harvesting the grain. They and the Bhuiyârs offer a pig and some liquor at the more important agricultural seasons. The Kharwârs sometimes call her Devî Dâî, or "Nurse Devî," and in times of trouble sprinkle rice and pulse in her name on the ground. When the crops are being sown they release a fowl as a scapegoat and pray—*Hê Dhartî Mahtârî! Kusal mangala rakhiyo! Harwâh, bail, sab bachen rahen* —"O Mother Earth! Keep in prosperity and protect the ploughmen and the oxen." In much the same spirit is the prayer of the peasant in Karnâl to Mother Earth:—*Sâh Bâdshâh sê surkhrû rakhiyê! Aur is men achchha nâj dê, to bâdshâh ko bhî paisa den, aur Sâh kâ bhi utar jâwê*—"Keep our rulers and bankers contented! Grant us a plentiful yield! So shall we pay our revenue and satisfy our banker!"[1]

SECRECY IN WORSHIP OF MOTHER EARTH.

We shall meet other instances in which secrecy is an essential element in these rural rites. This condition prevails almost universally. Notable, too, is the rule by which married women are excluded from a share in offerings to the Earth goddess.

THUNDER AND LIGHTNING.

As is natural, thunder and lightning are considered ill-omened. In the old mythology lightning (*vidyut*) was one of the weapons of the Maruts, and Parjanya was the deity who wielded the thunderbolt. Many legends tell that the soul of the first man came to earth in the form of the lightning. Thus Yama was the first man born of the thunderbolt, and he first trod the path of death and became regent of the dead. Many are the devices to scare the lightning demon. "During a thunderstorm it was a Greek custom to put out the fire, and hiss and cheep with the lips. The reason for the custom was explained by the Pythagoreans to be that by acting thus you scared the spirits in Tartarus, who were doubtless supposed to make the thunder and lightning. Similarly some of the Australian blacks, who attribute thunder to the agency of demons, and are much afraid of it, believe that they can dispel it by chanting some particular words and breathing hard; and it is a German superstition that the danger from a thunderstorm can be averted by putting out the fire. During a thunderstorm the Sakai of the Malay Peninsula run out of their

[1] "Settlement Report," 168.

houses and brandish their weapons to drive away the demons; and the Esthonians in Russia fasten scythes, edge upwards, over the door, that the demons, fleeing from the thundering god, may cut their feet if they try to seek shelter in the house. Sometimes the Esthonians, for a similar purpose, take all the edged tools in the house and throw them out into the yard. It is said that when the thunder is over, spots of blood are often found on the scythes and knives, showing that the demons have been wounded by them.

"So when the Indians of Canada were asked by the Jesuit missionaries why they planted their swords in the ground point upwards, they replied that the spirit of the thunder was sensible, and that if he saw the naked blades he would turn away and take good care not to approach their huts. This is a fair example of the close similarity of European superstitions to the superstitions of savages. In the present case the difference happens to be slightly in favour of the Indians, since they did not, like our European savages, delude themselves into seeing the blood of demons on the swords. The reason for the Greek and German custom of putting out the fire during a thunderstorm is probably a wish to avoid attracting the attention of the thunder demons. From a like motive some of the Australian blacks hide themselves during a thunderstorm, and keep absolutely silent, lest the thunder should find them out. Once during a storm a white man called out in a loud voice to a black fellow, with whom he was working, to put the saw under a log and seek shelter. He found that the saw had been already put aside, and the black fellow was very indignant at his master for speaking so loud. 'What for,' said he, in great wrath—'what for speak so loud? Now um thunder hear and know where um saw is.' And he went out and changed its hiding-place."[1]

All these precautions are well known to the people of Upper India. It is a very common habit to throw out axes and knives to scare the thunder demon, as we shall see is

[1] "Folk-lore," i. 153.

IMAGE OF GANGA MÂI.

To face I. 35.

the case with the evil spirit of hail. The rule of keeping quiet and muttering incantations under the breath is also familiar to them. They are particularly careful lest a first-born son may lean against anything and thus attract the demon on himself. Thunder in a clear sky is much dreaded, an idea which often appears in classical literature.[1]

EARTHQUAKES.

Earthquakes are also naturally an object of terror. Pythagoras believed that they were caused by dead men fighting beneath the earth. The common explanation of these occurrences in India is that Varâha, or the boar incarnation of Vishnu, who supports the earth, is changing the burden of the world from one tusk to another. By another account it is due to the great bull or elephant which supports the world. Derived from a more advanced theological stage is the theory that the earth shakes because it is over-burdened by the sins of mankind in this evil age. Colonel Dalton describes how a rumbling (probably caused by an earthquake) in the cave in which the bloodthirsty divinity of the Korwas was supposed to dwell, caused extreme terror among them.[2]

RIVER-WORSHIP.

High on the list of benevolent deities of Northern India are the great rivers, especially the Ganges and the Jumnâ, which are known respectively as Gangâ Mâî or "Mother Ganges" and Jumnâ jî or "Lady Jumnâ."

Gangâ, of course, in the mythologies has a divine origin. According to one account she flows from the toe of Vishnu, and was brought down from heaven by the incantations of the Saint Bhâgîratha, to purify the ashes of the sixty thousand sons of King Sâgara, who had been burnt up by the angry glance of Kapila, the sage. By another story she

[1] Virgil, "Georgics," i. 487; "Æneid," vii. 141; Horace, "Odes," i. 34, 5.

[2] "Descriptive Ethnology," 229.

descends in seven streams from Siva's brow. The descent of Gangâ disturbed the Saint Jahnu at his austerities, and in his anger he drank up the stream; but he finally relented, and allowed the river to flow from his ear. By a third account she is the daughter of Himavat, the impersonation of the Himâlayan range. Another curious tale, which must have been based on some Indian tradition, is found in Plutarch[1]—"The Ganges is a river of India, called so for the following reason:—The nymph Kalauria bore to Indus a son of notable beauty, by name Ganges, who in the ignorance of intoxication had connection with his mother. But when later on he learned the truth from his nurse, in the passion of his remorse he threw himself into the river Chliaros, which was called Ganges after him." Another legend again is found in the Mahâbhârata.[2] The wise Santanu goes to hunt on the banks of the Ganges and finds a lovely nymph, of whom he becomes enamoured. She puts him under the taboo that he is never to say anything to displease her, an idea familiar in the well-known Swan Maiden cycle of folk-tales. She bears him eight sons, of whom she throws seven into the river, and her husband dares not remonstrate with her. When she is about to throw away the last child he challenges her to tell him who she is and to have pity upon him. She then tells him that she is Gangâ personified, and that the seven sons are the divine Vasavas, who by being thrown into the river are liberated from the curse of human life. The eighth remains among men as Dyaus, the sky, in the form of the eunuch Bhîshma.

It is remarkable that, as in Plutarch's legend, the Jumnâ is connected with a tale of incest. Yamî or Yamunâ was the daughter of the Sun and sister of Yama, the god of death. They were the first human pair and the progenitors of the race of men. It is needless to say that similar traditions of brother and sister marriage are found in Egypt, Peru and elsewhere. Yamunâ, according to the modern story told on her banks, was unmarried, and hence some people will not drink from her because she was not purified

1 "Peri Potamôn."

2 i. 3888 sqq.

GANGES WATER BEARERS.

by the marriage rite, and so the water is heavy and indigestible. Another tale tells how Balarâma, in a state of inebriety, called upon her to come to him that he might bathe in her waters; and as she did not heed, he, in his rage, seized his ploughshare weapon, dragged her to him, and compelled her to follow him whithersoever he wandered through the forest. The river then assumed a human form and besought his forgiveness; but it was some time before she could appease the angry hero. This has been taken to represent the construction of some ancient canal from the river; but Mr. Growse shows that this idea is incorrect.[1]

The worship of Mother Ganges is comparatively modern. She is mentioned only twice in the Rig Veda, and then without any emphasis or complementary epithet. Apparently at this time the so-called Aryan invaders had not reached her banks.[2] There are numerous temples to Gangâ all along her banks, of which those at Hardwâr, Garhmuktesar, Soron, Mathura, Prayâg, and Benares are perhaps the most important in Upper India. She has her special festival on the seventh of the month of Baisâkh (May-June), which is celebrated by general bathing all along the banks of the sacred stream. Ganges water is carried long distances into the interior, and is highly valued for its use in sacrifices, as a remedy, a form of stringent oath, and a viaticum for the dying. The water of certain holy wells in Scotland[3] and elsewhere enjoys a similar value.

But it is by bathing in the sacred stream at the full moon, during eclipses, and on special festivals that the greatest efficacy is assured. On these occasions an opportunity is taken for making oblations to the sainted dead whose ashes have been consigned to her waters. Bathing is throughout India regarded as one of the chief means of religious advancement. The idea rests on a metaphor—as the body is cleansed from physical pollution, so the soul is

[1] "Mathura," 179 sq.

[2] Duncker, "History," iv. 11, note; Romesh Chandra Datt, "History of Civilization," i. 94.

[3] Gregor, "Folk-lore of North-East Scotland," 41.

purified from sin. The stock case of the merit of this religious bathing is that of King Trisanku, "he who had committed the three deadly sins," who is also known as Satyavrata. The legend appears in various forms. By one story he tried to win his way to heaven by a great sacrifice which his priest, Vasishtha, declined to perform. He then applied to Visvamitra, the rival Levite, who agreed to assist him. He was opposed by the sons of Vasishtha, whom he consumed to ashes. Finally, Trisanku was admitted to heaven, but he was forced by the angry saint to hang for ever with his head downwards. By another account he committed the deadly sins of running away with the wife of a citizen, offending his father, and killing in a time of famine Kâmadhenu, the wondrous cow of Vashishtha. By another story he killed a cow and a Brâhman and married his step-mother. At any rate he and the wicked Râja Vena were the types of violent sinners in the early legends; possibly they represent a revolt against the pretensions of the Brâhmans. At length the sage Visvamitra took pity upon him, and having collected water from all the sacred places in the world, washed him clean of his offences.

SPRINGS CONNECTED WITH THE GANGES.

Many famous springs are supposed to have underground connection with the Ganges. Such is that of Chângdeo in Khândesh, of which Abul Fazl gives an account, and that at Jahânpur in Alwar.[1] It was at the village of Bastali in the Karnâl District that the sage Vyâsa lived, and there the Ganges flowed into his well to save him the trouble of going to the river to bathe, bringing with her his loin cloth and water-pot to convince him that she was really the Ganges herself.[2]

SACRED RIVER JUNCTIONS.

When two sacred rivers combine their waters the junction (*Sangama*) is regarded as of peculiar sanctity.

[1] Jarrett, "Aîn-i-Akbari," ii. 224; "Râjputâna Gazetteer," iii. 219.
[2] "Karnâl Gazetteer," 31.

Such is the famous junction of the Ganges and Jumnâ at Prayâg, the modern Allahâbâd, which is presided over by the guardian deity Veni Mâdhava. The same virtue, but in a lesser degree, attaches to the junction of the Ganges and the Son or Gandak. In the Himâlayas cairns are raised at the junction of three streams, and every passer-by adds a stone. At the confluence of the Gaula and Baliya rivers in the Hills there is said to be a house of gold, but unfortunately it is at present invisible on account of some potent enchantment.[1] Bathing in such rivers is not only a propitiation for sin, but is also efficacious for the cure of disease. Even the wicked Râja Vena, who was, as we have seen, a type of old-world impiety, was cured, like Naaman the Syrian, of his leprosy by bathing in the Sâraswati, the lost river of the Indian desert.

Even minor streams have their sanctity and their legends. The course of the Sarju was opened by a Rishi, from which time dates the efficacy of a pilgrimage to Bâgheswar.[2] Râja Rantideva was such a pious king and offered up so many cattle in sacrifice, that his blood formed the river Chambal. Anasûyâ, the wife of Atri, was a daughter of the Rishi Daksha. She did penance for ten thousand years, and so was enabled to create the river Mandâkinî, and thus saved the land from famine. Her worship is localized at Ansuyaji in the Bânda District. The sacred portion of the Phalgu is said occasionally to flow with milk, though Dr. Buchanan was not fortunate enough to meet anyone who professed to have witnessed the occurrence.[3] The Narmadâ was wooed by the river Son, who proved faithless to her, and was beguiled by the Johilâ, a rival lady stream, who acted the part of the barber's wife at the wedding. The Narmadâ, enraged at her lover's perfidy, tore her way through the marble rocks at Jabalpur, and has worn the willow ever since.[4] She is now the great rival of Mother

[1] Buchanan, "Eastern India," i. 11; Madden, "Journal Asiatic Society, Bengal," 1847, 228, 400; Wright, "History of Nepâl," 154, 163.

[2] Madden, *loc. cit.*, 233.

[3] *Loc. cit.*, i. 14.

[4] Sleeman, "Rambles," i. 17.

Ganges. While in the case of the latter only the Northern (or as it is called the Kâsi or Benares bank) is efficacious for bathing or for the cremation of the dead, the Narmadâ is free from any restriction of the kind. The same is the case with the Son, at least during its course through the District of Mirzapur. By some the sanctity of the Narmadâ is regarded as superior even to that of the Ganges. While according to some authorities it is necessary to bathe in the Ganges in order to obtain forgiveness of sins, the same result is attained by mere contemplation of the Narmadâ. According to the Bhâvishya Purâna the sanctity of the Ganges will cease on the expiration of five thousand years of the Kali Yuga, or the fourth age of the world, which occurred in 1895, and the Narmadâ will take its place. The Ganges priests, however, repudiate this calumny, and it may safely be assumed that Mother Ganges will not abandon her primacy in the religious world of Hinduism without a determined struggle.[1]

ILL-OMENED STREAMS.

But all rivers are not beneficent. Worst of all is the dread Vaitaranî, the river of death, which is localized in Orissa and pours its stream of ordure and blood on the confines of the realm of Yama. Woe to the wretch who in that dread hour lacks the aid of the Brâhman and the holy cow to help him to the other shore. The name of one stream is accursed in the ears of all Hindus, the hateful Karamnâsa, which flows for part of its course through the Mirzapur District. Even to touch it destroys the merit of works of piety, for such is the popular interpretation of its name. No plausible reason for the evil reputation of this particular stream has been suggested except that it may have been in early times the frontier between the invading Aryans and the aborigines, and possibly the scene of a campaign in which the latter were victorious. The Karamâ tree is, however, the totem of the Drâvidian Kharwârs and

[1] "Central Provinces Gazetteer," 264.

Mânjhis, who live along its banks, and it is perhaps possible that this may be the real origin of the name, and that its association with good works (*karma*) was an afterthought.

The legend of this ill-omened stream is associated with that of the wicked king Trisanku, to whom reference has already been made. When the sage Visvamitra collected water from all the sacred streams of the world, it fell burdened with the monarch's sins into the Karamnâsa, which has remained defiled ever since. By another account, the sinner was hung up between heaven and earth as a punishment for his offences, and from his body drips a baneful moisture which still pollutes the water. Similar legends of the origin of rivers are not wanting in folk-lore. An Austrian story tells that all rivers take their origin from the tears shed by a giant's wife as she laments his death.[1] The same idea of a river springing from a corpse appears in one of the tales of Somadeva and in the twelfth novel of the Gesta Romanorum.[2] Nowadays no Hindu with any pretensions to personal purity will drink from this accursed stream, and at its fords many low caste people make their living by conveying on their shoulders their more scrupulous brethren across its waters.

ORIGIN OF RIVER-WORSHIP.

It is perhaps worth considering the possible origin of this river-worship. Far from being peculiar to Hinduism, it is common to the whole Aryan world. The prayer of the patient Odysseus[3] to the river after his sufferings in the deep is heard in almost the same language at every bathing Ghât in Upper India, from the source of Mother Ganges to where she joins the ocean. The river is always flowing, always being replenished by its tributary streams, and hence comes to be regarded as a thing of life, an emblem of eternal existence, a benevolent spirit which washes away the sins of humanity and supplies in a tropical land the chief needs of

[1] "Folk-lore," iii. 32. [2] "Katha Sarit Sâgara," i. 374.

[3] "Odyssey," v. 450; and for other instances see Tylor, "Primitive Culture," ii. 213; Campbell, "Notes," 325 sqq.

men. In a thirsty land the mighty stream of the Ganges would naturally arouse feelings of respect and adoration, not so much perhaps to those living on its banks and ever blessed by its kindly influence, as to the travel-worn pilgrim from the sandy steppes of Râjasthân or the waterless valleys of the Central Indian hills. We can hardly doubt that from this point of view Mother Ganges has been a potent factor in the spread of Hinduism. She became the handmaid of the only real civilization of which Hindustân could boast, and from her shrines bands of eager missionaries were ever starting to sow the seeds of the worship of the gods in the lands of the unbeliever.

The two great rivers of Upper India were, again, associated with that land of fable and mystery, the snowy range which was the home of the gods and the refuge of countless saints and mystics, who in its solitudes worked out the enigma of the world for the modern Hindu. They ended in the great ocean, the final home of the ashes of the sainted dead. Even the partially Hinduised Drâvidian tribes of the Vindhyan Plateau bring the bones of their dead relations to mingle with those of the congregation of the faithful, who have found their final rest in its waters since the world was young. The Ganges and the streams which swell its flood thus come to be associated with the deepest beliefs of the race, and it is hard to exaggerate its influence as a bond of union between the nondescript entities which go to make up modern Hinduism.

Again, much of the worship of rivers is connected with the propitiation of the water-snakes, demons and goblins, with which in popular belief many of them are infested. Such were Kâliyâ, the great black serpent of the Jumnâ, which attacked the infant Krishna; the serpent King of Nepâl, Karkotaka, who dwelt in the lake Nâgarâsa when the divine lotus of Adi Buddha floated on its surface.[1] At the temple of Triyugi Nârâyana in Garhwâl is a pool said to be full of snakes of a yellow colour which come out at the

[1] Growse, "Mathura," 55; Tod, "Annals," i. 675; Oldfield, "Sketches from Nepâl," ii. 204.

feast of the Nâgpanchamî to be worshipped. The Gârdevî, or river sprite of Garhwâl, is very malignant, and is the ghost of a person who has met his death by suicide, violence, or accident.[1] These malignant water demons naturally infest dangerous rapids and whirlpools, and it is necessary to propitiate them. Thus we learn that on the river Tâpti in Berâr timber floated down sometimes disappears in a subterraneous cavity; so before trying the navigation there the Gonds sacrifice a goat to propitiate the river demon.[2]

Another variety of these demons of water is the Nâga and his wife the Nâgin, of whom we shall hear more in connection with snake-worship. In the Sikandar, a tributary of the Son, is a deep water-hole where no one dares to go. The water is said to reach down as far as Pâtâla, or the infernal regions. Here live the Nâga and the Nâgin. In the middle of the river is a tree of the Kuâlo variety, and when ghosts trouble the neighbourhood an experienced Ojha or sorcerer is called, who bores holes in the bark of the tree and there shuts up the noxious ghosts, which then come under the rule of the Nâga and Nâgin, who are the supreme rulers of the ghostly band.

Another Mirzapur river, the Karsa, is infested by a Deo, or demon, known as Jata Rohini, or "Rohini of the matted locks." He is worshipped by the Baiga priest to ensure abundant rain and harvests and to keep off disease. The Baiga catches a fish which he presents to the Deo, but if any one but a Baiga dares to drink there, the water bubbles up and the demon sweeps him away.

Like this Deo of Mirzapur, most of these water demons are malignant and wait until some wretched creature enters their domains, when they seize and drag him away. Some of them can even catch the reflection of a person as he looks into water, and hence savages all over the world are very averse to looking into deep water-holes. Thus, the Zulus believe that there is a beast in the water which can seize the shadow of a man, and men are forbidden to lean over and

[1] Atkinson, "Himâlayan Gazetteer," ii. 788, 832.
[2] "Berar Gazetteer," 35.

look into a deep pool, lest their shadow should be taken away. There is a tale of the Godiva cycle in which a woman at Arles is carried off by a creature called a Drac and made to act as nurse to the demon's child.[1] In Scotland water-holes are known as "the cups of the fairies." And there is the Trinity well in Ireland, into which no one can gaze with impunity, and from which the river Boyne once burst forth in pursuit of a lady who had insulted it.[2]

In India, also, dangerous creatures of this kind abound. There is in Mirzapur a famous water-hole, known as Barewa. A herdsman was once grazing his buffaloes near the place, when the waters rose in anger and carried off him and his cattle. Nowadays the drowned buffaloes have taken the shape of a dangerous demon known as Bhainsâsura, or the buffalo demon, who now in company with the Nâga and the Nâgin lives in this place, and no one dares to fish there until he has propitiated the demons with the offering of a fowl, eggs, and a goat. Another kind of water demon attacks fishermen; it appears in the form of a turban which fixes itself to his hook and increases in length as he tries to drag it to the shore.

There is, again, the water-horse, with whom we are familiar in the "Arabian Nights," where he consorts with mares of mortal race. This creature is known in Kashmîr as the *Zalgur*.[3] The water-bull of Manxland is a creature of the same class, and they constantly appear through the whole range of Celtic folk-lore.[4] Such again is the Hydra of Greek mythology, and the Teutonic Nikke or Nixy, who has originated the legend of the Flying Dutchman, and in the shape of Old Nick is the terror of sailors. Like him is the Kelpie of

[1] "Folk-lore," i. 152, 209; iii. 72. [2] Rhys, "Lectures," 123.

[3] Knowles, "Folk-tales," 313.

[4] "Folk-lore," ii. 284, 509; Hunt, "Popular Romances," 194; Campbell, "Popular Tales," ii. 205; Conway, "Demonology," i. 110 sq.; Sir W. Scott, "Letters on Demonology," 85; Spencer, "Principles of Sociology," i. 219; Farrer, "Primitive Manners," 366; Aubrey, "Remaines," 30; Gordon Cumming, "From the Hebrides to the Himâlayas," i. 139; Tylor, "Primitive Culture," i. 109 sq.; ii. 208; Gregor, "Folk-lore," 66 sq.; Lady Wilde, "Legends," 216; Tawney, "Katha Sarit Sâgara," i. 58.

Scotland, a water-horse who is believed to carry off the unwary by sudden floods and devour them. Of the same kindred is the last of the dragons which St. Patrick chained up in a lake on the Galtee Mountains in Tipperary.

Many pools, again, in Northern India are infested by a creature known as the Bûrna, who is the ghost of a drowned person. He is always on the look-out for someone to take his place, so he drags in people who come to fish in his domains.[1] He is particularly feared by the Magahiya Doms, a caste of degraded nomadic gipsies who infest Gorakhpur and Behâr.

Many of these demons, such as the Nâga and Nâgin, have kingdoms and palaces stored with treasure under the water, and there they entice young men and maidens, who occasionally come back to their mortal kindred and tell them of the wonders which they have seen. These are akin to Morgan la Fay of the Orlando Innamorato, La Motte Fouqué's Undine, and they often merge into the mermaid of the Swan Maiden type of tale, who marries a mortal lover and leaves him at last because in his folly he breaks some taboo which is a condition of the permanence of their love.

But besides these dragons which infest rivers and lakes there are special water gods, many of which are the primitive water monster in a developed form. Such is Mahishâsura, who is the Mahishoba of Berâr, and like the Bhainsâsura already mentioned, infests great rivers and demands propitiation. According to the early mythology this Mahisha, the buffalo demon, was killed by Kârttikeya at the Krauncha pass in the Himâlaya, which was opened by the god to make a passage for the deities to visit the plains from Kailâsa. The Kols, again, have Nâga Era, who presides over tanks, wells, and any stagnant water, and Garha Era, the river goddess. "They," as Col. Dalton remarks, "are frequently and very truly denounced as the cause of sickness and propitiated with sacrifices to spare their victims."[2]

[1] Tylor, "Primitive Culture," i. 109.
[2] "Descriptive Ethnology, 188.

FLOODS AND DROWNING PEOPLE.

Floods are, as we have seen, regarded as produced by demoniacal agency. In the Panjâb, when a village is in danger of floods, the headman makes an offering of a cocoa-nut and a rupee to the flood demon. As in many other places the cocoa-nut represents the head of a human victim, which in olden times was the proper offering. He holds the offering in his hand and stands in the water. When the flood rises high enough to wash the offering from his hand, it is believed that the waters will abate. Some people throw seven handfuls of boiled wheat and sugar into the stream and distribute the remainder among the persons present. Some take a male buffalo, a horse, or a ram, and after boring the right ear of the victim, throw it into the water. If the victim be a horse, it should be saddled before it is offered. A short time ago, when the town and temples at Hardwâr were in imminent danger during the Gohna flood, the Brâhmans poured vessels of milk, rice and flowers into the waters of Mother Ganges and prayed to her to spare them.

In the same connection may be noticed the very common prejudice which exists in India against saving drowning people. This is familiar in Western folk-lore. It is supposed to be alluded to in the "Twelfth Night" of Shakespeare, and the plot of Sir W. Scott's "Pirate" turns upon it. Numerous instances of the same idea have been collected by Dr. Tylor and Mr. Conway.[1] Dr. Tylor considers that it is based upon the belief that to snatch a victim from the very clutches of the water spirit is a rash defiance of the deity which would hardly pass unavenged. Mr. Black[2] accounts for the idea on the ground that the spirits of people who have died a violent death may return to earth if they can find a substitute; hence the soul of the last dead man is insulted or injured by anyone preventing another from taking his place. This last theory is very common in Western folk-lore. Thus Lady Wilde writes from Ireland[3]:—"It is be-

[1] "Primitive Culture," i. 108 sq.; "Demonology," i. 205.

[2] "Folk Medicine," 28 sq.

[3] "Legends," 82 sq.

lieved that the spirit of the dead last buried has to watch in the churchyard until another corpse is laid there, or to perform menial offices in the spirit world, such as carrying wood and water, till the next spirit comes from earth. They are also sent on messages to earth, chiefly to announce the coming death of some relative, and at this they are glad, for their own time of peace and rest will come at last." So in Argyllshire,[1] it was believed that the spirit of the last interred kept watch around the churchyard until the arrival of another occupant, to whom its custody was transmitted. This, as we shall see in connection with the custom of barring the return of the ghost, quite agrees with popular feeling in India, and furnishes an adequate explanation of the prejudice against rescuing the drowning and incurring the wrath of the former ghost, who is thus deprived of the chance of release by making over his functions to a substitute.

KHWÂJA KHIZR, THE GOD OF WATER.

But besides these water spirits and local river gods, the Hindus have a special god of water, Khwâja Khizr, whose Muhammadan title has been Hinduised into Râja Kidâr, or as he is called in Bengal, Kâwaj or Pîr Badr. This is a good instance of a fact, which will be separately discussed elsewhere, that the Hindus are always ready to annex the deities and beliefs of other races.

According to the Sikandarnâma, Khwâja Khizr was a saint of Islâm, who presided over the well of immortality, and directed Alexander of Macedon in his vain search for the blessed waters. The fish is his vehicle, and hence its image is painted over the doors of both Hindus and Muhammadans, while it became the family crest of the late royal house of Oudh. Among Muhammadans a prayer is said to Khwâja Khizr at the first shaving of a boy, and a little boat is launched in a river or tank in his honour. The same rite is performed at the close of the rainy season, when it is supposed to have some connection with the saint Ilisha, that is

[1] Brand, "Observations," 480.

to say the prophet Elisha. Elisha, by the way, apparently from the miraculous way in which his bones revived the dead, has come down in modern times to Italy as a worker of miracles, and is known to the Tuscan peasant as Elisaeus.[1]

Another legend represents Khwâja Khizr to be of the family of Noah, who is also regarded by rural Muhammadans as a water deity in connection with the flood. Others connect him with St. George, the patron saint of England, who is the Ghergis of Syria, and according to Muhammadan tradition was sent in the time of the Prophet to convert the King of Maushil, and came to life after three successive martyrdoms. Others identify him with Thammuz, Tauz, or Adonis. Others call him the companion of Moses, and the commentator Husain says he was a general in the army of *Z*u'l Qarnain, "he of the horns," or Alexander the Great.[2]

Out of this jumble of all the mythologies has been evolved the Hindu god of water, the patron deity of boatmen, who is invoked by them to prevent their boats from being broken or submerged, or to show them the way when they have lost it. He is worshipped by burning lamps, feeding Brâhmans, and by setting afloat on a village pond a little raft of grass with a lighted lamp placed upon it. This, it may be noted, is one of the many ways in which the demon of evil or disease is sent away in many parts of the world.[3] Another curious function is, in popular belief, allotted to Khwâja Khizr, that of haunting markets in the early morning and fixing the rates of grain, which he also protects from the Evil Eye.[4]

THE FOLK-LORE OF WELLS.

In this connection some of the folk-lore of wells may be mentioned. The digging of a well is a duty requiring infinite

[1] Leland, "Etruscan Roman Remains," 242.

[2] Herklots, "Qânûn-i-Islâm," 21, 66 sq, 292; Hughes, "Dictionary of Islâm, s.v.

[3] Frazer, "Golden Bough," ii. 185.

[4] Ibbetson, "Panjâb Ethnography," 114; "Panjâb Notes and Queries," ii. 1; iii. 7; iv. 68.

care and caution. The work should begin on Sunday, and on the previous Saturday night little bowls of water are placed round the proposed site, and the one which dries up least marks the best site for the well, which reminds us of the fleece of Gideon. The circumference is then marked and they commence to dig, leaving the central lump of earth intact. They cut out this clod of earth last and in the Panjâb call it Khwâjajî, perhaps after Khwâja Khizr, the water god, worship it and feed Brâhmans. If it breaks it is a bad omen, and a new site will be selected a week afterwards. Further east when a man intends to sink a well he inquires from the Pandit an auspicious moment for commencing the work. When that hour comes he worships Gaurî, Ganesa, Sesha Nâga, the world serpent, the earth, the spade and the nine planets. Then facing in the direction in which, according to the directions of the Pandit, Sesha Nâga is supposed to be lying at the time, he cuts five clods with the spade. When the workmen reach the point at which the wooden well-curb has to be fixed, the owner smears the curb in five places with red powder, and tying Dûb grass and a sacred thread to it, lowers it into its place. A fire sacrifice is done, and Brâhmans are fed. When the well is ready, cow-dung, milk, cow urine, butter and Ganges water, leaves of the sacred Tulasî and honey are thrown in before the water is used.

But no well is considered lucky until the Sâlagrâma, or spiral ammonite sacred to Vishnu, is solemnly wedded to the Tulasî or basil plant, representing the garden which the well is intended to water. The rite is done according to the standard marriage formula : the relations are assembled ; the owner of the garden represents the bridegroom, while a kinsman of his wife stands for the bride. Gifts are given to Brâhmans, a feast is held in the garden, and both it and the well may then be used without danger. All this is on the same lines as many of the emblematical marriage rites which in other places are intended to promote the growth of vegetation.[1]

[1] Frazer, "Golden Bough," i. 102.

In Sirsa they have a legend that long ago, in time of drought, a headman of a village went to a Faqîr to beg him to pray for rain, and promised him his daughter in marriage if his prayer was successful. The rain came, but the headman would not perform his promise, and the Faqîr cursed the land, so that all the water became brackish. But he so far relented as to permit sweet water to flow on condition that it was given to all men free of cost. In one village the spring became at once brackish when a water-rate was levied, and turned sweet again when the tax was remitted. In another the brackish water became sweet at the intercession of a Faqîr. In the Panjâb there is a class of Faqîrs who are known as Sûnga, or "sniffers," because they can smell out sweet water underground. They work on much the same lines as their brethren in England, who discover springs by means of the divining rod.[1] In one of the tales of Somadeva we have a doll which can produce water at will, which is like Lucian's story of the pestle that was sent to fetch water. When the Egyptian sorcerer was away his pupil tried to perform the trick, but he did not know the charm for making the water stop, and the house was flooded. Then he chopped the pestle in two, but that only made matters worse, for both halves set to bring the water. This is somewhat like the magic quern of European folk-lore.[2]

The water of many wells is efficacious in the cure of disease. In Ireland, the first water drawn from a sacred well after midnight on May Eve is considered an effective antidote to witchcraft.[3] In India many wells have a reputation for curing barrenness, which is universally regarded as a disease, the work of supernatural agency. In India the water of seven wells is collected on the night of the Diwâlî, or feast of lamps, and barren women bathe in it as a means of procuring children. In a well in Orissa the priests throw betel-nuts into the mud, and barren women scramble for them. Those who find them will have their desire for

[1] "Sirsa Settlement Report," 178.
[2] "Katha Sarit Sâgara," i. 258; Clouston, "Popular Tales," i. 118.
[3] Lady Wilde, "Legends," 124.

children gratified before long.[1] For the same reason, after childbirth the mother is taken to worship the village well. She walks round it in the course of the sun and smears the platform with red lead, which is probably a survival of the orginal rite of blood sacrifice. In Dharwâr the child of a Brâhman is taken in the third month to worship water at the village well.[2] In Palâmau the Sârhul feast is observed in the month of Baisâkh (May), when dancing and singing goes on and the headmen entertain their tenants. The whole village is purified, and then they proceed to the village well, which is cleaned out, while the village Baiga does a sacrifice and every one smears the platform with red lead. No one may draw water from the well during the Sârhul.[3] Hydrophobia all over Northern India is cured by looking down seven wells in succession.

In the Panjâb the sites of deserted wells are discovered by driving about a herd of goats, which are supposed to lie down at the place where search should be made. Some people discover wells by dreams; others, as the Luniyas, a caste of navvies, are said, like the Faqîrs in Sirsa, to be able to discover by smell where water is likely to be found. I was once shown a well in the Muzaffarnagar district into which a Faqîr once spat, and for a long time after the visit of the holy man it ran with excellent milk. The supply had ceased, I regret to say, before my visit. The well of life which can survive even the ashes of a corpse is found throughout the Indian folk-tales.[4]

SACRED WELLS.

Sacred wells, of course, abound all over the country. Many of them are supposed to have underground connection with the Ganges or some other holy river. Many of

[1] Ball, "Jungle Life in India," 531; "Panjâb Notes and Queries," ii. 166; Temple, "Legends of the Panjâb," i. 2; Lady Wilde, "Legends," 236 sqq.

[2] Campbell, "Notes," 404.

[3] Forbes, "Settlement Report," 41.

[4] Knowles, "Folk-tales of Kashmîr," 504, with note; "Katha Sarit Sâgara," i. 499.

these are connected with the wanderings of Râma and Sîtâ after their exile from Ayodhya. Sîtâ's kitchen (Sîtâ kî rasoî) is shown in various places, as at Kanauj and Deoriya in the Allahâbâd District.[1] Her well is on the Bindhâchal hill in Mirzapur, and is a famous resort of pilgrims. There is another near Monghyr, and a third in the Sultânpur District in Oudh. The Monghyr well has been provided with a special legend. Sîtâ was suspected of faithlessness during her captivity in the kingdom of Râvana. She threw herself into a pit filled with fire, where the hot spring now flows, and came out purified. When Dr. Buchanan visited the place they had just invented a new legend in connection with it. Shortly before, it was said, the water became so cool as to allow bathing in it. The governor prohibited the practice, as it made the water so dirty that Europeans could not drink it. "But on the very day when the bricklayers began to build a wall in order to exclude the bathers, the water became so hot that no one could dare to touch it, so that the precaution being unnecessary, the work of the infidels was abandoned."[2]

At Benares are the Manikarnika well, which was produced by an ear-ring of Siva falling into it, and the Jnânavâpi, to drink of which brings wisdom. The well at Sihor in Râjputâna is sacred to Gautama, and is considered efficacious in the cure of various disorders. At Sarkuhiya in the Basti District is a well where Buddha struck the ground with his arrow and caused water to flow, as Moses did from the rock. There are, again, many wells which give omens. In the Middle Ages people used to resort to the fountain of Baranta in the Forest of Breclieu and fling water from a tankard on a stone close by, an act which was followed by thunder, lightning and rain.[3] At a Cornish well people used to go and inquire about absent friends. If the person "be living and in health, the still, quiet waters of the well pit will instantly bubble or boil up as a pot of clear, crystalline water; if sick, foul and puddled water; if dead, it will

[1] Führer, "Monumental Antiquities," 80, 134.
[2] "Eastern India," ii. 43.
[3] Rhys, "Lectures," 184.

neither boil nor bubble up, nor alter its colour or stillness."[1] Many other instances of the same fact might be given. So in Kashmîr, in one well water rushes out when a sheep or goat is sacrificed; another runs if the ninth of any month happen to fall on Friday; in a third, those who have any special needs throw in a nut; if it floats, it is considered an omen of success; if it sinks, it is considered adverse. At Askot, in the Himâlaya, there is a holy well which is used for divination of the prospects of the harvest. If the spring in a given time fills the brass vessel to the brim into which the water falls, there will be a good season; if only a little water comes, drought may be expected.[2]

HOT SPRINGS.

Hot springs are naturally regarded as sacred. We have already noticed an example in the case of Sîtâ's well at Monghyr. The holy tract in the hills, known as Vaishnava Kshetra, contains several hot springs, in which Agni, the fire god, resides by the permission of Vishnu. The hot springs at Jamnotri are occupied by the twelve Rishis who followed Mahâdeva from Lanka.[3]

WATERFALLS.

Waterfalls, naturally uncommon in the flat country of Upper India, are, as might have been expected, regarded with veneration, and the deity of the fall is carefully propitiated. The visitor to the magnificent waterfall in which the river Chandraprabha pours its waters over a sheer precipice three hundred feet high in its descent from the Vindhyan plateau to the Gangetic valley, will learn that it is visited by women, particularly those who are desirous of offspring. On a rock beside the fall they lay a simple offering consisting of a few glass bangles, ear ornaments

1 Hunt, "Popular Romances," 292.
2 Atkinson, "Himâlayan Gazetteer," ii. 793, 798.
3 Ibid., iii. 38.

made of palm leaves, and cotton waist strings. In Garhwâl there is a waterfall known as Basodhâra, which ceases to flow when it is looked at by an impure person.[1]

SACRED LAKES.

There are also numerous lakes which are considered sacred and visited by pilgrims. Such is Pushkar, or Pokhar, the lake *par excellence*, in Râjputâna. One theory of the sanctity of this lake is that it was originally a natural depression and enlarged at a subsequent date by supernatural agency. "Every Hindu family of note has its niche for purposes of devotion. Here is the only temple in India sacred to Brahma, the Creator. While he was creating the world he kindled the sacred fire; but his wife Sawantarî was nowhere to be found, and as without a woman the rites could not proceed, a Gûjar girl took her place. Sawantârî on her return was so enraged at the indignity that she retired to the height close by, known as Ratnagirî, or 'the hill of gems,' where she disappeared. On this spot a fountain gushed out, still called by her name, close to which is her shrine, not the least attractive in the precincts of Pokhar." Like many of these lakes, such as are known in Great Britain as the Devil's Punch-bowls, Pokhar has its dragon legend, and one of the rocks near the lake is known as Nâgpahâr, or "Dragon Hill." There is a similar legend attached to the Lonâr Lake in Berâr, which was then the den of the giant Lonâsura, whom Vishnu destroyed.[2]

Most famous of all the lakes is Mâna Sarovara in Tibet, about which many legends are told. "The lake of Mâna Sarovara was formed from the mind of Brahma, and thence derived its name. There dwell also Mahâdeva and the gods, and thence flow the Sarjû and other female rivers, and the Satadru (Satlaj) and other male rivers. When the earth of Mâna Sarovara touches any one's body, or when

[1] Atkinson, "Himâlayan Gazetteer," iii. 26.

[2] Tod, "Annals," i. 814 sq.; Conway, "Demonology," i. 113; "Berâr Gazetteer," 169.

any one bathes therein, he shall go to the Paradise of Brahma; and he who drinks its waters shall go to the Heaven of Siva, and shall be released from the sins of a hundred births; and even the beast which bears the name of Mâna Sarovara shall go to the Paradise of Brahma." It is said that the sons of Brahma, Marichi, Vasishtha and the rest of the sages proceeded to the north of Himâlaya and performed austerities on Mount Kailâsa, where they saw Siva and Pârvatî and remained for twelve years absorbed in meditation and prayer. There was very little rain and water was scanty. In their distress they appealed to Brahma. He asked them what their wishes might be. The Rishis replied, "We are absorbed in devotion on Kailâsa, and must always go thence to bathe in the Mandâkinî river; make a place for us to bathe in." Then Brahma, by a mental effort, formed the holy lake of Mânasa, and the Rishis worshipped the golden Linga which rose from the midst of the waters of the lake.[1]

So the Nainî Tâl Lake is sacred to Kâlî in one of her numerous forms. The goddess Sambrâ, the tutelary deity of the Chauhân Râjputs, converted a dense forest into a plain of gold and silver. But they, dreading the strife which such a possession would excite, begged the goddess to retract her gift, and she gave them the present lake of salt.[2] The people say that the Katûr valley was once a great lake where lived a Râkshasa named Râna who used to devour the inhabitants of the neighbouring villages. Indra's elephant Airâvata descended to earth at the place now known after him by the name Hâthi Chîna, and with his mighty tusks he burst the embankment of the lake and the water flowed away, so that the goddess Bhrawarî, whose shrine is there to this day, was enabled to destroy the monster.

THE LAKE OF THE FAIRY GIFTS.

In the Chânda District of the Central Provinces is the

[1] From the "Mânasa Khanda"; Atkinson, "Himâlayan Gazetteer," ii. 308.

[2] "Rajputâna Gazetteer," ii. 131.

lake of Taroba or Tadala, which is connected with an interesting series of folk-lore legends. A marriage procession was once passing the place, and, finding no water, a strange old man suggested that the bride and bridegroom should join in digging for a spring. They laughingly consented, and after removing a little earth a clear fountain gushed forth. As they were all drinking with delight the waters rose, and spreading over the land, overwhelmed the married pair. "But fairy hands soon constructed a temple in the depths, where the spirits of the drowned are supposed to dwell. Afterwards, on the lake side, a palm tree grew up, which appeared only during the day, sinking into the earth at twilight. One day a rash pilgrim seated himself on the tree and was borne into the skies, where the flames of the sun consumed him." This part of the story reads like a genuine solar myth. "The palm tree then shrivelled away into dust, and in its place appeared an image of the spirit of the lake, which is worshipped under the name of Taroba, or 'the palm-tree deity.' Formerly, at the call of pilgrims, all necessary vessels rose from the lake, and after being washed were returned to the waters. But an evil-minded man at last took those he had received to his house, and from that day the mystic provision wholly ceased."

This legend of the fairy gifts which are lost through the selfish greed of some mean-spirited man has been admirably illustrated by Mr. Hartland. It is also told of the Amner Lake in Elichpur, of the Karsota Lake in Mirzapur, and of many other places.[1]

Many of these lakes possess subaqueous palaces beneath their waters. At Cudden Point in Cornwall, the unhallowed revelry of a party of roisterers is heard from under the waves.[2] In one of Somadeva's stories the hero dives after a lady, and comes on a splendid temple of Siva; Sattvasila falls into the sea and finds a city with palaces of gold, supported on pillars of jewels; Yasahketu plunges into the sea and finds a city gleaming with palaces that had bright pillars of

[1] "Science of Fairy Tales," chapter vi.; "Berâr Gazetteer," 148.
[2] Hunt, "Popular Romances," 194.

precious stone, walls flashing with gold, and latticed windows of pearl. So in the sixth fable of the second chapter of the Hitopadesa, the hero dives into the water and sees a princess seated on a couch in a palace of gold, waited on by youthful sylphs. The sage Mandakarni alarmed the gods by his austerities, and Indra sent five of his fairies to beguile him. They succeeded, and now dwell in a house beneath the waters of the lake called from them Panchapsaras. At the Lake of Taroba, the tale of which has been already told, on quiet nights the country people hear faint sounds of drum and trumpet passing round the lake, and old men say that in one dry year when the waters sank low, golden pinnacles of a fairy temple were seen glittering in the depths. This is exactly the legend of Lough Neagh, immortalized by Thomas Moore.

THE SHÂHGARH LAKE.

A lake at Shâhgarh in the Bareilly District is the seat of another legend which appears widely in folk-lore. When Râja Vena ruled the land, he, like Buddha, struck by the inequality of human life, retired with his young wife Sundarî or Ketakî to live like a peasant. One day she went to the lake to draw water, and she had naught but a jar of unbaked clay and a thread of untwisted cotton. In the innocence of her heart she stepped into the lake, but the gods preserved her. After a time she wearied of this sordid life, and one morning she arrayed herself in her queenly robes and jewels, and going to the lake, as usual, stepped on the lotus petals. When she plunged in her jar it melted away, and the untwisted thread broke, and she herself sank beneath the water. But she was saved, and thenceforward learned the evil of vanity and pride in riches, and the strength of innocence and a pure mind. And the lotus pool, in honour of the good queen Sundarî, was called by all men the Rânî Tâl, or "the Queen's Tank," and is to be seen to this day just outside the town of Kâbar, though the lotus flowers have perished and the castle of Shâhgarh has sunk into dust.[1]

The same tale is told in Southern India of Renukâ, the mother of Parasurâma. In its Western form it is told in Switzerland of a pious boy who served a monastery, and in his innocence was able to carry water in a sieve without spilling a single drop.[2]

OTHER SACRED TANKS.

The number of lakes and tanks associated with some legend, or endued with some special sanctity of their own, is legion. Thus, the tank at Chakratîratha, near Nîmkhâr, marks the spot where the Chakra or discus of Vishnu fell during his contest with Asuras.[3] That near the Satopant glacier is said to be fathomless, and no bird can fly over it. Bhotiyas presents offerings to the lake, requesting the water spirit to keep the passes open and aid them in their dangerous journeys. As they are denied entrance into the temple of Badarinâth, it has for them all the virtue of Badarinâth itself.[4] Another famous tank is that at Amritsar, "the Lake of Immortality." A holy woman once took pity on a leper, and carried him to the banks of the tank. As he lay there a crow swooped into the water and came out a dove as white as snow. The leper saw the miracle, bathed, and was healed. The woman on her return could not recognize her friend, and withdrew in horror from his embraces. But the Guru Râm Dâs came and explained matters, and the grateful pair assisted him in embellishing the tank, which has become the centre of the Sikh religion. The Tadag Tâl in the Hills is sacred to Bhîm Sen, and the curious fish which it contains are said to be lice from the body of the hero.

[1] "Bareilly Settlement Report," 20; Führer, "Monumental Antiquities," 26; "Bhandâra Settlement Report," 47; Temple, "Legends of the Panjâb," i. 39.

[2] Oppert, "Ancient Inhabitants," 467; Grimm, "Household Tales," ii. 466.

[3] Führer, *loc cit.*, 290.

[4] "Himâlayan Gazetteer," iii. 27.

One day a Brâhman was passing the Mandkalla tank and saw a marriage party sitting before the wedding feast; but they were all most unaccountably silent and motionless. They asked him to join in the meal, and he did so with some misgivings, which were soon justified when he saw the heads of the whole party fall off before his eyes, and they soon disappeared.[1] The Râja Râma Chandra Sena was once hunting near the site of the present Dharâwat tank. He saw a crow drinking from a puddle, and, being in want of water, he ordered the courtiers to have a tank dug, the limits of which were to be the space that his horse would gallop round when released. Fortunately for them they selected a site close to some hills which checked the course of the horse. This reduced the tank to comparatively moderate dimensions.[2]

The tank at Lalitpur is famous for the cure of leprosy. One day, a Râja afflicted with the disease was passing by, and his Rânî dreamt that he should eat some of the confervæ on the surface. He ate it, and was cured; and next night the Rânî dreamt that there was a vast treasure concealed there, which when dug up was sufficient to pay the cost of excavation.[3] So, at Qasûr is the tank of the saint Basant Shâh, in which children are bathed to cure them of boils.

Of the Rin Mochan pool the Brâhmans say that any one who bathes there becomes free from debt.[4] Another at Pushkar turns red if the shadow of a woman during her menstrual period fall upon it.[5] Sîtâ proved her virtue by bathing in a tank. She prayed to Mother Earth, who appeared and carried her to the other bank, an incident of which a curious parallel is quoted by Mr. Clouston from the Gospel of the pseudo Mathew.[6] In the legend of Chyavana, as told in the Mahâbhârata, the three suitors of Sukanyâ bathed in a tank and came forth of a celestial beauty equal to hers. So in one of the Bengal folk-tales the old discarded

[1] "Archæological Reports," iv. 192.
[2] Ibid., viii. 39.
[3] Ibid., xxi. 175.
[4] Ibid., xiv. 76.
[5] Oppert, "Original Inhabitants," 289.
[6] "Popular Tales," i. 176.

wife bathes in a tank and recovers her youth and beauty.[1] It is a frequent condition imposed on visitors to these holy tanks that they should remove a certain quantity of earth and thus improve it.

Many tanks, again, are supposed to contain buried treasure which is generally in charge of a Yaksha. Hence such places are regarded with much awe. There is a tank of this kind in the Bijaygarh fort in the Mirzapur District, where many speculators have dug in vain; another forms an incident in Lâl Bihâri Dê's tale of Govinda Sâmanta.[2]

MOUNTAIN-WORSHIP; THE HIMÂLAYA.

"He who thinks of Himâchal (the Himâlaya), though he should not behold him, is greater than he who performs all worship at Kâsi (Benares); as the dew is dried up by the morning sun, so are the sins of mankind by the sight of Himâchal."[3] Such was the devotion with which the early Hindus looked on it as the home of the gods. Beyond it their fancy created the elysium of Uttara Kuru, which may be most properly regarded as an ideal picture created by the imagination of a life of tranquil felicity, and not as a reminiscence of any actual residence of the Kurus in the north.[4]

From early times the Himâlayan valleys were the resort of the sage and the ascetic. Almost every hill and river is consecrated by their legends, and the whole country teems with memories of the early religious life of the Hindu race. As in the mythology of many other peoples,[5] it was regarded as the home of the sainted dead, and the common source or origin of Hinduism. Its caves were believed to be the

[1] Lâl Bihâri Diê, "Folk-tales of Bengal," 281; "Berâr Gazetteer," 158, 176; "Panjâb Notes and Queries," iii. 42; Wright, "History of Nepâl," 135; "Bombay Gazetteer," v. 440; "Râjputana Gazetteer," ii. 220.

[2] i. 17.

[3] "Mânasa Khanda"; Atkinson, "Himâlayan Gazetteer," ii. 271.

[4] See the remarks by Lassen, quoted by Muir, "Ancient Sanskrit Texts," ii. 337.

[5] Spencer, "Principles of Sociology," i. 200 sq., 210, 336.

haunt of witches and fairies. Demons lurked in its recesses, as at the Blockberg, where, as Aubrey tells us, "the devils and witches do dance and feast."[1] Many of its most noted peaks are the home of the deities. Siva and Kuvera rest on Mount Kailâsa; Vaikuntha, the paradise of Vishnu, is on Mount Meru. The whole range is personified in Himavat, who is the father of Gangâ and Umâ Devî, who from her origin is known as Pârvatî, or "the mountaineer." One of the titles of Siva is Girisa, the "mountain god." His son Kârttikeya delights in the weird mountain heights.

MOUNTAIN-WORSHIP AMONG THE DRÂVIDIANS.

But, deeply rooted as the veneration for mountains is in the minds of the early Aryans, there is reason to suspect that this regard for mountains may be a survival from the beliefs of non-Aryan races whom the Hindus supplanted or absorbed. At any rate, the belief in the sanctity of mountains widely prevails among the non-Aryan or Drâvidian races. Most of these peoples worship mountains in connection with the god of the rain. The Santâls sacrifice to Marang Bura on a flat rock on the top of a mountain, and after feasting, work themselves up into a state of frenzy to charm the rain. The Korwas and Kûrs worship in the same way Mainpât, a plateau in the mountainous country south of the Son. The Nâgbansis and the Mundâri Kols worship a huge rock as the abode of the "great god," Baradeo.[2] So, in Garhwâl in the Chhipula pass is a shrine to the god of the mountain. At Tolma is a temple to the Himâlaya, and below Dungagiri in the same valley is a shrine in honour of the same peak.[3] In Hoshangâbâd in the Central Indian plateau, Sûryabhân or "Sun-rays" is a very common name for isolated round-peaked hills, on which the god is supposed to dwell, and among the Kurkus, Dungardeo, the mountain

[1] "Remaines," 18; Sir W. Scott, "Lectures on Demonology," 135.
[2] Dalton, "Descriptive Ethnology," 188, 210, 223, 230, 135, 186; Lubbock, "Origin of Civilization," 306.
[3] Atkinson, "Himâlayan Gazetteer," ii. 832.

god, resides on the nearest hill outside the village. He is worshipped every year at the Dasahra festival with a goat, two cocoa-nuts, five dates, with a ball of vermilion paste, and is regarded by them as their special god.[1] The idea that dwarfs, spirits, and fairies live on the tops of mountains is a common belief in Europe.

As in the Himâlaya, one of the main peaks, Nandâ Devî, has been identified with Pârvatî, the mountain goddess, so the aborigines of the Central Provinces have in Kattarpâr, the Kattipen of the Khândhs, a special deity of ravines, as Rhœa Sybeli was to the Etruscans.[2] In the Mirzapur hills the aboriginal tribes have an intense respect for mountains. On the Mâtra hill lives a Deo or demon known as Darrapât Deo. When Râvana abducted Sîtâ he is said to have kept her on this hill for some time, and her palanquin, turned into stone, is there to this day. No one ascends the mountain through fear of the demon, except an Ojha or sorcerer, who sacrifices a goat at the foot of the hill before he makes the attempt. So, in Garhwâl the peak of Barmdeo is sacred to Devî, and none can intrude with impunity. A Faqîr who ventured to do so in the days of yore was pitched across the river by the offended goddess.[3] On another Mirzapur hill, Chainpur, lives Kotî Rânî, who is embodied in the locusts which usually are found there. Similarly Pahâr Pando is a mountain deity of the Dharkârs, a sub-caste of the Doms. Bansaptî Mâî, who is half a forest and half a mountain goddess, lives on Jhurma hill, and if any one dares to sing in her neighbourhood, he becomes sick or mad. These mountain demons often take the form of tigers and kill incautious intruders on their domains. On the Aunri hill are two dreaded demons, Deorâsan and Birwat, the latter a Bîr or malignant ghost of some one who died a violent death. They rule the hail, and at harvest time the Baiga offers a goat, and spreading rice on the ground, prays—"O Lord

1 "Settlement Report," 121, 254.

2 Atkinson, *loc. cit.*, ii. 792; Hislop, "Papers," 14; Leland, "Etruscan Roman Remains," 139.

3 Atkinson, *loc. cit.*, iii. 48.

Mahâdeva! May this offering be effectual." Mangesar, the rugged peak which frowns over the valley of the Son, is a popular local god of the various Kolarian races, and a shrine to Bâba or Râja Mangesar, "the father and the king," is found in many of their villages.

RESPECT PAID TO THE VINDHYA AND KAIMÛR RANGES.

The Kaimûr and Vindhyan ranges also enjoy a certain amount of sanctity. On the latter the most famous shrines are those of Asthbhuja or "the eight-armed Devî," Sîtâkunda or the pool of Sîtâ, and the temple of Mahârânî Vindhyeswarî, the patron goddess of the range, built where it trends towards the Gangetic valley. She has travelled as far as Cutch, where she is worshipped under the corrupted name of Vinjân.[1] Her shrine has evil associations with traditions of human sacrifice, derived from the coarser aboriginal cultus which has now been adopted into Brâhmanism.[2] There the Thags used to meet and share their spoils with their patron goddess, and her Pandas or priests are so disorderly that a special police guard has to be posted at the shrine to ensure the peaceable division of the offerings among the sharers, who mortgage and sell their right to participate in the profits, like the advowson of a living in the English Church.

These two ranges, says the legend, are an offshoot from the Himâlaya. When Râma was building the bridge across the strait to Lanka, he sent his followers to Himâlaya to collect materials. They returned with a mighty burden, but meanwhile the hero had completed his task; so he ordered them to throw down their loads, and where the stones fell these ranges were produced. In the same way the Maniparvata at Ajudhya is said to have been dropped by Sugrîva, the monkey king of Kishkindhya, and the Irichh hills at Jhânsi are described to have been formed in the same way.

[1] "Bombay Gazetteer," v. 252.

[2] Human sacrifice to the Durgâ of the Vindhyas occurs often in Indian folk-lore. See Tawney, "Katha Sarit Sâgara," i. 64.

There is another legend of the Vindhyas told in the story of Nala and Damayantî. They were jealous of the Himâlaya, the peaks of which were each morning visited by the earliest rays of the rising sun. The sun, on being appealed to, declared that it was impossible for him to change his course. Immediately the Vindhyas swelled with rage, and rising in the heavens, intercepted the view of the sun, moon, and the constellations. The gods, alarmed, invoked the aid of the saint Agastya. He went, accompanied by his wife, and requested the Vindhyas to sink and let him pass to the south, and not rise till he returned. They agreed, and gave passage to the saint, but as he never came back they have never resumed their former height. Agastya finally settled on the Malayam or Potiyam mountain, not far from Cape Comorin. He now shines in the heavens as the regent of the star Canopus, and to him is ascribed almost all the civilization of Southern India. The legend possibly goes back to the arrival of the earliest Brâhmanic missionaries in Southern India, and the name of the range, which probably means "the divider," marked the boundary between the Aryan and Drâvidian peoples. A similar story is told of one of the ranges in Nepâl.[1]

OTHER FAMOUS HILLS.

A mention of some other famous hills in Northern India may close this account of mountain-worship. At Gaya is the Dharma Sila, or "rock of piety," which was once the wife of the saint Marîchi. The lord of the infernal regions, by order of Brahma, crushed it down on the head of the local demon.[2] The hills of Goghar kâ dhâr, in the Mundi State, have a reputation similar to that of the Brocken in the Hartz mountains on Wulpurgis night. On the 3rd of September the demons, witches, and magicians from the most distant parts of India assemble here and hold their revels, from

[1] Oppert, "Original Inhabitants," 24; Wright, "History of Nepâl," 178.

[2] Buchanan, "Eastern India," i. 51 sq.; Tawney, "Katha Sarit Sâgara," ii. 333.

which time it is dangerous for men to cross the mountains. The spirits of the Kulu range are said to wage war with those of the Goghar, and after a violent storm the peasants will show the traveller the stones which have been hurled from range to range. The last chief of Mundi was a mighty wizard himself. He had a little book of spells which the demons were forced to obey, and when he placed it in his mouth he was instantly transported where he pleased through the air.[1]

Another famous hill is that of Govardhan, near Mathura. This is the hill which Krishna is fabled to have held aloft on the tip of his finger for seven days, to protect the people of Braj from the tempests poured down on them by Indra when he was deprived of his wonted sacrifices. There is a local belief that as the waters of the Jumnâ are yearly decreasing in volume, so this hill is gradually sinking. Not a particle of stone is allowed to be removed from it, and even the road which crosses it at its lowest point, where only a few fragments of the rock crop up overground, had to be carried over them by a paved causeway.[2]

THE SPIRITS OF THE AIR.

"Aerial spirits or devils are such as keep quarter in the air, cause many tempests, thunder and lightnings, tear oaks, fire steeples, houses, strike men and beasts, make it rain wool, frogs, etc. They cause whirlwinds on a sudden, and tempestuous storms, which though our meteorologists refer to natural causes, yet I am of Bodin's mind that they are more often caused by those aerial devils in their several quarters."[3] This statement of Burton is a good summary of current Hindu opinion on this subject; and it is just this class of physical phenomena which civilized man admits to be beyond his control, that primitive races profess to be able to regulate. As Dr. Taylor puts it—"The rainfall is passing

[1] Griffin, "Râjas of the Panjâb."

[2] Growse, "Mathura," 278, where all the local legends are given in full.

[3] "Anatomy of Melancholy," 123.

from the region of the supernatural to join the tides and seasons in the realm of physical science."[1]

The old weather god was Indra, who wars with Vritra or Ahi, the dragon demon of drought, whom he compels to dispense the rain. He was revered as the causer of fertility, and feared as the lord of the lightning and the thunder. He has now been deposed from his pre-eminence, and is little more than a *roi fainéant*, who lives in a luxurious heaven of his own, solaced by the dances of the fairies who form his court, one of whom he occasionally bestows on some favoured mortal who wins his kindness or forces him to obey his orders. But his status is at present decidedly low, and it is remarkable in what a contemptuous way even so orthodox a poet as Tulasî Dâs speaks of him.[2] Mr. Wheeler[3] suggests that this degradation of Indra may possibly be due to the fact that he was a tribal god notoriously hostile to Brâhmans; and it is certainly very suggestive from this point of view that he has come to be regarded as the great deity of the Burman Buddhists. It is still further remarkable that at Benares, the headquarters of Brâhmanism, he has been replaced by a special rain god, Dalbhyeswara, who perhaps takes his name from Dalbhya, an ancient Rishi, who must be worshipped and kept properly dressed if the seasons are not to become unfavourable.[4]

BHÎMSEN, A WEATHER GODLING.

Bhîmsen, of whom more will be said later on, is regarded by the Gonds as a god of rain, and has a festival of four or five days' duration held in his honour at the end of the rainy season, when two poles about twenty feet high and five feet apart are set up with a rope attached to the top, by which the boys of the village climb up and then slide down the poles. This is apparently an instance of rude sympathetic magic, representing the descent of the rain.[5]

1 "Primitive Culture," ii. 261.
2 Growse, "Râmâyana," 318.
3 "History of India," chapter iii. 21, 330.
4 Sherring, "Sacred City," 129.
5 Hislop, "Papers," 18.

TANK OF BHÎMSEN, HARDWÂR.

DEMONIACAL CONTROL OF THE WEATHER.

It is an idea common to the beliefs of many races, that the spirits of the wind may be tied up in sacks and let out to injure an enemy and assist a friend. To this day the Lapps give their sailors magic sacks containing certain winds to secure them a safe journey.[1]

Another side of the matter may be illustrated from Marco Polo. "During the three months of every year that the Lord (Kublai Khân) resides at that place, if it should happen to be bad weather, there are certain crafty enchanters and astrologers in his train, who are such adepts in necromancy and the diabolical arts, that they are able to prevent any cloud or storm passing over the spot on which the Emperor's palace stands. Whatever they do in this way is by the help of the Devil; but they make those people believe that it is compassed by their own sanctity and the help of God. They always go in a state of dirt and uncleanness, devoid of respect for themselves or for those who see them, unkempt and sordidly attired." Timûr in his "Memoirs" speaks of the Indian Jâts using incantations to produce heavy rain, which hindered his cavalry from acting against them. A Yadachi was captured, and when his head had been taken off the storm ceased. Bâbar speaks of one of his early friends, Khwâjaka Mulai, who was acquainted with Yadagarî, or the art of bringing on rain and snow by incantations. In the same way in Nepâl the control of the weather is supposed to be vested in the Lamas.[2]

RAIN-MAKING AND NUDITY.

One very curious custom of rain-making has a series of remarkable parallels in Europe. In Servia, in time of drought, a girl is stripped and covered with flowers. She dances at each house, and the mistress steps out and pours a jar of water over her, while her companions sing rain

[1] "Folk-lore," iii. 541.

[2] Yule, "Marco Polo," i. 292, 301; Oldfield, "Sketches from Nepâl," ii. 6.

songs.[1] In Russia the women draw a furrow round the village, and bury at the juncture a cock, a cat, and a dog. "The dog is a demonic character in Russia, while the cat is sacred. The offering of both seems to represent a desire to conciliate both sides."[2] Mr. Conway thinks that the nudity of the women represents their utter poverty and inability to give more to conciliate the god of the rain; or that we have here a form of the Godiva and Peeping Tom legend, "where there is probably a distant reflection of the punishment sometimes said to overtake those who gazed too curiously upon the Swan Maiden with her feathers."[3]

The Godiva legend has been admirably illustrated by Mr. Hartland,[4] who comes to the conclusion that it is the survival of an annual rite in honour of a heathen goddess, and closely connected with those nudity observances which we are discussing. The difficulty is, however, to account for the nudity part of the ceremony. It may possibly be based on the theory that spirits dread indecency, or rather the male and female principles.[5]

This may be the origin of the indecencies of word and act practised at the Holî and Kajarî festivals in Upper India, which are both closely connected with the control of the weather. Among the Ramoshis of the Dakkhin the bridegroom is stripped naked before the anointing ceremony commences, and the same custom prevails very generally in Upper India. The Mhârs of Sholapur are buried naked, even the loin-cloth being taken off. Barren women worship a naked female figure at Bijapur. At Dayamava's festival in the Karnâtak, women walk naked to the temple where they make their vows; and the Mâng, who carries the scraps of holy meat which he scatters in the fields to promote fertility, is also naked.[6] The same idea of scaring evil

[1] "Notes and Queries," v. Ser. iii. 424; Farrer, "Primitive Manners," 70; Frazer, "Golden Bough," i. 16.

[2] Conway, "Demonology," i. 267.

[3] Ibid., 224.

[4] "Science of Fairy Tales," 71 sqq.

[5] Campbell, "Notes," 101 sq.

[6] "Bombay Gazetteer," xviii. 416; xxi. 180; "Journal Ethnological Society," N. S. i. 98. In the "Katha Sarit Sâgara," i. 154, the queen Kavalayavalî worships the gods stark naked.

spirits from temples possibly accounts for much of the obscene sculpture to be found on the walls of many Hindu shrines, and it may be noted in illustration of the same principle that in Nepâl temples are decorated with groups of obscene figures as a protection against lightning.[1]

RITES SPECIAL TO WOMEN.

Connected with the same principle it may be noted that in India, as in many other places, there are rites of the nature of the Bona Dea, in which only women take part, and from which males are excluded. In some of these rites nudity forms a part. Thus, in Italy, La Bella Marte is invoked when three girls, always stark naked, consult the cards to know whether a lover is true or which of them is likely to be married.[2] A number of similar usages have been discussed by Mr. Hartland. We have already noticed the custom of sun impregnation. Among Hindus, a woman who is barren and desires a child stands naked facing the sun and desires his aid to remove her barrenness. In one of the folk-tales the witch stands naked while she performs her spells.[3]

The rain custom in India is precisely the same as has been already illustrated by examples from Europe. During the Gorakhpur Famine in 1873-74, there were many accounts received of women going about with a plough by night, stripping themselves naked and dragging the plough over the fields as an invocation of the rain god. The men kept carefully out of the way while this was being done, and it was supposed that if the women were seen by the men the rite would lose its effect. Mr. Frazer on this remarks that "it is not said they plunge the plough into a stream or sprinkle it with water. But the charm would hardly be complete without it."[4] It was on my authority that the

[1] Wright, "History," 10.
[2] Leland, "Etruscan Roman Remains," 148, 301.
[3] "North Indian Notes and Queries," iii. 31, 35.
[4] "Golden Bough," i. 17; "Panjâb Notes and Queries," iii. 41, 115; Hartland, "Science of Fairy Tales," 84.

custom which Messrs. Frazer and Hartland quote was originally recorded, and I do not remember at the time hearing of this part of the ritual. Later inquiries do not point to it as part of the rite in Upper India.

It may be well to adduce other instances of this nudity rite. In Sirsa, when a horse falls sick, the cure is to kill a fowl or a he-goat and let its warm blood flow into the mouth of the animal; but if this cannot be done quickly, it is sufficient for a man to take off all his clothes and strike the horse seven times on the forehead with his shoe.[1] Here the nudity and the blows with the shoe are means to drive off the demon of disease. In Chhattarpur, when rain falls a woman and her husband's sister take off all their clothes and drop seven cakes of cow-dung into a mud reservoir for storing grain. If a man and his maternal uncle perform the same ceremony, it is equally effective; but as a rule women do it, and the special days for the rite are Sunday and Wednesday. Here we have the custom in process of modification, males, one of whom is a relation in the female line, being substituted for the female officiants.

Another similar means of expelling the demon of disease is given by Mrs. Fanny Parkes in her curious book entitled "Wanderings of a Pilgrim in search of the Picturesque."[2] "The Hindu women in a most curious way propitiate the goddess who brings cholera into the bâzâr. They go out in the evening, about 7 p.m., sometimes two or three hundred at a time, each carrying a *lota* or brass vessel filled with sugar, water, cloves, etc. In the first place they make *pûjâ*; then, stripping off their sheets and binding their sole petticoat round their waists, as high above the knee as it can be pulled up, they perform a most frantic sort of dance, forming themselves into a circle, while in the centre of the circle about five or six women dance entirely naked, beating their hands together over their heads, and then applying them behind with a great smack that keeps time with the

[1] "Settlement Report," 207.

[2] I cannot procure this book. The quotation is from "Calcutta Review," xv. 486.

music, and with the song they scream out all the time, accompanied by native instruments played by men who stand at a distance, to the sound of which these women dance and sing, looking like frantic creatures. The men avoid the place where the ceremony takes place, but here and there one or two men may be seen looking on, whose presence does not seem to molest the nut-brown dancers in the least; they shriek and sing and dance and scream most marvellously." Here we find the rule of privacy at these nudity rites slightly modified.

Another instance of the nudity rite in connection with cattle disease comes from Jâlandhar.[1] "When an animal is sick the remedy is for some one to strip himself and to walk round the patient with some burning straw or cane fibre in his hands."

Nudity also appears to be in some places a condition of the erection of a pinnacle on a Hindu temple. "The Temple of Arang in Râêpur district and that at Deobalada were built at the same time. When they were finished and the pinnacles (*kalas*) had to be put on, the mason and his sister agreed to put them on simultaneously at an auspicious moment. The day and hour being fixed by Brâhmans, the two, stripping themselves naked, *according to custom on such occasions*, climbed up to the top. As they got up to the top each could see the other, and each through shame jumped down into the tank close to their respective temples, where they still stand turned into stone, and are visible when the tank water falls low in seasons of drought."[2]

Of the regular nudity rite in case of failure of rain, we have a recent instance from Chunâr in the Mirzapur district. "The rains this year held off for a long time, and last night (24th July, 1892) the following ceremony was performed secretly. Between the hours of 9 and 10 p.m. a barber's wife went from door to door and invited all the women to join in ploughing. They all collected in a field from which all males were excluded. Three women from a cultivator's

[1] "Settlement Report," 135.
[2] Cunningham, "Archæological Reports," vii. 162.

family stripped off all their clothes; two were yoked to a plough like oxen, and a third held the handle. They then began to imitate the operation of ploughing. The woman who had the plough in her hand shouted, 'O Mother Earth! bring parched grain, water and chaff. Our bellies are bursting to pieces from hunger and thirst.' Then the landlord and village accountant approached them and laid down some grain, water and chaff in the field. The women then dressed and went home. By the grace of God the weather changed almost immediately, and we had a good shower."[1] Here we see the ceremony elaborately organized; the privacy taboo is enforced, and the ritual is in the nature of sympathetic magic, intended to propitiate Mother Earth.

The nudity rite for the expulsion of disease is also found in Madras. "The image of Mariyamma, cut out of Margosa wood, is carried from her temple to a stone called a Buddukal, in the centre of the village, on the afternoon of the first day of the feast. A rounded stone, about six inches above the ground and about eight inches across, is to be seen just inside the gate of every village. It is what is called the Baddukal or navel stone; it is worshipped in times of calamity, especially during periods of cattle disease; often women passing it with water pour a little on it, and every one on first going out of the village in the morning is supposed to give it some little tribute of attention. The following day all men and women of Sûdra castes substitute garments of leaves of the Margosa, little branches tied together, for their ordinary clothes, and thus attired go with music to the goddess."[2] Here the dress may imply some form of nudity rite, or may be a reminiscence of the time when, like the Juângs of Chota Nâgpur, they wore leaf aprons.

There can be little doubt that rites of this kind largely prevail in India, but, as might naturally be expected, they are very carefully concealed, and it is extremely difficult to obtain precise information about them.

[1] "North Indian Notes and Queries," i. 210.
[2] Oppert, "Original Inhabitants," 476, quoting Mr. Fawcett.

OTHER RITES TO BRING RAIN.

Besides these nudity rites there are many ways of causing rain to fall. In Kumaun when rain fails they sink a Brâhman up to his lips in a tank, and there he goes on repeating the name of Râja Indra, the god of rain, for a day or two, when rain is sure to fall; or they dig a trench five or six feet deep and make a Brâhman or a Jogi sit in it, when the god, in pity for the holy man, will relent and give rain. Another plan is to hang a frog with his mouth open on a bamboo, and the deity pities him and brings the rain.[1] In Mirzapur they turn a plough upside down and bury it in a field, rub the lingam of Mahâdeva with cow-dung, and offer water at the grave of a Brahm or bachelor Brâhman.

Among the Bhîls in time of drought women and girls go out dancing and singing with bows and arrows in their hands, and seizing a buffalo belonging to another village, sacrifice it to the goddess Kâlî. The headman of the village to which the animal belongs seldom objects to the appropriation of it. If he does, the women by abusing and threatening to shoot him always have their own way.[2] Analogous to this regular rain sacrifice is the custom at Ahmadnagar, where on the bright 3rd of Baisâkh (April-May) the boys of two neighbouring villages fight with slings and stones. The local belief is that if the fight be discontinued, rain fails, or if rain does fall that it produces a plague of rats.[3] At Ahmadâbâd, again, there is a city headman, known as the Nagar Seth or "chief man of the town." When rain holds off he has to perambulate the city walls, pouring out milk to appease Râja Indra.[4] Here we reach the "sympathetic magic" type of observance under which most of the other practices may be classed, though here and there we seem to find the germ of the principle of vicarious sacrifice. Thus in the Panjâb the village girls pour down on an old woman as she passes some cow-dung dissolved in water; or an old woman is made to sit down under the

1 "North Indian Notes and Queries," iii. 134.

2 "Bombay Gazetteer," iii. 221.

3 "Indian Antiquary," v. 5.

4 "Bombay Gazetteer," iv. 114.

house-roof spout and get a wetting when it rains. Here the idea must be that her sufferings in some way propitiate the angry god. In the Muzaffarnagar District, if rain fails, they worship Râja Indra and read the story of the Megha Râja, or king of the rain. In his name they give alms to the poor and release a young bull or buffalo. Crushed grain is cooked on the edge of a tank in his honour and in the name of the rain god Khwâja Khizr, and some offering is made to Bhûmiya, the lord of the soil. In Chhattarpur, on a wall facing the east, they paint two figures with cow-dung—one representing Indra and the other Megha Râja, with their legs up and their heads hanging down. It is supposed that the discomfort thus caused to them will compel them to grant the boon of rain. The Mirzapur Korwas, when rain fails, get the Baiga to make a sacrifice and prayer to Sûraj Deota, the Sun godling.

Another common plan in Upper India is for a gang of women to come out to where a man is ploughing and drive him and his oxen by force back to the village, where he and his cattle are well fed. Another device is to seize the blacksmith's anvil and pitch it into a well or the village tank. We have already given instances of the connection of wells with rainfall, such as the case of the well in Farghâna which caused rain if defiled.[1] Mr. Gomme has collected several European instances of the same belief.[2] The anvil is probably used for this purpose because it is regarded as a sort of fetish, and the blacksmith himself is, as we shall see later on, considered as invested with supernatural powers.

In the Panjâb, apparently on the principle of vicarious sacrifice to which reference has been already made, an earthen pot of filth is carried to the door of some old woman cursed with a bad temper, and thrown down at her threshold, which is a sacred place. If she then falls into a rage and gives vent to her feelings in abusive language, the rain will come down. The old woman is considered a

[1] Jarrett, "Aîn-i-Akbari," ii. 408, quoting Alberuni, chapter viii.
[2] "Ethnology in Folk-lore," 94.

sort of witch, and if she is punished the influence which restrains the rain will be removed.[1]

There are numerous instances in which the king is held responsible for a failure of the rain. In Kângra there are some local gods whose temples are endowed with rent-free lands. When rain is wanted, these deities are ordered to provide it; and if they fail, they have to pay a fine into the Râja's treasury. This is the way the Chinese treat their gods who refuse to do their duty.[2]

The song of Alha and Udal, which describes the struggle between the Hindus and the early Muhammadan invaders, is sung in Oudh to procure rain. In the Hills smart showers are attributed to the number of marriages going on at the time in the plains. The bride and bridegroom, as we shall see in the legend of Dulha Deo, are particularly exposed to the demoniacal influence of the weather. In the Eastern Districts of the North-Western Provinces the people will not kill wolves, as they say that wherever there falls a drop of a wolf's blood the rain will be deficient.

To close this catalogue of devices to procure rain, we may note that it is a common belief that sacred stones are connected with rainfall. In the temple of Mars at Rome there was a great stone cylinder which, when there was a drought, was rolled by the priests through the town.[3] In Mingrelia, to get rain they dip a holy image in water daily till it rains. In Navarre the image of St. Peter was taken to a river, where some prayed to him for rain, but others called out to duck him in the water.[4] A stone in the form of a cross at Iona was used for the same purpose.[5] So in India the relics of Gautama Buddha were believed to have the same influence.[6] In Behâr in seasons of drought a holy stone, known as Nârâyana Chakra, is kept in a vessel of water; sometimes a piece of plantain leaf on which are written the names of one hundred and eight villages beginning with the letter *K* and

1 "Panjâb Notes and Queries," i. 102.
2 Ibid., ii. 41; Lyall, "Asiatic Studies," 136.
3 Leland, "Etruscan Roman Remains," 369.
4 "Golden Bough," i. 14.
5 Brand, "Observations," 753.
6 Beal, "Fah Hian," 78.

not ending in Pur is thrown into the water.[1] In the same way the lingam of Mahâdeva, a thirsty deity, who needs continual cooling to relieve his distress, must be kept continually moist to avoid drought. Not long ago when rain failed at Mirzapur, the people contributed to maintain a gang of labourers who brought water to pour on a famous lingam. The same custom prevails in Samoa.[2] There, when rain was excessive, the stone representing the rain-making god was laid by the fire and kept warm till fine weather set in; but in time of drought the priest and his followers, dressed up in fine mats, went in procession to the stream, dipped the stone, and prayed for a shower.

DEVICES TO CAUSE RAIN TO CEASE.

In England when rain is in excess the little children sing, "Rain! Rain! Go away! Come again on a Saturday!"

In India there are many devices intended to secure the same object. One is the reverse of the nudity charm which we have already discussed. In Madras, a woman, generally an ugly widow, is made to dance, sometimes naked, with a burning stick in her hand and facing the sky. This is supposed to disgust Varuna, the sky god, who shrinks away from such a sight and withholds the rain.[3] Other devices have the same object, to put pressure on the deities who are responsible for the excessive rain. Thus, in Muzaffarnagar the Muni or Rishi Agastya, who is a great personage in early folk-lore, is supposed to have power to stop the rain. When rain is in excess they draw a figure of him on a loin cloth and put it out in the rain. Some paint his figure on the outside of the house and let the rain wash it away. This generally brings him to his senses and he gives relief. Another practice, which is believed to be employed by evil-minded people who are selfishly interested in a drought, is to light a lamp with melted butter and put it outside when

[1] "Panjâb Notes and Queries," iv. 218.
[2] Turner, "Samoa," 45.
[3] "North Indian Notes and Queries," i. 101; Aubrey, "Remaines," 180; Henderson, "Folk-lore of the Northern Counties," 24.

the rain-clouds collect. The rain god is afraid to put out the sacred light, and retires. Another way in use in the Panjâb is to give an unmarried girl some oil and get her to pour it on the ground, saying, "If I pour not out the oil, mine the sin ; if thou disperse not the clouds, thine the sin." In Mirzapur it is considered a good plan to name twenty-one men who are blind of an eye, and consequently ill-omened, and make twenty-one knots in a cord and tie it under the eaves of the house. In Kumaun many devices are used to effect the same result. Some hot oil is poured into the left ear of a dog. When the pain makes him yell it is believed that Râja Indra takes pity on him and stops the rain. Another plan is very like the Mirzapur device. Five, seven, or eleven grains of Urad pulse are placed in a piece of cloth, wrapped up and tied with a treble cord. Each grain bears the name of a blind person, known to the man who is carrying out the rite. This is known as the "binding of the blind men." The packet is either buried under the eaves of a house where the water drips, or put in a tree. The object is to excite the compassion of Râja Indra by their sufferings. Others take seven pieces of granite, seven grains of mustard, and seven bits of goat-dung, parch them in an oven, and then put them under the drip of the eaves. These represent the demons, who are enemies of Indra, and he is so pleased at their discomfiture that he disperses the clouds. Others fix up a harrow perpendicularly where four roads meet. As this instrument is always used in a horizontal position, this indicates that gross injustice is being done to the world, and the rain god relents. Others when the thunder roars in the rain-clouds invoke the saint Agastya, who once drank up all the waters of the world in four sips ; so all the clouds fear him and disperse when he is invoked.

Another favourite plan is to fee a Brâhman to make sixty holes in a piece of wood and run a string through all of them. While he is thus "binding up the rain" he recites spells in honour of the Sun godling, Sûraj Nârâyan, who is moved to interfere. Others take a piece of unleavened bread, go into the fields and place it on the ground; or taking some sugar, rice, and other articles ordinarily used in worship to a place where four roads meet, defile them in a particularly disgusting way. On such substances the rain is ashamed to fall. In Bombay a leaf-plate filled with cooked rice and curds is placed in some open spot where the rain can see it and avoid it. If the rain should persist in coming, a live coal is laid on a tile and placed in some open place, where it is implored to swallow the hateful rain. All these practices are magic of the ordinary sympathetic kind.[1]

Rain-clouds are supposed also to be under the influence of the Evil Eye, and will blow over without giving rain if the malicious glance falls upon them. Hence, when rain is needed, if any one runs out of a house bareheaded while it is raining, he is ordered in at once, or he is told to put on his cap or turban, for a bareheaded man is apt to wish involuntarily that the rain may cease, and thus injure his neighbours.

Everywhere it is believed that the Banya or cornchandler, who is interested in high prices, buries some water in an earthen pot in order to stop the rain.

HAIL AND WHIRLWIND.

The hail and the whirlwind are, like most of the natural phenomena which we have been discussing, attributed to demoniacal agency. The Maruts who ride on the whirlwind and direct the storm hold a prominent place in the Veda, where they are represented as the friends and allies of Indra. Another famous tempest demon was Trinâvartta, who assumed the form of a whirlwind and carried off the infant Krishna, but was killed by the child.

Mr. Leland[2] tells a curious Italian story of a peasant who killed the church sexton with his billhook because he stopped ringing the bell and thus allowed the hail to injure his vines. This illustrates a well-known principle that demons, and in particular the demon who brings the hail, can be scared by

[1] Aubrey, "Remaines," 180; Henderson, "Folk-lore," 24; "Panjâb Notes and Queries," i. 65, 75, 109, 126.

[2] "Etruscan Roman Remains," 217.

noise. Thus Aubrey tells us:[1]—"At Paris, when it begins to thunder and lighten, they do presently ring out the great bell at the Abbey of St. Germain, which they do believe makes it cease. When it thundered and lightened they did ring St. Adelm's bell in Malmesbury Abbey. The curious do say that the ringing of bells exceedingly disturbs spirits." Hence one plan of driving away the hail is to take out an iron griddle-plate and beat it with a bamboo. Here the use of iron, a well-known demon scarer, increases the efficacy of the rite. It is also an improvement if this be done by a virgin, and in some places it is considered sufficient if when the hail falls an unmarried girl is sent out with an iron plate in her hand. Possibly following out the same train of ideas, the Kharwârs of Mirzapur, when hail falls, throw into the courtyard the wooden peg of the corn-mill, which, as we shall see, is considered possessed of certain magical powers.

In Muzaffarnagar, when hail begins they pray at once to two noted demons, Ismâîl Jogi and Nonâ Chamârin, and ring a bell in a Saiva temple to scare the demon.

Another method is to put pressure on the hail demon by the pretence of sheer physical pain. Thus in Multân it is believed that if you can catch a hailstone in the air before it reaches the ground and cut it in two with a pair of scissors the hail will abate.[2] Not long ago a lady at Namî Tâl, when a hailstorm came on, saw her gardener rush into the kitchen and bring out the cook's chopper, with which he began to make strokes on the ground where the hail was falling. It appeared on inquiry that he believed that the hail would dread being cut and cease to fall.[3] In Kumaun, where hail is much dreaded, there are many devices of the same kind. Some put an axe in the open air with the edge turned up, so that the hailstones may be cut in pieces and cease falling. Another plan is to spit at the hail as it falls, or to sprinkle the hailstones with blood drawn from some famous magician, a rite which can hardly be anything but a survival of human sacrifice. A third device is to call an enchanter and make

[1] Brand, "Observations," 431. [2] "Archæological Reports," v. 136.
[3] "North Indian Notes and Queries," i. 13.

him blow a conch-shell in the direction of the hail. Others put a churn in the open air when the rain is falling, in the belief that when the hailstones touch it they will become as soft as butter. Others, again, when hail falls, send out a wizard or one possessed by some deity and make him beat the hailstones with a shoe.[1]

There are, again, certain persons specially in charge of the hail. Thus, "at the town of Cleonæ in Argolis there were watchmen maintained at the public expense to look out for hailstorms. When they saw a hail-cloud approaching they made a signal, whereupon the farmers turned out and sacrificed lambs and fowls. They believed that when the clouds had tasted the blood they would turn aside and go somewhere else. If any man was too poor to afford a lamb or a fowl, he pricked his finger with a sharp instrument and offered his own blood to the clouds; and the hail, we are told, turned aside from his fields as readily as from those where it had been propitiated with the blood of victims."[2] In the same way the duty of charming away the hail is, in Kumaun, entrusted to a certain class of Brâhmans known as Woli or Oliya (*ola*, "hail"). Their method is to take a dry gourd, which they fill with pebbles, grains of Urad pulse, mustard, goat-dung and seeds of cotton. This is then tied by a triple cord to the highest tree on a mountain overhanging the village. Until the crops are cut the Oliya goes to this place every day and mutters his incantations. If the crops are reaped without disaster of any kind he is liberally remunerated.[3]

As has been already said, whirlwinds are the work of demons. The witches in Macbeth meet in thunder, lightning and rain, they can loose and bind the winds and cause vessels to be tempest-tossed at sea. The same principle was laid down by Pythagoras;[4] and Herodotus[5] describes the people of Psylli marching in a body to fight the south wind

[1] "North Indian Notes and Queries," iii. 135.
[2] "Folk-lore," i. 162.
[3] "North Indian Notes and Queries," iii. 106.
[4] "Folk-lore," i. 149. [5] Ibid., iv. 173.

which had dried up their water-tanks. In Ireland it is believed that a whirlwind denotes that a devil is dancing with a witch; or that the fairies are rushing by, intent on carrying off some victim to fairyland. The only help is to fling clay at the passing wind, and the fairies will be compelled to drop the mortal child or the beautiful young girl they have abducted.[1] A gentleman at Listowel not long ago was much astonished when a cloud of dust was being blown along a road to see an old woman rush to the side and drag handfuls of grass out of the fence, which she threw in great haste into the cloud of dust. He inquired and learned that this was in order to give *something* to the fairies which were flying along in the dust. So in Italy, Spolviero is the wind spirit which flies along in the dust eddies.[2]

In the Panjâb Pheru[3] is the deity of the petty whirlwinds which blow when the little dust-clouds rise in the hot weather. He was a Brâhman, and a long story is told of him, how he worshipped Sakhi Sarwar, was made Governor of Imânâbâd by Akbar, but he abandoned the saint and returned to his caste, whereupon he was afflicted with leprosy. When he repented he was cured by eating some magical earth and believed in the saint till he died. His shrine is at Miyânkê, in the Lahore District, and when a Panjâbi sees a whirlwind he calls out, *Bhâi Pheru, teri kâr*—"May Bhâi Pheru protect us!" Another whirlwind demon, the saint Rahma, was once neglected at the wheat harvest, and he raised a whirlwind which blew for nine days in succession, and wrought such damage in the threshing-floors that since then his shrine receives the appropriate offerings. On the same principle whirlwinds are called in Bombay Bagâlya or devils.[4]

Among the Mirzapur Korwas, when a dust-storm comes, the women thrust the house broom, which, as we shall see, is a demon scarer, into the thatch, so that it may not be

[1] Lady Wilde, "Legends," 128; "Folk-lore," i. 149, 153; iv. 351.
[2] Leland, "Etruscan Roman Remains," 79.
[3] Temple, "Legends of the Panjâb," ii. 104 sqq.; iii. 301.
[4] "North Indian Notes and Queries," i. 39; Forbes, "Oriental Memoirs," i. 205.

blown away. The Pankas in the same way make their women hold the thatch and throw the rice mortar and the flour-mill pivot into the courtyard. The wind is ashamed of being defeated by the power of women and ceases to blow.

AEROLITES.

All over the world people say that if when a meteor or falling star darts across the sky they can utter a wish before it disappears, that wish will be granted. The old Norsemen believed that it implied that a dragon was flashing through the air. In Italy[1] the sight of such a body is a cure for blear eyes. In India it is believed that the residence of a soul in heaven is proportionate to the charities done by him on earth, and when his allotted period is over he falls as an aerolite. A falling star means that the soul of some great man is passing through the air, and when people see one of these stars they thrust their five fingers into their mouths to prevent their own souls from joining his company. Many of these aerolites are worshipped as lingams in Saiva shrines. One which fell at Sîtâmarhi in Bengal in 1880, has now been deified, and is worshipped as Adbhût-nâtha, or "the miraculous god."[2]

[1] Leland, *loc. cit.*, 272.

[2] "Archæological Reports," xvi. 32.

CHAPTER II.

THE HEROIC AND VILLAGE GODLINGS.

Arma procul currusque virum miratur inanes.
Stant terrâ defixæ hastæ, passimque soluti
Per campum pascuntur equi.

Æneid, vi. 652-654.

THE HEROIC GODLINGS.

NEXT to these deities which have been classed as the godlings of nature, come those which have a special local worship of their own. The number of these godlings is immense, and their functions and attributes so varied, that it is extremely difficult to classify them on any intelligible principle. Some of them are pure village godlings, of whom the last Census has unearthed an enormous number all through Northern India. Some of them, like Hanumân or Bhîmsen, are survivals in a somewhat debased form of the second-rate deities or heroes of the older mythology. Some have risen to the rank, or are gradually being elevated to the status, of national deities. Some are in all probability the local gods of the degraded races, whom we may tentatively assume to be autochthonous. Many of these have almost certainly been absorbed into Brâhmanism at a comparatively recent period. Some are in process of elevation to the orthodox pantheon. But it will require a much more detailed analysis of the national faith than the existing materials permit, before it will be possible to make a final classification of this mob of deities on anything approaching a definite principle.

The deities of the heroic class are as a rule benignant, and

G 2

are generally worshipped by most Hindus. Those that have been definitely promoted into the respectable divine cabinet, like Hanumân, have Brâhmans or members of the ascetic orders as their priests, and their images, if not exactly admitted into the holy of holies of the greater shrines, are still allotted a respectable position in the neighbourhood, and receive a share in the offerings of the faithful.

The local position of the shrine very often defines the status of the deity. To many godlings of this class is allotted the duty of acting as warders (dwârapâla) to the temples of the great gods. Thus, at the Ashthbhuja hill in Mirzapur, the pilgrim to the shrine of the eight-armed Devî meets first on the road an image of the monkey god Hanumân, before he comes into the immediate presence of the goddess. So at Benares, Bhaironnâth is chief police-officer (Kotwâl) or guardian of all the Saiva temples. Similarly at Jageswar beyond Almora we find Kshetrapâl, at Badarinâth Ghantakaran, at Kedârnâth Bhairava, and at Tungnâth Kâl Bhairon.[1] In many places, as the pilgrim ascends to the greater temples, he comes to a place where the first view of the shrine is obtained. This is known as the Devadekhnî or spot from which the deity is viewed. This is generally occupied by some lower-class deity, who is just beginning to be considered respectable. Then comes the temple dedicated to the warden, and lastly the real shrine itself. There can be little doubt that this represents the process by which gods which are now admittedly within the inner circle of the first class, such as the beast incarnations of Vishnu, the elephant-headed Ganesa, and the Sâktis or impersonations of the female energies of nature, underwent a gradual elevation.

This process is actually still going on before our eyes. Thus, the familiar Gor Bâba, a deified ghost of the aboriginal races, has in many places become a new manifestation of Siva, as Goreswara. Similarly, the powerful and malignant goddesses, who were by ruder tribes propitiated with the sacrifice of a buffalo or a goat, have been annexed to

[1] Atkinson, "Himâlayan Gazetteer," ii. 762.

HANUMÂN AS A WARDEN.

Brâhmanism as two of the numerous forms of Durgâ Devî, by the transparent fiction of a Bhainsâsurî or Kâlî Devî. In the case of the former her origin is clearly proved by the fact that she is regarded as a sort of tribal deity of the mixed tribe of Kânhpuriya Râjputs in Oudh. Similarly Mahâmâî, or the "Great Mother," a distinctively aboriginal goddess whose shrine consists of a low flat mound of earth with seven knobs of coloured clay at the head or west side, has been promoted into the higher pantheon as Jagadambâ Devî, or "Mother of the World." Her shrine is still a simple flat mound of earth with seven knobs at the top, and a flag in front to the east.[1] More extended analysis will probably show that the obligations of Brâhmanism to the local cultus are much greater than is commonly supposed.

HANUMÂN.

First among the heroic godlings is Hanumân, "He of the large jaws," or, as he is generally called, Mahâbîr, the "great hero," the celebrated monkey chief of the Râmâyana, who assisted Râma in his campaign against the giant Râvana to recover Sîtâ. Hardly any event in his mythology, thanks to the genius of Tulasî Dâs, the great Hindi poet of Hindustân, is more familiar to the Hindu peasant than this. It forms the favourite subject of dramatic representation at the annual festival of the Dasahra. There Hanumân, in fitting attire, marches along the stage at the head of his army of bears and monkeys, and the play ends with the destruction of Râvana, whose great body, formed of wickerwork and paper, is blown up with fireworks, amid the delighted enthusiasm of the excited audience.

It is almost certain that the worship of Hanumân does not come down from the earliest ages of the Hindu faith, though it has been suggested that he is the legitimate descendant of Vrisha-kapi, the great monkey of the Veda.[2] Besides being a great warrior he was noted for his skill in magic, grammar and

[1] Cunningham, "Archæological Reports," xvii. 141.
[2] Barth, "Religions of India," 265.

the art of healing. Many local legends connect him with sites in Northern India. Hills, like the Vindhya and that at Govardhan, are, as we have seen, attributed to him or to his companions. The more extreme school of modern comparative mythologists would make out that Hanumân is only the impersonation of the great cloud-monkey which fights the sun.[1]

But the fact of monkey-worship is susceptible of a much simpler explanation. The ape, from his appearance and human ways, is closely associated with man. It is a belief common to all folk-lore that monkeys were once human beings who have suffered degradation,[2] and according to one common belief stealers of fruit become monkeys in their next incarnation. But the common theory that the monkey is venerated in memory of the demigod Hanumân is, as Sir A. Lyall[3] remarks, "plainly putting the cart before the horse, for the monkey is evidently at the bottom of the whole story. Hanumân is now generally supposed to have been adopted into the Hindu heaven from the non-Aryan or aboriginal idolaters; though, to my mind, any uncivilized Indian would surely fall down and worship at first sight of an ape. Then there is the modern idea that the god was really a great chief of some such aboriginal tribe as those which to this day dwell almost like wild creatures in the remote forests of India; and this may be the nucleus of fact in the legend regarding him. It seems as if hero-worship and animal-worship had got mixed up in the legend of Hanumân."

At the same time, it must be remembered that the so-called Aryans enjoy no monopoly of his worship. He is sometimes like a tribal godling of the aboriginal Suiris, and the wild Bhuiyas of Keunjhar identify him with Borâm, the Sun godling.[4] It is at least a possible supposition that his worship may have been imported into Brâhmanism from some such source as these.

[1] Gubernatis, "Zoological Mythology," ii. 99 sq.
[2] See instances collected by Tylor, "Primitive Culture," i. 376 sqq.
[3] "Asiatic Studies," 13 sq.
[4] Buchanan, "Eastern India," i. 467; Dalton, "Descriptive Ethnology," 147.

HANUMAN AND HIS PRIEST.

I. 87

HANUMÂN AS A VILLAGE GODLING.

But whatever may be the origin of the cult, the fact remains that he is a great village godling, with potent influence to scare evil spirits from his votaries. His rude image, smeared with oil and red ochre, meets one somewhere or other in almost every respectable Hindu village. One of his functions is to act as an embodiment of virile power. He is a giver of offspring, and in Bombay women sometimes go to his temple in the early morning, strip themselves naked, and embrace the god.[1] Mr. Hartland has collected many instances of similar practices. Thus a cannon at Batavia used to be utilized in the same way; and at Athens there is a rock near the Callirrhoe, whereon women who wish to be made fertile rub themselves, calling on the Moirai to be gracious to them.[2]

On the same principle he is, with Hindu wrestlers, their patron deity, his place among Musalmâns being taken by 'Ali. Their aid is invoked at the commencement of all athletic exercises, and at each wrestling school a platform is erected in their honour. Tuesday is sacred to Mahâbîr and Friday to 'Ali. Hindu wrestlers on Mahâbîr's day bathe in a river in the morning, and after bathing dress in clean clothes. Then taking a jar of water, some incense, sweets, and red or white flowers, they repair to the wrestling school, bow down before the platform and smear it with cow-dung or earth. After this the sweets are offered to Mahâbîr and verses are recited in his honour. Then they do the exercise five times and bow before the platform. When the service is over they smear their bodies with the incense, which is supposed to give them strength and courage. Care is taken that no woman sees the athletes exercising, lest she should cast the Evil Eye upon them.

One special haunt of the monkey deity is what is known as the Bandarpûnchh or "monkey tail" peak in the Himâlayas. They say that every year in the spring a single

[1] Campbell, "Notes," 260.

[2] "Legend of Perseus," i. 173.

monkey comes from Hardwâr to this peak and remains there twelve months, when he makes way for his successor.

Hanumân is a favourite deity of the semi-Hinduized Drâvidian races of the Vindhya-Kaimûr plateau. "The most awe-inspiring of their tremendous rocks are his fanes; the most lovely of their pools are sacred by virtue of the tradition of his having bathed in them." He was known as Pawan-kâ-pût, or "son of the wind," which corresponds to his older title of Marutputra, or "son of the wind god." And the Bhuiyas of Sinhbhûm, who are, as Colonel Dalton gravely remarks, "without doubt the apes of the Râmâyana," call themselves Pawan-bans, or "sons of the wind," to this day.[1] But in the plains his chief function is as a warden or guardian against demoniacal influence, and at the Hanumângarhi shrine at Ajudhya he is provided with a regular priesthood consisting of Khâki ascetics.

The respect paid to the monkey does not need much illustration. The ordinary monkey of the plains (*Macacus Rhesus*) is a most troublesome, mischievous beast, and does enormous mischief to crops, while in cities he is little short of a pest. But his life is protected by a most effective sanction, and no one dares to injure him.

General Sleeman[2] tells a story of a Muhammadan Nawâb of Oudh, who was believed to have died of fever, the result of killing a monkey. "Mumtâz-ud-daula," said his informant, "might have been King of Oudh had his father not shot that monkey." In the Panjâb an appeal to the monkey overcomes the demon of the whirlwind. There is a Bombay story that in the village of Makargâon, whenever there is a marriage in a house, the owner puts outside the wedding booth a turban, a waist-cloth, rice, fruits, turmeric, and betel-nuts for the village monkeys. The monkeys assemble and sit round their Patel, or chief. The chief tears the turban and gives a piece to each of them, and the other things are divided. If the householder does not present these offerings they ascend the booth and defile the wedding feast.

[1] "Descriptive Ethnology," 140.
[2] "Journey through Oudh," ii. 133.

He has then to come out and apologize, and when he gives them the usual gifts they retire.[1] The feeding of monkeys is part of the ritual at the Durgâ Temple at Benares, and there, too, there is a king of the monkeys who is treated with much respect. Instances of Râjas carrying out the wedding of a monkey at enormous expense are not unknown. Where a monkey has been killed it is believed that no one can live. His bones are also exceedingly unlucky, and a special class of exorcisers in Bihâr make it their business to ascertain that his bones do not pollute the ground on which a house is about to be erected.[2]

The worship of Hanumân appears, if the Census returns are to be trusted, to be much more popular in the North-West Provinces than in the Panjâb. In the former his devotees numbered about a million, and in the latter less than ten thousand persons. But the figures are probably open to question, as he is often worshipped in association with other deities.

WORSHIP OF BHÎMSEN.

Another of these beneficent guardians or wardens is Bhîmsen, "he who has a terrible army." He has now in popular belief very little in common with the burly hero of the Mahâbhârata, who was notorious for his gigantic strength, great animal courage, prodigious appetite and irascible temper; jovial and jocular when in good humour, but abusive, truculent and brutal when his passions were roused.[3] He is now little more than one of the wardens of the house or village.

In parts of the Central Provinces he has become degraded into a mere fetish, and is represented by a piece of iron fixed in a stone or in a tree.[4] Under the name of Bhîmsen or Bhîmpen, his worship extends from Berâr to the extreme east of Bastar, and not merely among the Hinduized

[1] Campbell, "Notes," 260.

[2] Buchanan, "Eastern India," ii. 141 sq.; "Panjâb Notes and Queries," iv. 9.

[3] Dowson, "Classical Dictionary," s.v.

[4] "Gazetteer," 323.

aborigines, who have begun to honour Khandoba, Hanumân, Ganpati and their brethren, but among the rudest and most savage tribes. He is generally adored under the form of an unshapely stone covered with vermilion, or of two pieces of wood standing from three to four feet out of the ground, which are possibly connected with the phallic idea, towards which so many of these deities often diverge. Bhiwâsu, the regular Gond deity, is identical with him. Mr. Hislop[1] mentions a large idol of him eight feet high, with a dagger in one hand and a javelin in the other. He has an aboriginal priest, known as Bhûmak, or "he of the soil," and the people repair to worship on Tuesdays and Saturdays, offering he-goats, hogs, hens, cocks and cocoa-nuts. The headman of the village and the cultivators subscribe for an annual feast, which takes place at the commencement of the rains, when the priest takes a cow from the headman by force and offers it to the godling in the presence of his congregation. The Mâriya Gonds worship him in the form of two pieces of wood previous to the sowing of the crops. The Naikudê Gonds adore him in the form of a huge stone daubed with vermilion. Before it a little rice is cooked. They then besmear the stone with vermilion and burn resin as incense in its honour, after which the victims—sheep, hogs and fowls—with the usual oblation of spirits, are offered. The god is now supposed to inspire the priest, who rolls his head, leaps frantically round and round, and finally falls down in a trance, when he announces whether Bhîmsen has accepted the service or not. At night all join in drinking, dancing and beating drums. Next morning the congregation disperses. Those who are unable to attend this tribal gathering perform similar rites at home under the shade of the Mahua tree (*Bassia latifolia*).[2]

PILLAR-WORSHIP OF BHÎMSEN.

The local worship of Bhîmsen beyond the Drâvidian tract is specially in the form of pillars, which are called Bhîmlâth

[1] "Papers," 16.

[2] Ibid., 23 sq.

or Bhîmgada, "Bhîm's clubs." Many of these are really the edict pillars which were erected by the pious Buddhist King Asoka, but they have been appropriated by Bhîmsen. Such are the pillars in the Bâlaghât District of the Central Provinces and at Kahâon in Gorakhpur. At Devadhâra, in the Lower Himâlaya, are two boulders, the uppermost of which is called Ransila, or "the stone of war." On this rests a smaller boulder, said to be the same as that used by Bhîmsen to produce the fissures in the rocks; in proof of which the print of his five fingers is still pointed out, as they show the hand-mark of the Giant Bolster in Cornwall.[1]

Bhîmsen is one of the special gods of the Bhuiyas of Keunjhar, and they consider themselves to be descended from him, as he is the brother of Hanumân, the founder of their race. According to the Hindu ritual he has his special feast on the Bhaimy Ekâdashî, or eleventh of the bright fortnight in the month of Mâgh. The Bengal legend tells that Bhîmsen, the brother of Yudishthira, when he was sent to the snowy mountains and lay benumbed with cold, was restored by the Saint Gorakhnâth, and made king of one hundred and ten thousand hills, stretching from the source of the Ganges to Bhutân. Among other miracles Bhîmsen and Gorakhnâth introduced the sacrifice of buffaloes in place of human beings, and in order to effect this Bhîmsen thrust some of the flesh down the throat of the holy man. So though they have both lost caste in consequence, they are both deified. The saint is still the tutelary deity of the reigning family of Nepâl, and all over that kingdom and Mithila Bhîmsen is a very common object of worship. That mysterious personage Gorakhnâth flits through religious legend and folk-lore from post-Vedic to mediæval times; and little has yet been done to discover the element of historical truth which underlies an immense mass of the wildest fiction.[2]

[1] Madden, "Journal Asiatic Society Bengal," 1848, p. 600; Hunt, "Popular Romances," 73.

[2] Buchanan, "Eastern India," iii. 38.

WORSHIP OF BHÎSHMA.

In about the same rank as Bhîmsen is Bhîshma, "the terrible one," another hero of the Mahâbhârata. To the Hindu nowadays he is chiefly known by the tragic circumstances of his death. He was covered all over by the innumerable arrows discharged at him by Arjuna, and when he fell from his chariot he was upheld from the ground by the arrows and lay as on a couch of darts. This Sara-sayya or "arrow-bed" of Bhîshma is probably the origin of the Kantaka-sayya or "thorn-couch" of some modern Bairâgis, who lie and sleep on a couch studded with nails. He wished to marry the maiden Satyavatî, but he gave her up to his father Sântanu, and Bhîshma elected to live a single life, so that his sons might not claim the throne from his step-brethren. Hence, as he died childless and left no descendant to perform his funeral rites, he is worshipped with libations of water on the Bhíshma Ashtamî, or 23rd of the month of Mâgh; but this ceremony hardly extends beyond Bengal.

In Upper India five days in the month of Kârttik (November-December) are sacred to him. This is a woman's festival. They send lamps to a Brâhman's house, whose wife during these five days must sleep on the ground, on a spot covered with cow-dung, close to the lamps, which it is her duty to keep alight. The lamps are filled with sesamum oil, and red wicks wound round sticks of the sesamum plant rest in the lamp saucers. A walnut, an âonla (the fruit of the emblic myrobolon), a lotus-seed, and two copper coins are placed in each lamp. Each evening the women come and prostrate themselves before the lamps or walk round them. They bathe on each day of the feast before sunrise, and are allowed only one meal in the day, consisting of sugar-cane, sweet potatoes and other roots, with meal made of amarinth seed, millet and buckwheat cakes, to which the rich add sugar, dry ginger, and butter. They drink only milk. Of course the Brâhman gets a share of these good things, to which the rich contribute in addition a lamp-saucer made of silver, with a golden wick, clothes, and money.

At the early morning bath of the last day five lighted lamps made of dough are placed, one at the entrance of the town or village, others at the four cross-roads, under the Pîpal or sacred fig tree, at a temple of Siva, and at a pond. This last is put in a small raft made of the leaves of the sugar-cane, and floated on the water. A little grain is placed beside each lamp. After the lamps handed over to the Brâhman have burnt away or gone out, the black from the wicks is rubbed on the eyes and fingers of the worshippers, and their toe-nails are anointed with the remainder of the oil. All the articles used in the worship are well-known scarers of demons, and there can be little doubt that the rite is intended to conciliate Bhîshma in his character of a guardian deity, and induce him to ward off evil spirits from the household of the worshipper.

There is a curious legend told to explain the motive of the rite. A childless Râja once threatened to kill all his queens unless one of them gave birth to a child. One of the Rânîs who had a cat, announced that she had been brought to bed of a girl, who was to be shut up for twelve years, a common incident in the folk-tales.[1] This was all very well, but the supposed princess had to be married, and here lay the difficulty. Now this cat had been very attentive during this rite in honour of Bhîshma, keeping the wicks alight by raising them from time to time with her paws, and cleaning them on her body. So the grateful godling turned her into a beautiful girl, but her tail remained as before. However, the bridegroom's friends admired her so much that they kept her secret at the wedding, and so saved the Rânî from destruction, and when the time came for the bride to go to her husband her tail dropped off too. So Hindu ladies use the oil and lamp-black of Bhîshma's feast day as valuable aids to beauty. Such cases of animal transformation constantly appear in the folk-tales. In one of the Kashmîr stories a cat, by the advice of Pârvatî, rubs herself with oil and is turned into a girl; but she does not rub a small patch

[1] Frazer, "Golden Bough," ii. 225 sqq.; "Panjâb Notes and Queries," iii. 181 sq.

between her shoulders, and this remained covered with the cat's fur.[1]

The worship of the heroes of the Mahâbhârata does not prevail widely, unless we have a survival of it in the worship of the Pânch Pîr. At the last Census in the North-Western Provinces less than four thousand persons declared themselves worshippers of the Pândavas. The number in the Panjâb is even smaller.

WORSHIP OF THE LOCAL GODLINGS.

We now come to the local or village godlings, a most nondescript collection of deities, possessing very various attributes. There is good reason to believe that most of these deities, if not all, belong to the races whom it is convenient to call non-Aryan, or at least outside Brâhmanism, though some of them may have been from time to time promoted into the official pantheon. But Dr. Oppert,[2] writing of Southern India, remarks that "if the pure Vedic doctrine has been altered by the influx of non-Aryan tenets, so have also the latter undergone a change by coming in contact with Aryan ideas, and not only have males intruded into the once exclusive female circle of the Grâmadevatâs, but also a motley of queer figures have crept in, forming indeed a very strange gathering. The Grâmadevatâ-prathishtha mentions as Grâmadevatâs the skull of Brahma, the head of Vishnu, the skull of Renukâ, the figure of Draupadî, the body of Sîtâ, the harassing followers of Siva (the Pramathas), the attendants of Vishnu (Pârishadas), demons, Yoginîs, various kinds of Sâktis made of wood, stone, or clay; persons who were unsuccessful in their devotional practice, Sunasepha, Trisanku, Ghatotkacha, and others; Devakî's daughter, multiform Durgâs and Sâktis; Pûtanâ and others who kill children; Bhûtas, Pretas, and Pisâchas; Kûsmânda, Sâkinî, Dâkinî, Vetâlas, and others; Yakshas, Kirâtadevî, Sabarî, Rudra, one hundred millions of forms of Rudra; Mâtangî,

[1] Knowles, "Folk-tales from Kashmîr," 10.
[2] "Original Inhabitants," 455.

Syâmalâ, unclean Ganapati, unclean Chândalî, the goddess of the liquor pot (Surabhandeswarî), Mohinî, Râkshasi, Tripurâ, Lankhinî, Saubhadevî, Sâmudrikâ, Vanadurgâ, Jaladurgâ, Agnidurgâ, suicides, culprits, faithful wives, the goddesses of matter, goddesses of qualities, and goddesses of deeds, etc." Through such a maze as this it is no easy task to find a clue.

The non-Brâhmanic character of the worship is implied by the character of the priesthood. In the neighbourhood of Delhi, where the worship of Bhûmiya as a local godling widely prevails, the so-called priest of the shrine, whose functions are limited to beating a drum during the service and receiving the offerings, is usually of the sweeper caste. Sîtalâ, the small-pox goddess, is very often served by a Mâli, or gardener. Sir John Malcolm notes that the Bhopa of Central India, who acts as the village priest, is generally drawn from some menial tribe.[1] In the hill country of South Mirzapur, the Baiga who manages the worship of Gansâm, Râja Lâkhan, or the aggregate of the local deities, known as the Dih or Deohâr, is almost invariably a Bhuiyâr or a Chero, both semi-savage Drâvidian tribes. Even the shrine erected in honour of Nâhar Râo, the famous King of Mandor, who met in equal combat the chivalrous Chauhân in the pass of the Aravalli range, is tended by a barber officiant.[2] Though the votaries of the meaner godling are looked on with some contempt or pity by their more respectable neighbours, little active hostility or intolerance is exhibited. More than this, the higher classes, and particularly their women, occasionally join in the worship of the older gods. At weddings and other feasts their aid and protection are invoked. Every woman, no matter what her caste may be, will bow to the ghosts which haunt the old banyan or pîpal tree in the village, and in time of trouble, when the clouds withhold the rain, when the pestilence walketh in darkness, and the murrain devastates the herds, it is to the patron deities of the village that they appeal for assistance.

[1] "Central India," ii. 206.

[2] Tod. "Annals," i. 67 ; for other examples see Buchanan, "Eastern India," ii. 131, 352, 478 ; "Central Provinces Gazetteer," 110.

VILLAGE SHRINES.

The shrine of the regular village godling, the Grâmadevatâ or Ganwdevatâ, is generally a small square building of brick masonry, with a bulbous head and perhaps an iron spike as a finial. A red flag hung on an adjoining tree, often a pîpal, or some other sacred fig, or a nîm, marks the position of the shrine. In the interior lamps are occasionally lighted, fire sacrifices (*homa*) made and petty offerings presented. If a victim is offered, its head is cut off outside the shrine and perhaps a few drops of blood allowed to fall on the inner platform, which is the seat of the godling. These shrines never contain a special image, such as are found in the temples of the higher gods. There may be a few carved stones lying about, the relics of some dismantled temple, but these are seldom identified with any special deity, and villagers will rub a projecting knob on one of them with a little vermilion and oil as an act of worship.

Speaking of this class of shrine in the Panjâb, Mr. Ibbetson writes:[1] "The Hindu shrine must always face east, while the Musalmân shrine is in the form of a tomb and faces the south. This sometimes gives rise to delicate questions. In one village a section of the community had become Muhammadan. The shrine of the common ancestor needed rebuilding, and there was much dispute as to its shape and aspect. They solved the difficulty by building a Musalmân grave facing south, and over it a Hindu shrine facing east. In another village an Imperial trooper was once burnt alive by the shed in which he was sleeping catching fire, and it was thought best to propitiate him by a shrine, or his ghost might become troublesome. He was by religion a Musalmân, but he had been burnt, not buried, which seemed to make him a Hindu. After much discussion the latter opinion prevailed, and a Hindu shrine with an eastern aspect now stands to his memory."

To the east of the North-Western Provinces the village shrines are much less substantial erections. In the Gangetic

[1] "Panjâb Ethnography," 114.

A VILLAGE SHRINE.

valley, where the population has been completely Hinduized, the shrine of the collective village deities, known as the Deohâr, consists of a pile of stones, some of which may be the fragments of a temple of the olden days, collected under some ancient, sacred tree. The shrine is the store-house of anything in the way of a curious stone to be found in the village, water-worn pebbles or boulders, anything with eccentric veining or marking. Here have been occasionally found celts and stone hatchets, relics of an age anterior to the general use of iron. In the same way in some European countries the celt or stone arrow-head is worn as an amulet.

Little clay images of elephants and horses are often found near these shrines. Some villagers will say that these represent the equipage (*sawârî*) of the deity; others explain them by the fact that a person in distress vows a horse or an elephant to the god, and when his wishes are realized, offers as a substitute this trumpery donation. It was a common practice to offer substitutes of this kind. Thus when an animal could not be procured for sacrifice, an image of it in dough or wax was prepared and offered as a substitute.[1] We shall meet later on other examples of substitution of the same kind. On the same principle women used to give cakes in the form of a phallus to a Brâhman.[2] At these shrines are also found curious little clay bowls with short legs which are known as kalsa. The kalsa or water jar is always placed near the pole of the marriage shed, and the use of these beehive-shaped vessels at village shrines is found all along the hills of Central India.[3] On the neighbouring trees are often hung miniature cots, which commemorate the recovery of a patient from small-pox or other infectious disease.

Among the semi-Hinduized Drâvidian races of the Vindhyan range, many of whom worship Gansâm or Râja Lâkhan, the shrine usually consists of a rude mud building or a structure made of bamboo and straw, roofed with a coarse

[1] Frazer, "Golden Bough," ii. 83.
[2] Tawney, "Katha Sarit Sâgara," i. 8.
[3] "Bombay Gazetteer," iii. 220; "Râjputâna Gazetteer," iii. 65.

thatch, which is often allowed to fall into disrepair, until the godling reminds his votaries of his displeasure by an outbreak of epidemic disease or some other misfortune which attacks the village. The shrine is in charge of the village Baiga, who is invariably selected from among some of the ruder forest tribes, such as the Bhuiya, Bhuiyâr or Chero. Inside is a small platform known as "the seat of the godling" (*Devatâ kâ baithak*), on which are usually placed some of the curious earthen bowls already described, which are made specially for this worship, and are not used for domestic purposes. In these water is placed for the refreshment of the godling, and they thus resemble the funeral vases of the Greeks. In ordinary cases the offering deposited on the platform consists of a a thick griddle cake, a little milk, and perhaps a few jungle flowers; but in more serious cases where the deity makes his presence disagreeably felt, he is propitiated with a goat, pig, or fowl, which is decapitated outside the shrine, with the national and sacrificial axe. The head is brought inside dripping with blood, and a few drops of blood are allowed to fall on the platform. The head of the victim then becomes the perquisite of the officiating Baiga, and the rest of the meat is cooked and eaten near the shrine by the adult male worshippers, married women and children being carefully excluded from a share in the offering. The special regard paid to the head of the victim is quite in consonance with traditions of European paganism and folk-lore in many countries.[1] Lower south, beyond the river Son, the shrine is of even a simpler type, and is there often represented by a few boulders near a stream, where the worshippers assemble and make their offerings.

The non-Brâhmanic character of the worship is still further marked by the fact that no special direction from the homestead is prescribed in selecting the site for the shrine. No orthodox Hindu temple can be built south of the village site, as this quarter is regarded as the realm of Yama, the god of death; here vagrant evil spirits prowl and

[1] Gomme, "Ethnology in Folk-lore," 34 sq.

consume or defile the offerings made to the greater gods. In the more Hinduized jungle villages some attempt is occasionally made to conform to this rule, and sometimes, as in the case of the more respectable Hindu shrines, the door faces the east. But this rule is not universal, and the site of the shrine is often selected under some suitable tree, whatever may be its position as regards the homestead, and it very often commemorates some half-forgotten tragedy, where a man was carried off by a tiger or slain or murdered, where he fell from a tree or was drowned in a watercourse. Here some sort of shrine is generally erected with the object of appeasing the angry spirit of the dead man.

These shrines have no idol, no bell to scare vagrant ghosts and awake the godling to partake of the offerings or listen to the prayers of his votaries. If he is believed to be absent or asleep, a drum is beaten to awaken or recall him, and this answers the additional purpose of scaring off intruding spirits, who are always hungry and on the watch to appropriate the offerings of the faithful. Here are also none of the sacrificial vessels, brazen lamps and cups, which are largely used in respectable fanes for waving a light before the deity as part of the service, or for cooling the idol with libations of water, and the instrument used for sacrificing the victim is only the ordinary axe which the dweller in the jungle always carries.

There is one special implement which is very commonly found in the village shrines of the hill country south of the Ganges. This is an iron chain with a heavy knob at the end, to which a strap, like a Scotch tawse, is often attached. The chain is ordinarily three and a half feet long, the tawse two feet, and the total weight is about seven pounds. This is known as the Gurda; it hangs from the roof of the shrine, and is believed to be directly under the influence of the deity, so that it is very difficult to procure a specimen. The Baiga priest, when his services are required for the exorcism of a disease ghost, thrashes himself on the back and loins with his chain, until he works himself up to the proper degree of religious ecstasy.

Among the more primitive Gonds the chain has become a godling and is regularly worshipped. In serious cases of epilepsy, hysteria, and the like, which do not readily yield to ordinary exorcism, the patient is taken to the shrine and severely beaten with the holy chain until the demon is expelled. This treatment is, I understand, considered particularly effective in the case of hysteria and kindred ailments under which young women are wont to suffer, and like the use of the thong at the Lupercalia at Rome, a few blows of the chain are considered advisable as a remedy for barrenness. The custom of castigating girls when they attain puberty prevails among many races of savages.[1]

IDENTIFICATION OF THE LOCAL GODLING.

The business of selecting a site for a new village or hamlet is one which needs infinite care and attention to the local godlings of the place. No place can be chosen without special regard to the local omens. There is a story told of one of the Gond Râjas of Garh Mandla, whose attention was first called to the place by seeing a hare, when pursued by his dogs, turn and chase them. It struck him that there must be much virtue in the air of a place where a timid animal acquired such courage.[2] The site of the settlement of Almora is said to have been selected by one of the kings before whom in this place a hare was transformed into a tiger.[3] Similar legends are told of the foundation of many forts and cities.

But it is with the local godlings that the founder of a new settlement has most concern. The speciality of this class of godlings is that they frequent only particular places. Each has his separate jurisdiction, which includes generally one or sometimes a group of villages. This idea has doubtless promoted the rooted disinclination of the Hindu to leave his home and come into the domain of a fresh set of

[1] Frazer "Golden Bough," ii. 233.
[2] "Bhandâra Settlement Report," 51.
[3] Ganga Datt Upreti, "Folk-lore of Kumaun," Introduction, vii.

godlings with whom he has no acquaintance, who have never received due propitiation from him or his forefathers, and who are hence in all probability inimical to him. But people to whom the local godling of their village has shown his hostility by bringing affliction upon them for their neglect of his service, can usually escape from his malignity by leaving his district. This habit of emigration to escape the malignity of the offended godling doubtless accounts for many of the sites of deserted villages, which are scattered all over the country. We say that they were abandoned on account of a great famine or a severe epidemic, but to the native mind these afflictions are the work of the local deity, who could have warded them off had he been so disposed. Hence when a settlement is being founded it is a matter of prime necessity that the local godling or group of godlings should be brought under proper control and carefully identified, so as to ensure the safety and prosperity of the settlement. The next and final stage is the establishment of a suitable shrine and the appointment of a competent priest.

There are, as might have been expected, many methods of identifying and establishing the local gods. Thus in North Oudh, when a village is founded the site is marked off by cross stakes of wood driven into the ground, which are solemnly worshipped on the day of the completion of the settlement, and then lapse into neglect unless some indication of the displeasure of the god again direct attention to them. These crosses, which are called Daharchandî, are particularly frequent and well-marked in the villages occupied by the aboriginal Thârus in the sub-Himâlayan Tarâî, where they may be found in groups of ten or more on the edge of the cultivated lands. So, among the Santâls, a piece of split bamboo, about three feet high, is placed in the ground in an inclined position and is called the Sipâhî or sentinel of the hamlet; among the Gonds two curved posts, one of which is much smaller than the other, represent the male and female tutelary gods.[1]

[1] Dalton, "Descriptive Ethnology," 220, 281.

In the Eastern Districts of the North-Western Provinces a more elaborate process is carried out, which admirably illustrates the special form of local worship now under consideration. When the site of a new settlement is selected, an Ojha is called in to identify and mark down the deities of the place. He begins by beating a drum round the place for some time, which is intended to scare vagrant, outsider ghosts and to call together the local deities. All the people assemble, and two men, known as the Mattiwâh and the Pattiwâh, "the earth man" and "the leaf man," who represent the gods of the soil and of the trees, soon become filled with the spirit and are found to be possessed by the local deities. They dance and shout for some time in a state of religious frenzy, and their disconnected ejaculations are interpreted by the Ojha, who suddenly rushes upon them, grasps with his hands at the spirits which are supposed to be circling round them, and finally pours through their hands some grains of sesamum, which is received in a perforated piece of the wood of the Gûlar or sacred fig-tree. The whole is immediately plastered up with a mixture of clay and cow-dung, and the wood is carefully buried on the site selected for the Deohâr or local shrine. By this process the deities are supposed to be fastened up in the sacred wood and to be unable to do any mischief, provided that the usual periodical offerings are made in their honour.

This system does not seem to prevail among the Drâvidian races of the Vindhyan plateau. Some time ago I discussed the matter with Hannu Baiga, the chief priest of the Bhuiyas beyond the Son, and he was pleased to express his unqualified approval of the arrangement. Indeed, he promised to adopt it himself, but unfortunately Hannu, who was a mine of information on the religion and demonology of his people, died before he could apply this test to the local deities of his parish. His wife has died also, and I understand that he is known to be the head of all the Bhûts or malignant ghosts of the neighbourhood, while his wife rules all the Churels who infest that part of the country.

At the same time, to an ordinary Baiga the plan would

hardly be as comfortable as the present arrangement. It would not suit him to have the local ghosts brought under any control, because he makes his living by doing the periodical services to propitiate them. Nowadays he believes fully in the influence of the magic circle and of spirituous liquor as ghost scarers. Both these principles will be discussed elsewhere. So he is supposed once a year at least, or oftener in case of pestilence or other trouble, to perambulate all round the village boundary, sprinkling a line of spirits as he walks. The idea is to form a magic circle impervious to strange and, in the nature of the case, necessarily malignant ghosts, who might wish to intrude from outside; and to control the resident local deities, and prevent them from contracting evil habits of mischief by wandering beyond their prescribed domains.

The worst about this ritual is that the Baiga is apt to be very deliberate in his movements, and to drink the liquor on the road and to spoil the symmetry of the circle during his fits of intoxication. I know of one disreputable shepherd who was upwards of a fortnight getting round an ordinary sized village, and the levy on his parishioners to pay the wine bill was, as may easily be imagined, a very serious matter, to say nothing of several calamities, which occurred to the inhabitants in their unprotected state owing to his negligence. At present the feeling in his parish is very strong against him, and his constituents are thinking of removing him, particularly as he has only one eye. This is a very dangerous deformity in ordinary people, but in a Baiga, who is invested with religious functions, it is most objectionable, and likely to detract from his efficiency.

In Hoshangâbâd a different system prevails. When a new village is formed by the aboriginal Kurkus, there is no difficulty in finding the abode of the godling Dûngar Devatâ and Mâtâ, because you have only to look for and discover them upon their hill and under their tree. But Mutua Devatâ has generally to be created by taking a heap of stones from the nearest stream and sacrificing a pig and seven chickens to him. "There is one ceremony, however, which is worth notice, not so much as being distinctively Kurku, as illustrating the sense of mystery and chance which in the native mind seems to be connected with the idea of measurement, and which arises probably from the fact that with superficial measures, by heaping lightly or pressing down tight, very different results can be obtained. A measure is filled up with grain to the level of the brim, but no head is poured on, and it is put before Mutua Devatâ. They watch it all night, and in the morning pour it out, and measure it again. If the grain now fills up the measure and leaves enough for a head to it, and still more, if it brims and runs over, this is a sign that the village will be very prosperous, and that every cultivator's granaries will run over in the same way. But it is an evil omen if the grain does not fill up to the level of the rims of the vessel. A similar practice obtains in the Narmadâ valley when they begin winnowing, and some repeat it every night while the winnowing goes on."[1]

The same custom prevails among the Kols and kindred races in Mirzapur, who make the bride and bridegroom carry it out as an omen of their success or failure in life. By carefully packing and pressing down the grain, any chance of an evil augury is easily avoided. We shall see later on that measuring the grain is a favourite device intended to save it from the depredations of evil-minded ghosts.

WORSHIP OF DWÂRA GUSÂÎN.

A typical case of the worship of a local godling is found among the Malers of Chota Nâgpur. His name is Dwàra Gusâîn, or "Lord of the house door." "Whenever from some calamity falling upon the household, it is considered necessary to propitiate him, the head of the family cleans a place in front of his door, and sets up a branch of the tree called Mukmum, which is held very sacred; an egg is placed near the branch, then a hog is killed and friends feasted; and

[1] "Settlement Report," 257.

SHRINE OF BHÛMIYA WITH SWÂSTIKA.

when the ceremony is over the egg is broken and the branch placed on the suppliant's house."[1] Dwâra Gusâîn is now called Bârahdvâri, because he is supposed to live in a temple with twelve doors and is worshipped by the whole village in the month of Mâgh.[2] The egg is apparently supposed to hold the deity, and this, it may be remarked, is not an uncommon folk-lore incident.[3]

WORSHIP OF BHÛMIYA.

One of the most characteristic of the benevolent village godlings is Bhûmiya—"the godling of the land or soil" (*bhûmi*). He is very commonly known as Khetpâl or Kshetrapâla, "the protector of the fields"; Khera or "the homestead mound"; Zamîndâr or "the landowner"; and in the hills Sâim or Sâyam, "the black one" (Sanskrit *syâma*). In the neighbourhood of Delhi he is a male godling; in Oudh Bhûmiyâ is a goddess and is called Bhûmiyâ Rânî or "soil queen." She is worshipped by spreading flat cakes and sweetmeats on the ground, which having been exposed some time to the sun, are eventually consumed by the worshipper and his family. The rite obviously implies the close connection between the fertility of the soil and sunshine.

To the west of the Province the creation of Bhûmiya's shrine is "the first formal act by which the proposed site of a village is consecrated, and when two villages have combined their homesteads for greater security against the marauders of former days, the people of the one which moved still worship at the Bhûmiya of the deserted site. Bhûmiya is worshipped after the harvests, at marriages, and on the birth of a male child; and Brâhmans are commonly fed in his name. Women often take their children to the shrine on Sundays, and the first milk of a cow or buffalo is always offered there."[4] Young bulls are sometimes released

[1] Dalton, "Descriptive Ethnology," 268.
[2] Risley, "Tribes and Castes of Bengal," ii. 58.
[3] Temple, "Wideawake Stories," 399.
[4] Ibbetson, "Panjâb Ethnography," 114; "Oudh Gazetteer," i. 518.

in his honour, and the term *Bhûmiya sând* has come to be equivalent to our "parish bull."

In the Hills he is regarded by some as a beneficent deity, who does not, as a rule, force his worship on anyone by possessing them or injuring their crops. When seed is sown, a handful of grain is sprinkled over a stone in the field nearest to his shrine, in order to protect the crop from hail, blight, and the ravages of wild animals, and at harvest time he receives the first-fruits to protect the garnered grain from rats and insects. He punishes the wicked and rewards the virtuous, and is lord of the village, always interested in its prosperity, and a partaker in the good things provided on all occasions of rejoicing, such as marriage, the birth of a son, or any great good fortune. Unlike the other rural deities, he seldom receives animal sacrifices, but is satisfied with the humblest offering of the fruits of the earth.[1]

In Gurgâon, again, he is very generally identified with one of the founders of the village or with a Brâhman priest of the original settlers. The special day for making offerings to him is the fourteenth day of the month. Some of the Bhûmiyas are said to grant the prayers of their votaries and to punish severely those who offend them. He visits people who sleep in the vicinity of his shrine with pains in the chest, and one man who was rash enough to clean his teeth near his shrine was attacked with sore disease. Those Bhûmiyas who thus bear the reputation of being revengeful and vicious in temper are respected, and offerings to them are often made, while those who have the character of easy good-nature are neglected.[2]

In parts of the Panjâb[3] Khera Devatâ or Chânwand is identified with Bhûmiya; according to another account she is a lady and the wife of Bhûmiya, and she sometimes has a special shrine, and is worshipped on Sunday only. To illustrate the close connection between this worship of Bhûmiya as the soil godling with that of the sainted dead, it may be noted that in some places the shrine of Bhûmiya is identified with

[1] Atkinson, "Himâlayan Gazetteer," ii. 825.
[2] Channing, "Settlement Report," 34.
[3] Maclagan, "Panjâb Census Report," 103 sq.

the Jathera, which is the ancestral mound, sacred to the common ancestor of the village or tribe. One of the most celebrated of these Jatheras is Kâla Mahar, the ancestor of the Sindhu Jâts, who has peculiar influence over cows, and to whom the first milk of every cow is offered. The place of the Jathera is, however, often taken by the Theh or mound which marks the site of the original village of the tribe.

But Bhûmiya, a simple village godling, is already well on his way to promotion to the higher heaven. In Patna some have already begun to identify him with Vishnu. In the Hills the same process is going on, and he is beginning to be known as Sâim, a corruption of Svayambhuva, the Bauddha form now worshipped in Nepâl. In the plains he is becoming promoted under the title of Bhûmîsvara Mahâdeva and his spouse Bhûmîsvarî Devî, both of whom have temples at Bânda.[1] In the Hills it is believed that he sometimes possesses people, and the sign of this is that the hair of the scalplock becomes hopelessly entangled. This reminds us of that very Mab "that plaits the manes of horses in the night and bakes the elflocks in foul sluttish hairs, which once untangled much misfortune bodes."

It was a common English belief that all who have communication with fairies find their hair all tied in double knots.[2] As we shall see later on, the hair is universally regarded as an entry for spirits, perhaps, as Mr. Campbell suggests, because it leads to the opening in the skull through which the dying spirit makes its exit. Hence many of the customs connected with letting the hair loose, cutting it off or shaving.

No less than eighty-five thousand persons declared themselves, at the last census, to be worshippers of Bhûmiya in the North-Western Provinces, while in the Panjâb they numbered only one hundred and sixty-three.

WORSHIP OF BHAIRON.

Bhûmiya, again, is often confounded with Bhairon, another warden godling of the land; while, to illustrate the

[1] Führer, "Monumental Antiquities," 146.
[2] Sir W. Scott, "Letters on Demonology," 143.

extraordinary jumble of these mythologies, Bhairon, who is almost certainly the Kâro Bairo (Kâl Bhairon) of the Bhuiyas of Keunjhar, is identified by them with Bhîmsen.[1]

Bhairon has a curious history. There is little doubt that he was originally a simple village deity; but with a slight change of name he has been adopted into Brâhmanism as Bhairava, "the terrible one," one of the most awful forms of Siva, while the female form Bhairavî is an equivalent for Devî, a worship specially prevalent among Jogis and Sâktas. On the other hand, the Jainas worship Bhairava as the protector or agent of the Jaina church and community, and do not offer him flesh and blood sacrifices, but fruits and sweetmeats.[2]

In his Saiva form he is often called Svâsva, or "he who rides on a dog," and this vehicle of his marks him down at once as an offshoot from the village Bhairon, because all through Upper India the favourite method of conciliating Bhairon is to feed a black dog until he is surfeited.

One of his distinctive forms is Kâl Bhairon, or Kâla Bhairava, whose image depicted with his dog is often found as a sort of warden in Saiva temples. One of his most famous shrines is at Kalinjar, of which Abul Fazl says "marvellous tales are related."[3] He is depicted with eighteen arms and is ornamented with the usual garlands of skulls, with snake earrings and snake armlets and a serpent twined round his head. In his hands he holds a sword and a bowl of blood. In the Panjâb he is said to frighten away death, and in Râjputâna Col. Tod calls him "the blood-stained divinity of war."[4] The same godling is known in Bombay as Bhairoba, of whom Mr. Campbell[5] writes—"He is represented as a standing male figure with a trident in the left hand and a drum (*damaru*) in the right, and encircled with a serpent. When thus represented he is called Kâla Bhairava. But generally he is represented by a rough stone covered over with oil and red lead. He is said to be

[1] Dalton, "Descriptive Ethnology," 147.
[2] Wilson, "Essays," i. 21; "Bombay Gazetteer," xvi. 568.
[3] Jarrett, "Aîn-i-Akbari," ii. 159; Führer, "Monumental Antiquities," 153.
[4] "Annals," ii. 15.
[5] "Notes," 147.

very terrible, and, when offended, difficult to be pleased. By some he is believed to be an incarnation of Siva himself, and by others as a spirit much in favour with the god Siva. He is also consulted as an oracle. When anyone is desirous of ascertaining whether anything he is about to undertake will turn out according to his wishes, he sticks two unbroken betel-nuts, one on each breast of the stone image of Bhairava, and tells it, if his wish is to be accomplished, that the right or left nut is to fall first. It is said, like other spirits, Bhairava is not a subordinate of Vetâla, and that when he sets out on his circuit at night, he rides a black horse and is accompanied by a black dog."

In the Panjâb he[1] is usually represented as an inferior deity, a stout black figure, with a bottle of wine in his hand; he is an evil spirit, and his followers drink wine and eat meat. One set of ascetics, akin to the Jogis, besmear themselves with red powder and oil and go about begging and singing the praises of Bhairon, with bells or gongs hung about their loins and striking themselves with whips. They are found mainly in large towns, and are not celibates. Their chief place of pilgrimage is the Girnâr Hill in Kâthiawâr. That very old temple, the Bhairon Kâ Asthân near Lahore, is so named from a quaint legend regarding Bhairon, connected with its foundation. In the old days the Dhînwâr girls of Riwâri used to be married to the godling at Bandoda, but they always died soon after, and the custom has been abandoned. We shall meet later on other instances of the marriage of girls to a god.

As a village godling Bhairon appears in various forms as Lâth Bhairon or "Bhairon of the club," which approximates him to Bhîmsen, Battuk Bhairon or "the child Bhairon," and Nand Bhairon, in which we may possibly trace a connection with the legend of the divine child Krishna and his foster-father Nanda. In Benares, again, he is known as Bhaironnâth or "Lord Bhairon," and Bhût Bhairon, "Ghost Bhairon," and he is regarded as the deified magis-

[1] Maclagan, "Panjâb Census Report," 107.

trate of the city, who guards all the temples of Siva and saves his votaries from demons.[1]

But in his original character as a simple village godling Bhairon is worshipped with milk and sweetmeats as the protector of fields, cattle and homestead. Some worship him by pouring spirits at his shrine and drinking there; and on a new house being built, he is propitiated to expel the local ghosts. He is respected even by Muhammadans as the minister of the great saint Sakhi Sarwar, and in this connection is usually known as Bhairon Jati or "Bhairon the chaste."[2] But as we have seen, he is becoming rapidly promoted into the more respectable cabinet of the gods, and his apotheosis will possibly finally take place at the great Saiva shrine of Mandhâta on the Narmadâ, with which a local legend closely connects him.[3] All over Northern India his stone fetish is found in close connection with the images of the greater gods, to whom he acts the part of guardian, and this, as we have already seen, probably marks a stage in his promotion.

He has, according to the last census, only five thousand followers in the Panjâb, as compared with one hundred and and seventy-five thousand in the North-Western Provinces.

WORSHIP OF GANESA.

On pretty much the same stage as these warden godlings whom we have been considering is Ganesa, whose name means "lord of the Ganas" or inferior deities, especially those in attendance on Siva. He is represented as a short, fat man, of a yellow colour, with a protuberant belly, four hands, and the head of an elephant with a single tusk. Pârvatî is said to have formed him from the scurf of her body, and so proud was she of her offspring that she showed him to the ill-omened Sani, who when he looked at him reduced his head to ashes. Brahma advised her to replace the head with the first she could find, and the first she found

[1] Sherring, "Sacred City," 119.
[2] "Panjâb Notes and Queries," i. 35.
[3] "Central Provinces Gazetteer," 259.

GANESA.

I. 110.

was that of an elephant. Another story says that Ganesa's head was that of the elephant of Indra, and that one of his tusks was broken off by the axe of Parasurâma. Ganesa is the god of learning, the patron of undertakings and the remover of obstacles. Hence he is worshipped at marriages, and his quaint figure stands over the house door and the entrance of the greater temples. But there can be little doubt that he, too, is an importation from the indigenous mythology. His elephant head and the rat as his vehicle suggest that his worship arose from the primitive animal cultus.

THE WORSHIP OF THE GREAT MOTHERS.

From these generally benevolent village godlings we pass on to a very obscure form of local worship, that of the Great Mothers. It prevails both in Aryan and Semetic lands,[1] and there can be very little doubt that it is founded on some of the very earliest beliefs of the human race. No great religion is without its deified woman, the Virgin, Mâyâ, Râdhâ, Fâtimah, and it has been suggested that the cultus has come down from a time before the present organization of the family came into existence, and when descent through the mother was the only recognized form.[2]

We have already met instances of this mother-worship in the case of Gangâ Mâî, "Mother Ganges," and Dhartî Mâtâ, "the Earth Mother." We shall meet it again in Sîtalâ Mâtâ, "the small-pox Mother."

In the old mythology Aditî, or infinite space, was regarded as the Eternal Mother, and Prâkritî was the Eternal Mother, capable of evolving all created things out of herself, but never so creating unless united with the eternal spirit principle embodied in the Eternal Male, Parusha. There appears to have been a tendency on the part of the Indo-Germanic race to look upon their deities as belonging to

[1] For the Celtic Mothers see Rhys, "Lectures," 100, 899; for Arabia, Robertson-Smith, "Kinship," 179.

[2] Lubbock, "Origin of Civilization," 146; Starke, "Primitive Family," 17 sqq.; Letourneau, "Sociology," 384.

both sexes at once, and hence the dualistic idea in Brâhmanism of Ardhanari, or the androgynous Siva.[1]

We shall meet later on with the ghost of the unpurified mother, the Churel, which is based on a different but cognate association of ideas. Akin to this, again, is the worship of the Satî, or model wife, to which we shall refer again, and that of the Chȃran women of Gujarât, who were obliged to immolate themselves to prevent outrage from the Kolis and other freebooters.

This worship, probably derived from one of the so-called non-Aryan races, was subsequently developed into that of the female energies of the greater gods, a Brâhmânî of Brahma, Indrânî of Indra, and so on; and thus the simple worship of the mother has developed and degenerated into the abominations of the Tantras. These mothers are usually regarded as eight in number, the Ashta Mâtrî, but the enumeration of them varies. Sometimes there are only seven—Brâhmî or Brahmânî, Maheshvarî, Kaumârî, Vaishnavî, Vârâhî, Indrânî or Aindrânî, or Mahendrî and Châmundâ. Sometimes the number is nine—Brahmânî, Vaishnavî, Raudrî, Vârâhî, Narasinhikâ, Kaumârî, Mahendrî, Châmundâ, Chandikâ. Sometimes sixteen—Gaurî, Padmâ, Sachî, Medhâ, Savitrî, Vijayâ, Jayâ, Devasenâ, Svadhâ, Svâhâ, Sântî, Pushtî, Dhritî, Tushtî, Atmadevatâ, Kuladevatâ.[2] They are closely connected with the worship of Siva and are attendants on his son Skanda, or Kârttikeya, and rise in the later mythology to a much greater number.

MOTHER-WORSHIP IN GUJARÂT.

But it is in Gujarât that this form of worship prevails most widely at the present day. Sir Monier-Williams enumerates about one hundred and forty distinct Mothers,

[1] Benfey, "Panchatantra," i. 41-52; quoted by Tawney, "Katha Sarit Sâgara," ii. 638.

[2] Monier-Williams, "Sanskrit Dictionary, s.v. Mâtrî"; for the Nepâl enumeration, Oldfield, "Sketches," i. 151; for Bombay, "Gazetteer," xvii. 715. In the "Katha Sarit Sâgara" (i. 552), Nârâyanî is their leader. There is a very remarkable story of the gambler who swindled the Divine Mothers (ibid., ii. 574 sqq.).

besides numerous varieties of the more popular forms. They are probably all local deities of the Churel type, who have been adopted into Brâhmanism. Some are represented by rudely carved images, others by simple shrines, and others are remarkable for preferring empty shrines, and the absence of all visible representations. Each has special functions. Thus one called Khodiâr, or "mischief," is said to cause trouble unless propitiated; another called Antâî causes and prevents whooping cough; another named Berâî prevents cholera; another called Marakî causes cholera; Hadakâî controls mad dogs and prevents hydrophobia; Asapurâ, represented by two idols, satisfies the hopes of wives by giving children. Not a few are worshipped either as causing or preventing demoniacal possession as a form of disease. The offering of a goat's blood to some of these Mothers is regarded as very effectual. A story is told of a Hindu doctor who cured a whole village of an outbreak of violent influenza, attributed to the malignant influence of an angry Mother goddess, by simply assembling the inhabitants, muttering some cabalistic texts, and solemnly letting loose a pair of scapegoats in a neighbouring wood as an offering to the offended deity. One of these Mothers is connected with the curious custom of the Couvade, which will be discussed later on.[1] Another famous Gujarât Mother is Ambâ Bhavânî. On the eighth night of the Naurâtra the Râna of Danta attends the worship, fans the goddess with a horsehair fly-flapper, celebrates the fire sacrifice, and fills with sweetmeats a huge cauldron, which, on the fall of the garland from the neck of the goddess, the Bhîls empty. Among the offerings to her are animal sacrifice and spirituous liquor. The image is a block of stone roughly hewn into the semblance of a human figure.[2]

MOTHER-WORSHIP IN UPPER INDIA.

In the Hills what is known as the Mâtrî Pûjâ is very popular. The celebrant takes a plank and cleans it with

[1] Campbell, "Notes," 311; "Athenæum," 6th December, 1879; "Folk-lore Record," iii. Part i. 117 sqq.
[2] "Bombay Gazetteer," v. 432 sq.

rice flour. On it he draws sixteen figures representing the Mâtrîs, and to the right of them a representation of Ganesa. Figures of the sun and moon are also delineated, and a brush made of sacred grass is dipped in cow-dung and the figures touched with it. After the recital of verses, a mixture of sugar and butter is let drop on the plank, three, five, or seven times. The celebrant then marks the forehead of the person for whose benefit the service is intended with a coin soaked in butter, and keeps the money as his fee. The service concludes with a waving of lamps to scare vicious ghosts, singing of hymns and offering of gifts to Brâhmans.[1]

At Khalâri, in the Râêpur District of the Central Provinces, is a Satî pillar worshipped under the name of Khalârî Mâtâ. According to the current legend Khalârî Mâtâ often assumes a female human form and goes to the adjacent fairs, carrying vegetables for sale. Whoever asks any gift from her receives it. Once a young man returning from a fair was overtaken by a strange woman on the road, who said she was going to see her sister. She asked him to go in front, and said that she would follow. Not wishing to allow a beautiful young woman to travel alone at night, he hid himself among some bushes. Presently he heard a great jingling noise and saw a four-armed woman go up the steep, bare hill and disappear. It was quite certain that this was Khalârî Mâtâ herself.[2]

In many parts of the plains, Mâyâ, the mother of Buddha, has been introduced into the local worship as the Gânwdevî, or village goddess. Her statues, which are very numerous in some places, are freely utilized for this purpose. In the same way a figure of the Buddha Asvaghosha is worshipped at Deoriya in the Allahâbâd District as Srinagarî Devî.[3]

THE JUNGLE MOTHERS.

As an instance of another type of Mother-worship we may take Porû Mâî of Nadiya. She is "represented by a

[1] Atkinson, "Himâlayan Gazetteer," ii. 884.
[2] Cunningham, "Archæological Reports," vii. 158.
[3] Growse, "Mathura," 116, 125; Führer, "Monumental Antiquities" 27, 132.

little piece of rough black stone painted with red ochre, and placed beneath the boughs of an ancient banyan tree. She is said to have been in the heart of the jungles, with which Nadiya was originally covered, and to have suffered from the fire which Râja Kâsi Nâth's men lighted to burn down the jungle."[1] She is, in fact, a Mother goddess of the jungle, of whom there are numerous instances. In the North-Western Provinces she is usually known as Banspatî or Bansapatî Mâî (Vanaspatî, "mistress of the wood"). Agni, the fire god, is described in the Rig Veda as "the son of the Vanaspatis," or the deities of the large, old forest trees.[2] Another name for her in the Western Districts is Âsarorî, because her shrine is a pile of pebbles (*rorî*) in which her votaries have confidence (*âsâ*) that it will protect them from harm. The shrine of the jungle mother is usually a pile of stones and branches to which every passer-by contributes. When she is displeased she allows a tiger or a leopard to kill her negligent votary. She is the great goddess of the herdsmen and other dwellers in the forest, and they vow to her a cock, a goat, or a young pig if she saves them and their cattle from beasts of prey. Sometimes she is identified with the Churel, more often with a Havva or Bhût, the spirit, usually malignant, of some one who has met untimely death in the jungle. Akin to her is the Ghataut of Mirzapur, who is the deity of dangerous hill passes (*ghât*) and is worshipped in the same way, and Baghaut, the ghost of a man who was killed by a tiger (*bâgh*). These all, in the villages along the edge of the jungle, merge in character and function with the divine council, or Deohâr, of the local gods.

OTHER MOTHER GODDESSES.

Another of these divine mothers, Mâtâ Januvî or Janamî, the goddess of births, is a sort of Juno Lucina among the Râjputs, like the Greek Ilithyia, or the Carmenta of the Romans. Her power rests in a bead, and all over Northern

[1] Bholanâth Chandra, "Travels of a Hindu," i. 38.
[2] "Rig Veda," viii. 23, 25.

India midwives carry as a charm to secure easy delivery a particular sort of bead, known as Kailâs Maura, or "the crown of the sacred mountain Kailâsa." Difficult parturition is a disease caused by malignant spirits, and numerous are the devices to cure it. The ancient Britons, we are told,[1] used to bind a magic girdle, impressed with numerous mystical figures, round the waist of the expectant mother, and the jewel named Aetites, found in the eagle's nest, applied to the thigh of one in labour, eases pain and quickens delivery. Sir W. Scott[2] had a small stone, called a toad-stone, which repelled demons from lying-in women.

On the sacred plain of Kurukshetra there once stood a fort, known as Chakravyûha, and to the moderns as Chakâbu Kâ Qila, from which to the present day immense ancient bricks are occasionally dug. Popular belief ascribes great efficacy to these bricks, and in cases of protracted labour, one of them is soaked in water, which is given to the patient to drink. Sometimes an image of the fort, which is in the form of a labyrinth or maze, is drawn on a dish, which is first shown to the mother and then washed in water, which is administered to the woman. All through Nepâl and the neighbouring districts, the local rupee, which is covered with Saiva emblems, is used in the same way, and Akbar's square rupee, known as the Châryârî, because it bears the names of the four companions (Châr-Yâr) of the Prophet, is credited with the same power. There are numerous Mantras or mystic formulæ which are used for the same purpose.

Dread famine has become a goddess under the title of Bhûkhî Mâtâ, the "hunger Mother," who, like all the deities of this class, is of a lean and starved appearance.[3] An interesting ceremony for the exorcism of the hunger Mother is recorded from Bombay. The people subscribed to purchase ten sheep, fifty fowls, one hundred cocoanuts, betel nuts, sugar, clarified butter, frankincense, red powder, turmeric, and flowers. A day previous to the commence-

[1] Brand, "Observations," 331. [2] "Border Minstrelsy," 466.
[3] Tod, "Annals," ii. 363 sq., 763; Conway, "Demonology," i. 54.

ment of the ceremony, all the inhabitants of the village, taking with them their clothes, vessels, cattle, and other movable goods, left their houses and encamped at the gate or boundary of the village. At the village gate a triumphal arch was erected, and it was adorned with garlands of flowers and mango leaves covered with red powder and turmeric. All these things are, as we shall see, well known as scarers of demons. The villagers bathed, put on new clothes, and then a procession was formed. On coming to the triumphal arch the whole procession was stopped. A hole was dug in the ground, and the village watchman put in it the head of a sheep, a cocoanut, betel nuts, with leaves and flowers. The arch was then worshipped by each of the villagers. The village watchman first entered the arch, and he was followed by the villagers with music, loud cheering, and clapping of hands. The whole party then went to the village temple, bowed to the village god, and went to their respective houses. The blood of the ten sheep and fifty fowls was offered to the village god, and the flesh was distributed among the people. A dinner was given to Brâhmans and the rite came to an end.[1] The idea of the sanctity of the arch is probably based on the same principle as that of perforated stones, to which reference will be made in another connection.

Greatest of all the mother goddesses of the Râjputs is Mâmâ Devî, the mother of the gods. She is thus on the same plane as Cybele Rhea and Demeter, the Corn Mother, who gives the kindly increase of the fruits of the earth. In one of her temples she is represented in the midst of her numerous family, including the greater and the minor divinities. Their statues are all of the purest marble, each about three feet high and tolerably executed, though evidently since the decline of the art.[2]

WORSHIP OF GANSÂM DEO.

We now come to consider some divinities special to the Drâvidian races, who touch on the North-Western Provinces

[1] Campbell, "Notes," 145. [2] Tod, "Annals," i. 708; ii. 670.

to the south, across the Kaimûr and Vindhyan ranges, the physical as well as the ethnical frontier between the valleys of the Ganges and Jumnâ and the mountain country of Central India. The chief Gond deity is Gansâm Deo. Some vague attempt has been made to elevate him into the pantheon of Brâhmanism, and his name has been corrupted into Ghanasyâma, which means in Sanskrit, "black like the heavy rain clouds of the rainy season," and is an epithet of Râma and of Krishna. One legend derives him from an actual Gond chieftain, just as many of the local godlings whom we shall consider afterwards have sprung from real living persons of eminence, or those who have lost their lives in some exceptional way. It is said that this chieftain was devoured by a tiger soon after his marriage. As might have been expected, his spirit was restless, and one year after his death he visited his wife and she conceived by him. Instances of such miraculous conceptions are common in folk-lore.[1] "The descendants of this ghostly embrace are, it is said, living to this day at Amoda, in the Central Provinces. He, about the same time, appeared to many of his old friends, and persuaded them that he could save them from the maws of tigers and other calamities, if his worship were duly inaugurated and regularly performed; and in consequence of this, two festivals in the year were established in his honour; but he may be worshipped at any time, and in all sickness and misfortunes his votaries confidently appeal to him."[2]

In the Hill country of Mirzapur, the shrine of Gansâm is about one hundred yards from the village site and without any ornamentation. Both inside and outside is a platform of mud, on which the deity can rest when so disposed. The only special offerings to him are the curious water-pots (*kalsa*) already described, and some rude clay figures of horses and elephants, which are regarded as the equipage (*sawârî*) of the deity. In the Central Provinces, "a bamboo with a red or yellow flag tied to the end is planted in one

[1] Hartland, "Legend of Perseus," i. chap. iv.
[2] Dalton, "Descriptive Ethnology," 232.

corner, an old withered garland or two is hung up, a few blocks of rough stone, some smeared with vermilion, are strewn about the place which is specially dedicated to Gansâm Deo."[1]

WORSHIP OF DÂNTAN DEO AND LALITÂ.

To the east of the Mirzapur District, there is a projecting mass of rock, which, looked at from a particular place, bears a rude resemblance to a hideous, grinning skull, with enormous teeth. This has come to be known as Dântan Deo or "the deity of the teeth," and is carefully propitiated by people when they are sick or in trouble. Akin to this deity is Lalitâ, who is worshipped to the west of the Province. She is the sister of Kâlî, and brings bad dreams. Her speciality is her long teeth, and she has sometimes a curious way of blowing up or inflating the bodies of people who do not pay her due respect.

WORSHIP OF DÛLHA DEO, THE BRIDEGROOM GODLING.

Another great godling of the Drâvidian races is Dûlha Deo, "the bridegroom godling." In his worship we have an echo of some great tragedy, which still exercises a profound influence over the minds of the people.

The bridegroom on his way to fetch the bride, is, by established Hindu custom, treated with special reverence, and this unfortunate bridegroom, whose name is forgotten, is said to have been killed by lightning in the midst of his marriage rejoicings, and he and his horse were turned into stone. In fact, like Ganymede or Hylas, he was carried off by the envy or cruel love of the merciless divine powers.

He is now one of the chief household deities of the Drâvidian people. Flowers are offered to him on the last day of Phâlgun (February), and at marriages a goat. Among some of the Gond tribes he has the first place, and is iden-

[1] "Gazetteer," 276.

tified with Pharsipen, the god of war. In the native States of Rîwa and Sarguja, even Brâhmans worship him, and his symbol or fetish is the battle-axe, the national weapon of the Drâvidian races, fastened to a tree. In Mirzapur he is pre-eminently the marriage godling. In the marriage season he is worshipped in the family cook-room, and at weddings oil and turmeric are offered to him. When two or three children in the same hamlet are being married at the same time, there is a great offering made of a red goat and cakes; and to mark the benevolent character of the deity as a household godling, the women, contrary to the usual rule, are allowed a share of the meat. This purely domestic worship is not done by the Baiga or devil priest, but by the Tikâit or eldest son of the family. He is specially the tribal god of the Ghasiyas, who pour a little spirits in the cook-room in honour of him and of deceased relatives. The songs in his honour lay special stress on the delicacies which the house-mother prepares for his entertainment. Among the Kharwârs, when the newly married pair come home, he is worshipped near the family hearth. A goat is fed on rice and pulse, and its head is cut off with an axe, the worshipper folding his hands and saying, "Take it, Dûlha Deo!"

On the day when this worship is performed, the ashes of the fireplace are carefully removed with the hands, a broom is not used, and special precautions are taken that none of the ashes fall on the ground.

General Sleeman gives the legend of Dûlha Deo in another form.

"In descending into the valley of the Narmadâ over the Vindhya range from Bhopâl, one may see on the side of the road, upon a spur of the hill, a singular pillar of sandstone rising in two spires, one turning and rising above the other to the height of some twenty to thirty feet. On the spur of a hill, half a mile distant, is another sandstone pillar not quite so high. The tradition is that the smaller pillar was the affianced bride of the larger one, who was a youth of a family of great eminence in those parts. Coming with his uncle to pay his first visit to his bride in the marriage procession, he grew more and more impatient as he approached nearer and nearer, and she shared the feeling. At last, unable to restrain himself, he jumped from his uncle's shoulders, and looked with all his might towards the place where his bride was said to be seated. Unhappily she felt no less impatient than he did, and they saw each other at the same moment. In that moment the bride, bridegroom, and uncle were, all three, converted into pillars, and there they stand to this day, a monument to warn mankind against an inclination to indulge in curiosity. It is a singular fact that in one of the most extensive tribes of the Gond population, to which this couple is said to have belonged, the bride always, contrary to the usual Hindu custom, goes to the bridegroom in procession to prevent a recurrence of this calamity."[1]

This legend is interesting from various points of view. In the first place it is an example of a process of thought of which we shall find instances in dealing with fetishism, whereby a legend is localized in connection with some curious phenomenon in the scenery, which attracts general attention. Secondly, we have an instance of the primitive taboo which appears constantly in folk-lore, where, as in the case of Lot's wife, the person who shows indiscreet curiosity by a look is turned into stone or ashes.[2] Thirdly, it may represent a survival of a custom not uncommon among primitive races, where the marriage capturing is done, not by the bridegroom, but by the bride. Thus, among the Gâros, all proposals of marriage must come from the lady's side, and any infringement of the custom can only be atoned for by liberal presents of beer given to her relations by the friends of the bridegroom, who pretends to be unwilling and runs away, but is caught and subjected to ablution, and then taken, in spite of the resistance and counterfeited grief and lamentations of the

[1] "Rambles and Recollections," i. 123.

[2] Stokes, "Indian Fairy Tales," 140 sqq.; Temple, "Wideawake Stories," 109, 302; "Indian Antiquary," iv. 57; Grimm, "Household Tales," ii. 400.

parents, to the bride's house.[1] It may then reasonably be expected that this custom of marriage prevailed among some branches of the Gond tribe, and that as they came more and more under Hindu influence, an unorthodox ritual prevailing in certain clans was explained by annexing the familiar legend of Dûlha Deo.

[1] Dalton, "Descriptive Ethnology," 64; other instances in Westermarck, "History of Human Marriage, 158 sq.

CHAPTER III.

THE GODLINGS OF DISEASE.

Καὶ γὰρ τοῖσι κακὸν χρυσόθρονος Ἄρτεμις ὦρσεν
Χωσαμένη ὃ οἱ οὔτι θαλύσια γουνῷ ἀλωῆς
Οἰνεὺς ῥέξ.

Iliad ix. 533-535.

We now come to consider a class of rural godlings, the deities who control disease.

The Demoniacal Theory of Disease.

It is a commonplace of folk-lore and the beliefs of all savage races that disease and death are not the result of natural causes, but are the work of devils and demons, witchcraft, the Evil Eye, and so forth. It is not difficult to understand the basis on which beliefs of this class depend. There are certain varieties of disease, such as hysteria, dementia, epilepsy, convulsions, the delirium of fever, which in the rural mind indicate the actual working of an evil spirit which has attacked the patient. There are, again, others, such as cholera, which are so sudden and unexpected, so irregular in their appearances, so capricious in the victims which they select, that they naturally suggest the idea that they are caused by demons. Even to this day the belief in the origin of disease from spirit possession is still common in rural England. Fits, the falling sickness, ague, cramp, warts, are all believed to be caused by a spirit entering the body of the patient. Hence comes the idea that the spirit which is working the mischief can be scared by a charm or by the exorcism of a sorcerer. They say to the ague, "Ague! farewell till we meet in hell," and to the cramp, "Cramp! be thou faultless, as Our Lady was when she bore Jesus."

It is needless to say that the same theory flourishes in rural India. Thus, in Râjputâna,[1] sickness is popularly attributed to Khor, or the agency of the offended spirits of deceased relations, and for treatment they call in a "cunning man," who propitiates the Khor by offering sweetmeats, milk, and similar things, and gives burnt ash and black pepper sanctified by charms to the patient. The Mahadeo Kolis of Ahmadnagar believe that every malady or disease that seizes man, woman, child, or cattle is caused either by an evil spirit or by an angry god. The Bijapur Vaddars have a yearly feast to their ancestors to prevent the dead bringing sickness into the house.[2]

Further east in North Bhutân all diseases are supposed to be due to possession, and the only treatment is by the use of exorcisms. Among the Gâros, when a man sickens the priest asks which god has done it. The Kukis and Khândhs believe that all sickness is caused by a god or by an offended ancestor.[3]

So among the jungle tribes of Mirzapur, the Korwas believe that all disease is caused by the displeasure of the Deohâr, or the collective village godlings. These deities sometimes become displeased for no apparent reason, sometimes because their accustomed worship is neglected, and sometimes through the malignity of some witch. The special diseases which are attributed to the displeasure of these godlings are fever, diarrhœa and cough. If small-pox comes of its own accord in the ordinary form, it is harmless, but a more dangerous variety is attributed to the anger of the local deities. Cholera and fever are regarded as generally the work of some special Bhût or angry ghost. The Kharwârs believe that disease is due to the Baiga not having paid proper attention to Râja Chandol and the other tutelary godlings of the village. The Pankas think that

[1] "Gazetteer," i. 175.

[2] "Bombay Gazetteer," xvii. 200; xxiii. 12; Campbell, "Notes, 12 sqq.

[3] Dalton, "Descriptive Ethnology,' 97, 60, 46.

disease comes in various ways—sometimes through ghosts or witches, sometimes because the godlings and deceased ancestors were not suitably propitiated. All these people believe that in the blazing days of the Indian summer the goddess Devî flies through the air and strikes any child which wears a red garment. The result is the symptoms which less imaginative people call sunstroke. Instances of similar beliefs drawn from the superstitions of the lower races all over the country might be almost indefinitely extended. Even in our own prayers for the sick we pray the Father "to renew whatsoever has been decayed by the fraud and malice of the Devil, or by the carnal will and frailness" of the patient.

Leprosy is a disease which is specially regarded as a punishment for sin, and a Hindu affected by this disease remains an outcast until he can afford to undertake a purificatory ceremony. Even lesser ailments are often attributed to the wrath of some offended god or saint. Thus, in Satâra, the King Sateswar asked the saint Sumitra for water. The sage was wrapped in contemplation, and did not answer him. So the angry monarch took some lice from the ground and threw them at the saint, who cursed the King with vermin all over his body. He endured the affliction for twelve years, until he was cured by ablution at the sacred fountain of Devrâshta.[1] As we shall see, the Bengâlis have a special deity who rules the itch.

From ideas of this kind the next stage is the actual impersonation of the deity who brings disease, and hence the troop of disease godlings which are worshipped all over India, and to whose propitiation much of the thoughts of the peasant are devoted.

SÎTALÂ, THE GODDESS OF SMALL-POX.

Of these deities the most familiar is Sîtalâ, "she that loves the cool," so called euphemistically in consequence of the fever whîch accompanies small-pox, the chief infant

[1] "Bombay Gazetteer," xix. 465.

plague of India, which is under her control. Sîtalâ has other euphemistic names. She is called Mâtâ, "the Mother" *par excellence;* Jag Rânî, "the queen of the world;" Phapholewâlî, "she of the vesicle;" Kalejewâlî, "she who attacks the liver," which is to the rustic the seat of all disease. Some call her Mâhâ Mâî, "the great Mother." These euphemistic titles for the deities of terror are common to all the mythologies. The Greeks of old called the awful Erinyes, the Eumenides, "the well-meaning." So the modern Greeks picture the small-pox as a woman, the enemy of children, and call her Sunchoremene, "indulgent," or "exorable," and Eulogia, "one to be praised or blessed;" and the Celts call the fairies "the men of peace" and "the good people," or "good neighbours."[1]

In her original form as a village goddess she has seldom a special priest or a regular temple. A few fetish stones, tended by some low-class menial, constitute her shrine. As she comes to be promoted into some form of Kâlî or Devî, she is provided with an orthodox shrine. She receives little or no respect from men, but women and children attend her service in large numbers on "Sîtalâ's seventh," Sîtalâ Kî Saptamî, which is her feast day. In Bengal she is worshipped on a piece of ground marked out and smeared with cow-dung. A fire being lighted, and butter and spirits thrown upon it, the worshipper makes obeisance, bowing his forehead to the ground and muttering incantations. A hog is then sacrificed, and the bones and offal being burnt, the flesh is roasted and eaten, but no one must take home with him any scrap of the victim.[2]

Two special shrines of Sîtalâ in Upper India may be specially referred to. That at Kankhal near Hardwâr has a curious legend, which admirably illustrates the catholicity of Hinduism. Here the local Sîtalâ has the special title of Turkin, or "the Muhammadan lady." There was once a

[1] Grimm, "Teutonic Mythology," ii. 1161; Tylor, "Early History," 143; Spencer, "Principles of Sociology," i. 229; Sir W. Scott, "Lectures on Demonology," 105.

[2] Risley, "Tribes and Castes of Bengal," i. 179.

SHRINE OF SĪTALA AND DISEASE GODLINGS.

p. 126.

princess born to one of the Mughal Emperors, who, according to the traditions of the dynasty, when many of the chief ladies of the harem were of Hindu birth, had a warm sympathy for her ancestral faith. So she made a pilgrimage to Hardwâr, and thence set off to visit the holy shrines situated in the upper course of the Ganges. When she reached the holy land of Badarinâth, the god himself appeared to her in a dream, and warned her that she being a Musalmân, her intrusion into his domains would probably encourage the attacks of the infidel. So he ordered her to return and take up her abode in Kankhal, where as a reward for her piety she should after her death become the guardian goddess of children and be deified as a manifestation of Sîtalâ. So after her death a temple was erected on the site of her tomb, and she receives the homage of multitudes of pilgrims. There is another noted shrine of Sîtalâ at Râêwala, in the Dehra Dûn District. She is a Satî, Gândharî, the wife of Dhritarâshtra, the mother of Duryodhana. When Dhritarâshtra, through the force of his divine absorption, was consumed with fire at Sapta-srota, near Hardwâr, Gândhâri also jumped into the fire and became Satî with her husband. Then, in recognition of her piety, the gods blessed her with the boon that in the Iron Age she should become the guardian deity of children and the goddess of small-pox in particular. Another noted Sîtalâ in this part of the country is the deity known as Ujalî Mâtâ, or "the White Mother," who has a shrine in the Muzaffarnagar District. Here vast crowds assemble, and women make vows at her temple for the boon of sons, and when a child is born they take it there and perform their vow by making the necessary offering to the goddess. One peculiarity of the worship of the Kankhal goddess and of Ujalî Mâtâ is that calves are released at her shrine. This can hardly be anything else but a survival of the rite of cattle slaughter, and this is one of many indications that the worship of Sîtalâ is a most primitive cult, and probably of indigenous origin.

Sîtalâ, according to one story, is only the eldest of a band of seven sisters, by whom the pustular group of diseases is supposed to be caused. So the charmer Lilith has twelve daughters, who are the twelve kinds of fevers, and this arrangement of diseases or evil spirits in categories of sevens or twelves is found in the Chaldaic magic.[1] Similarly in the older Indian mythology we have the seven Mâtrîs, the seven oceans, the seven Rishis, the seven Adityas and Dânavas, and the seven horses of the sun, and numerous other combinations of this mystic number. One list gives their names as Sîtalâ, Masânî, Basanti, Mahâ Mâî, Polamdê, Lamkariyâ, and Agwânî.[2] We shall meet Masânî or Masân, the deity of the cremation ground, in another connection. Basantî is the "yellow goddess," so called probably on account of the colour of the skin in these diseases. Mahâ Mâî is merely "the great Mother." Polamdê is possibly "she who makes the body soft or flabby," and Lamkariyâ, "she that hasteneth." Agwânî is said to mean "the leader," and by one account, Agwân, who has twenty-five thousand votaries, according to the last census returns, in the North-West Provinces, is the son of Râja Ben, or Vena, and the brother of the small-pox sisters. At Hardwâr they give the names of the seven sisters as Sîtalâ, Sedalâ, Runukî, Jhunukî, Mihilâ, Merhalâ, and Mandilâ, a set of names which smacks of some modification of an aboriginal cultus.

Their shrines cluster round the special shrine of Sîtalâ, and the villagers to the west of the North-West Provinces call them her Khidmatgârs, or body servants. Round many of the shrines again, as at Kankhal, we find a group of minor shrines, which by one explanation are called the shrines of the other disease godlings. Villagers say that when disease appears in a family, the housewife comes and makes a vow, and if the patient recovers she makes a little shrine to the peculiar form of Devî which she considers responsible for the illness. The Brâhmans say that these minor shrines are in honour of the Yoginîs, who are usually

[1] Leland, "Etruscan Roman Remains," 153.
[2] Ibbetson, "Panjâb Ethnography," 114.

said to number eight—Mârjanî, Karpûratilakâ, Malayagandhinî Kauamudikâ, Bherundâ, Mâtâlî, Nâyakî, Jayâ or Subhâchârâ, Sulakshanâ and Sunandâ. In the Gurgaon District, accompanying images of Sîtalâ, is one of Sedhu Lâla, who is inferior to her, yet often worshipped before her, because he is regarded as her servant and intercessor. Copper coins are thrown behind her shrine into a saucer, which is known as her Mâlkhâna or Treasury. Rice and other articles of food are placed in front of her shrine, and afterwards distributed to Chamârs, the currier caste, and to dogs.[1]

Like so many deities of this class Sîtalâ is on the way to promotion to the higher heaven. In some places she is identified with Kâlikâ Bhavânî, and one list of the seven small-pox sisters gives their names as Sîtalâ, Phûlmatî, Chamariyâ, Durgâ Kâlî, Mahâ Kâlî, and Bhadrâ Kâlî. This has obviously passed through the mill of Brâhmanism. Of these, Chamariyâ is doubtless allied to Châmar, who is a vaguely described low-caste deity, worshipped in the North-Western Provinces. Some say he is the ghost of a Chamâr, or worker in leather, who died an untimely death. Chamariyâ is said to be the eldest and Phûlmatî the youngest sister of Sîtalâ. She, by the common account, takes her name from the pustules (*phûl*) of the disease. She brings the malady in its mildest form, and the worst variety is the work of Sîtalâ in person. She lives in the Nîm tree, and hence a patient suffering from the disease is fanned with its leaves. A very bad form of confluent small-pox is the work of Chamariyâ, who must be propitiated with the offering of a pig through a Chamâr or other low-caste priest. The influence of Kâlî in her threefold form is chiefly felt in connection with other pustular diseases besides small-pox. Earthenware images of elephants are placed at her shrine, and her offerings consist of cakes, sweetmeats, pigs, goats, sheep, and black fowls. Bhadrâ Kâlî is the least formidable of all. The only person who has influence over Kâlî is the Ojha, or sorcerer, who, when

[1] "Indian Antiquary," viii. 211.

cholera and similar epidemics prevail, collects a subscription and performs a regular expiatory service.

CONNECTION OF SÎTALÂ WITH HUMAN SACRIFICE.

In her form as household goddess, Sîtalâ is often known as Thandî, or "the cool one," and her habitation is in the house behind the water-pots, in the cold, damp place where the water drips. Here she is worshipped by the house-mother, but only cold food or cold water is offered to her.

There is, however, a darker side to the worship of Sîtalâ and the other disease godlings than this mild household service. In 1817 a terrible epidemic of cholera broke out at Jessore. "The disease commenced its ravages in August, and it was at once discovered that the August of this year had five Saturdays (a day under the influence of the ill-omened Sani). The number five being the express property of the destructive Siva, a mystical connection was at once detected, the infallibly baneful influence of which it would have been sacrilege to question. On the night of the 27th a strange commotion spread through the villages adjacent to the station. A number of magicians were reported to have quitted Marelli with a human head in their possession, which they were to be directed by the presence of supernatural signs to leave in a certain, and to them unknown, village. The people on all sides were ready by force to arrest the progress of these nocturnal visitors. For the prophecy foretold that wherever the head fell, the destroying angel terminating her sanguinary course would rest, and the demon of death, thus satisfied, would refrain from further devastation in that part of the country. Dr. Tytler says that on that night, while walking along the road, endeavouring to allay the agitation, the judge and he perceived a faint light arising from a thick clump of bamboos. Attracted to the spot, they found a hut which was illuminated, and contained images of five Hindu gods, one of which was Sîtalâ, the celebrated and formidable Aulâ Bîbî,

'Our Lady of the Flux,' an incarnation of Kâlî, who it is believed is one day to appear riding on a horse for the purpose of slaughtering mankind, and of setting the world on fire. In front of the idol a female child about nine years of age lay on the ground. She was evidently stupefied with intoxicating drugs, and in this way prepared to answer responses to such questions as those initiated into the mysteries should think proper to propose."[1] There is much in this statement which is open to question, and it seems doubtful whether, as Dr. Chevers is disposed to believe, the case was really one of intended human sacrifice.

SMALL-POX WORSHIP IN BENGAL.

In Bengal the divine force antagonistic to Sîtalâ is Shashthî, "goddess of the sixth," who is regarded as the special guardian of children. The worship of Shashthî rests on a physiological fact, which has only recently been applied to explain this special form of worship. The most fatal disease of Indian children is a form of infantile lock-jaw, which is caused by the use of a coarse, blunt instrument, such as a sickle, for severing the umbilical cord. This disease usually makes its appearance between the sixth and twelfth day of the life of the child, and hence we have the formal rites of purification from the birth pollution performed as the Chhathî on the sixth and the Barahî on the twelfth day after delivery.

"In Bengal when small-pox rages, the gardeners are busiest. As soon as the nature of the disease is determined, the physician retires and a gardener is summoned. His first act is to forbid the introduction of meat, fish, and all food requiring oil or spices for its preparation. He then ties a lock of hair, a cowry shell, a piece of turmeric, and an article of gold on the right wrist of the patient. (The use of these articles as scarers of evil spirits will be considered later on.) The sick person is then laid on the Majhpatta, the young and unexpanded leaf of the plantain tree, and

[1] Chevers, "Medical Jurisprudence for India," 415 sq.

milk is prescribed as the sole article of food. He is fanned with a branch of the sacred Nîm (*Azidirachta Indica*), and any one entering the chamber is sprinkled with water. Should the fever become aggravated and delirium ensue, or if the child cries much and sleeps little, the gardener performs the Mâtâ Pûjâ. This consists in bathing an image of the goddess causing the disease, and giving a draught of the water to drink. To relieve the irritation of the skin, pease meal, turmeric, flour or shell sawdust is sprinkled over the body. If the eruption be copious, a piece of new cloth in the figure of eight is wrapped round the chest and shoulders. On the night between the seventh and eighth days of the eruption, the gardener has much to do. He places a water-pot in the sick-room, and puts on it rice, a cocoanut, sugar, plantains, a yellow rag, flowers, and a few Nîm leaves. Having mumbled several spells (*mantra*), he recites the tale (*qissa*) of the particular goddess, which often occupies several hours. When the pustules are mature, the gardener dips a thorn of the Karaunda (*Carissa*) in sesamum oil and punctures each one. The body is then anointed with oil, and cooling fruits are given. When the scabs have peeled off, another ceremony called Godâm is gone through. All the offerings on the water-pot are rolled in a cloth and fastened round the waist of the patient. The offerings are the perquisite of the gardener, who also receives a fee. Government vaccinators earn a considerable sum yearly by executing the Sîtalâ worship, and when a child is vaccinated, a portion of the service is performed"—a curious compromise between the indigenous faith and European medical science.[1]

The special Tirhût observance of the Jur Sîtal or "small-pox fever" feast will be more conveniently considered in connection with other usages of the same kind.

MÂTANGÎ SAKTÎ AND MASÂN.

We have already seen that Sîtalâ is in the stage of promotion to the Brâhmanical heaven. Here her special name

[1] Risley, "Tribes and Castes," ii. 62.

is Mâtangî Saktî, a word which has been connected with Mâtâ and Masân, but really refers to Durgâ-Devî in her terrible elephant form. Masân or Masânî is quite a different goddess. She resides at the Masân or cremation ground, and is greatly dreaded. The same name is in the eastern district of the North-Western Provinces applied to the tomb of some low-caste man, very often a Teli or oilman, or a Dhobi or washerman, both of whose ghosts are generally obnoxious. Envious women will take the ashes from a cremation ground and throw them over an enemy's child. This is said to cause them to be "under the influence of the shadow" (Sâya, Chhâya) and to waste away by slow decline. This idea is familiar in folk-lore. All savages believe that their shadow is a part of themselves, that if it be hurt the owner of it will feel pain, that a man may lose his shadow altogether and thus be deprived of part of his soul and strength, and that vicious people, as in the present case, can fling their shadow upon you and cause you injury.[1]

Mâtangî Saktî, again, appears in at least eight forms—Raukâ Devî, Ghraukâ Devî, Melâ Devî, Mandlâ Devî, Sîtalâ Devî, Durgâ Devî and Sankarâ Devî, a collection of names which indicates the extraordinary mixture of beliefs, some of them importations from the regular mythology, but others obscure and local manifestations of the deity, out of which this worship has been developed. She is described as having ears as large as a winnowing fan, projecting teeth, a hideous face with a wide open mouth. Her vehicle is the ass, an animal very often found in association with shrines of Sîtalâ. She carries a broom and winnowing fan with which she sifts mankind, and in one hand a pitcher and ewer. This fan and broom are, as we shall see later on, most powerful fetishes. All this is sheer mythology at its lowest stage, and represents the grouping of various local fetish beliefs on the original household worship.

[1] Spencer, "Principles of Sociology," i. 115; Frazer, "Golden Bough," i. 141 sqq.

JOURNEY FORBIDDEN DURING AN EPIDEMIC OF SMALL-POX.

During a small-pox epidemic no journey, not even a pilgrimage to a holy shrine, should be undertaken. Gen. Sleeman[1] gives a curious case in illustration of this: "At this time the only son of Râma Krishna's brother, Khushhâl Chand, an interesting boy of about four years of age, was extremely ill of small-pox. His father was told that he had better defer his journey to Benares till the child should recover; but he could neither eat nor sleep, so great was his terror lest some dreadful calamity should befall the whole family before he could expiate a sacrilege which he had committed unwittingly, or take the advice of his high priest, as to the best manner of doing so, and he resolved to leave the decision to God himself. He took two pieces of paper and having caused *Benares* to be written on one and *Jabalpur* on the other, he put them both in a brass vessel. After shaking the vessel well, he drew forth that on which Benares had been written. 'It is the will of God,' said Râma Krishna. All the family who were interested in the preservation of the poor boy implored him not to set out, lest the Devî who presides over small-pox should be angry. It was all in vain. He would set out with his household god, and unable to carry it himself, he put it upon a small litter upon a pole, and hired a bearer to carry it at one end while he supported the other. His brother Khushhâl Chand sent his second wife at the same time with offerings to the Devî, to ward off the effects of his brother's rashness from the child. By the time his brother had got with his god to Adhartâl, three miles from Jabalpur, he heard of the death of his nephew. But he seemed not to feel this slight blow in the terror of the dreadful, but undefined, calamity which he felt to be impending over him and the whole family, and he went on his road. Soon after, an infant son of his uncle died of the same disease, and the whole town at once became divided into two parties—those who held that the child had been killed by the Devî as a punishment for Râma Krishna's

[1] "Rambles and Recollections," i. 207.

presuming to leave Jabalpur before they recovered, and those who held that they were killed by the god Vishnu himself for having deprived him of one of his arms. Khushhâl Chand's wife sickened on the road and died before reaching Mirzapur; and as the Devî was supposed to have nothing to say to fevers, this event greatly augmented the advocates of Vishnu."

OBSERVANCES DURING SMALL-POX EPIDEMICS.

In the Panjâb when a child falls ill of small-pox no one is allowed to enter the house, especially if he have bathed, washed, or combed his hair, and if any one does come in, he is made to burn incense at the door. Should a thunder-storm come on before the vesicles have fully come out, the sound is not allowed to enter the ear of the sick child, and metal plates are violently beaten to drown the noise of the thunder. For six or seven days, when the disease is at its height, the child is fed with raisins covered with silver leaf. When the vesicles have fully developed it is believed that Devî Mâtâ has come. When the disease has abated a little, water is thrown over the child. Singers and drummers are summoned and the parents make with their friends a procession to the temple of Devî, carrying the child dressed in saffron-coloured clothes. A man goes in advance with a bunch of sacred grass in his hands, from which he sprinkles a mixture of milk and water. In this way they visit some fig-tree or other shrine of Devî, to which they tie red ribbons and besmear it with red lead, paint and curds.[1]

One method of protecting children from the disease is to give them opprobrious names, and dress them in rags. This, with other devices for disease transference, will be discussed later on. We have seen that the Nîm tree is supposed to influence the disease; hence branches of it are hung over the door of the sick-room. Thunder disturbs the goddess in possession of the child, so the family flour-mill, which, as as we shall see, has mystic powers, is rattled near the child.

[1] Nûr Ahmad Chishti, *Yâdgâr-i-Chishti*.

Another device is to feed a donkey, which is the animal on which Sîtalâ rides. This is specially known in the Panjâb as the Jandî Pûjâ.[1] In the same belief that the patient is under the direct influence of the goddess, if death ensues the purification of the corpse by cremation is considered both unnecessary and improper. Like Gusâîns, Jogis, and similar persons who are regarded as inspired, those who die of this disease are buried, not cremated. As Sir A. C. Lyall observes,[2] "The rule is ordinarily expounded by the priests to be imperative, because the outward signs and symptoms mark the actual presence of divinity; the small-pox is not the god's work, but the god himself manifest; but there is also some ground for concluding that the process of burying has been found more wholesome than the hurried and ill-managed cremation, which prevails during a fatal epidemic." Gen. Sleeman gives an instance of an outbreak of the disease which was attributed to a violation of this traditional rule.[3]

MINOR DISEASE GODLINGS.

There are a number of minor disease godlings, some of whom may be mentioned here. The Benares godling of malaria is Jvaraharîsvara, "the god who repels the fever." The special offering to him is what is called Dudhbhanga, a confection made of milk, the leaves of the hemp plant and sweetmeats. Among the Kols of Chaibâsa, Bangara is the godling of fever and is associated with Gohem, Chondu, Negra and Dichali, who are considered respectively the godlings of cholera, the itch, indigestion and death. The Bengâlis have a special service for the worship of Ghentu, the itch godling. The scene of the service is a dunghill. A broken earthenware pot, its bottom blackened with constant use for cooking, daubed white with lime, interspersed with a few streaks of turmeric, together with a branch or two of the Ghentu plant, and last, not least, a broomstick of the genuine palmyra or cocoanut stock, serve

[1] "Panjâb Notes and Queries," iii. 42, 167.
[2] "Asiatic Studies," 57 sq.
[3] "Rambles and Recollections," i. 208.

as the representation of the presiding deity of itch. The mistress of the family, for whose benefit the worship is done, acts as priestess. After a few doggrel lines are recited, the pot is broken and the pieces collected by the children, who sing songs about the itch godling.[1]

Some of these godlings are, like Shashthî, protectors of children from infantile disorders. Such are in Hoshangâbâd Bijaysen, in whose name a string, which, as we shall see, exercises a powerful influence over demons, is hung round the necks of children from birth till marriage, and Kurdeo, whose name represents the Kuladevatâ, or family deity. Among the Kurkus he presides over the growth and health of the children in three or four villages together.[2] Acheri, a disease sprite in the Hills, particularly favours those who wear red garments, and in his name a scarlet thread is tied round the throat as an amulet against cold, and goitre. Ghanta Karana, "he who has ears as broad as a bell," or "who wears bells in his ears," is another disease godling of the Hills. He is supposed to be of great personal attractions, and is worshipped under the form of a water jar as the healer of cutaneous diseases. He is a gate-keeper, or, in other words, a godling on his promotion, in many of the Garhwâl temples.[3]

Among the Kurkus of Hoshangâbâd, Mutua Deo is represented by a heap of stones inside the village. His special sacrifice is a pig, and his particular mission is to send epidemics, and particularly fevers, in which case he must be propitiated with extraordinary sacrifices.[4]

One of the great disease Mothers is Marî Bhavânî. She has her speciality in the regulation of cholera, which she spreads or withholds according to the attention she receives. They tell a curious story about her in Oudh. Safdar Jang, having established his virtual independence of the Mughal Empire, determined to build a capital. He selected as the

[1] "Calcutta Review," xviii. 68.
[2] Hoshangâbâd "Settlement Report," 119, 255.
[3] Atkinson, "Himâlayan Gazetteer," ii. 833, 816 sq.
[4] "Settlement Report," 254 sq.

site for it the high bank of the Gûmti, overlooking Pâparghât in Sultânpur. And but for the accident of a sickly season, that now comparatively unknown locality might have enjoyed the celebrity which afterwards fell to the lot of Faizâbâd. The fort was already begun when the news reached the Emperor, who sent his minister a khilat, to all outward appearance suited to his rank and dignity. The royal gift had been packed up with becoming care, and its arrival does not seem to have struck Safdar Jang as incompatible with the rebellious attitude which he had assumed. The box in which it was enclosed was opened with due ceremony, when it was discovered that the Emperor, with grim pleasantry, had selected as an appropriate gift an image of Marî Bhavânî. The mortality which ensued in Safdar Jang's army was appalling, and the site was abandoned, Marî Bhavânî being left in sole possession. Periodical fairs are now held there in her honour.[1]

HARDAUL LÂLA, THE CHOLERA GODLING.

But the great cholera godling of Northern India is Hardaul, Hardaur, Harda, Hardiya or Hardiha Lâla. It is only north of the Jumnâ that he appears to control the plague, and in Bundelkhand, his native home, he seems to have little connection with it. With him we reach a class of godlings quite distinct from nearly all those whom we have been considering. He is one of that numerous class who were in their lifetime actual historical personages, and who from some special cause, in his case from the tragic circumstances of his death, have been elevated to a seat among the hosts of heaven. Hardaur Lâla, or Dîvân Hardaur, was the second son of Bîr Sinha Deva, the miscreant Râja of Orchha, in Bundelkhand, who, at the instigation of Prince Jahângîr, assassinated the accomplished Abul Fazl, the litterateur of the court of Akbar.[2] His brother Jhajhâr, or Jhujhâr, Sinh succeeded to the throne

[1] Sultânpur, "Settlement Report," 42.
[2] Blochmann, "Aîn-i-Akbari," Introduction, xxiv.

on the death of his father; and after some time suspecting Hardaur of undue intimacy with his wife, he compelled her to poison her lover with all his companions at a feast in 1627 A.D.

After this tragedy it happened that the daughter of the Princess Kanjâvatî, sister of Jhajhâr and Hardaur, was about to be married. Her mother, according to the ordinary rule of family etiquette, sent an invitation to Jhajhâr Sinh to attend the wedding. He refused with the mocking taunt that she would be wise to invite her favourite brother Hardaur. Thereupon, she in despair went to his cenotaph and lamented his wretched end. Hardaur from below answered her cries, and promised to attend the wedding and make all the necessary arrangements. The ghost kept his promise, and arranged the marriage ceremony as befitted the honour of his house.

Subsequently he is said to have visited the bedside of the Emperor Akbar at midnight, and besought him to issue an order that platforms should be erected in his name, and honour be paid to him in every village of the Empire, promising that if he were duly propitiated, no wedding should ever be marred with storm or rain, and that no one who before eating presented a share of his meal to him, should ever want for bread. Akbar, it is said, complied with these requests, and since then the ghost of Hardaul has been worshipped in nearly every village in Northern India. But here, as in many of these legends, the chronology is hopeless. Akbar died in 1605 A.D., and the murder of Hardaul is fixed in 1627.

He is chiefly honoured at weddings, and in the month of Baisâkh (May), when the women, particularly those of the lower classes, visit his shrine and eat the offerings presented to him. The shrine is always erected outside the hamlet, and is decorated with flags. On the day but one before the arrival of a wedding procession, the women of the family worship Hardaul, and invite him to the ceremony. If any signs of a storm appear, he is propitiated with songs, one of the best known of which runs thus—

Lâla! Thy shrine is in every hamlet!
Thy name throughout the land!
Lord of the Bundela land!
May God increase thy fame!

Or in the local patois—

Gânwân chauntra,
Lâla desan nâm:
Bundelê des kê Raiya,
Râû kê.
Tumhârî jay rakhê
Bhagwân!

Many of these shrines have a stone figure of the hero represented on horseback, set up at the head or west side of the platform. From his birthplace Hardaul is also known as Bundela, and one of the quarters in Mirzapur, and in the town of Brindaban in the Mathura District, is named after him.[1]

But while in his native land of Bundelkhand Hardaul is a wedding godling, in about the same rank as Dulha Deo among the Drâvidian tribes, to the north of the Jumnâ it is on his power of influencing epidemics of cholera that his reputation mainly rests. The terrible outbreak of this pestilence, which occurred in the camp of the Governor-General, the Marquess Hastings, during the Pindâri war, was generally attributed by the people to the killing of beef for the use of the British troops in the grove where the ashes of Hardaul repose. Sir C. A. Elliott remarks that he has seen statements in the old official correspondence of 1828 A.D., when we first took possession of Hoshangâbâd, that the district officers were directed to force the village headmen to set up altars to Hardaul Lâla in every village. This was part of the system of "preserving the cultivators," since it was found that they ran away, if their fears of epidemics were not calmed by the respect paid to the local gods. But in Hoshangâbâd, the worship of Hardaul Lâla has fallen into great neglect in recent times, the repeated

[1] The chief authorities for Hardaul are Cunningham, "Archæological Reports," xvii. 162 sqq.: V. A. Smith, "Journal Asiatic Society of Bengal," 1875.

recurrence of cholera having shaken the belief in the potency of his influence over the disease.[1]

EXORCISM OF THE CHOLERA DEMON.

Mention has been already made of the common belief in an actual embodiment of pestilence in a human or ghostly form. A disease so sudden and mysterious as cholera is naturally capable of a superstitious explanation of this kind. Everywhere it is believed to be due to the agency of a demon, which can be expelled by noise and special incantations, or removed by means of a scapegoat. Thus, the Muhammadans of Herat believed that a spirit of cholera stalked through the land in advance of the actual disease.[2] All over Upper India, when cholera prevails, you may see fires lighted on the boundaries of villages to bar the approach of the demon of the plague, and the people shouting and beating drums to hasten his departure. On one occasion I was present at such a ceremonial while out for an evening drive, and as we approached the place the grooms advised us to stop the horses in order to allow the demon to cross the road ahead of us without interruption.

This expulsion of the disease spirit is often a cause of quarrels and riots, as villages who are still safe from the epidemic strongly resent the introduction of the demon within their boundaries. In a recent case at Allahâbâd a man stated that the cholera monster used to attempt to enter his house nightly, that his head resembled a large earthen pot, and that he and his brother were obliged to bar his entrance with their clubs. Another attributed the immunity of his family to the fact that he possessed a gun, which he regularly fired at night to scare the demon. Not long ago some men in the same district enticed the cholera demon into an earthen pot by magical rites, and clapping on the lid, formed a procession in the dead of night for the purpose of carrying the pot to a neighbouring village, with

[1] "Settlement Report," 451 sq.
[2] Ferrier, "Caravan Journeys," 451 sq.

which their relations were the reverse of cordial, and burying it there secretly. But the enemy were on the watch, and turned out in force to frustrate this fell intent. A serious riot occurred, in the course of which the receptacle containing the evil spirit was unfortunately broken and he escaped to continue his ravages in the neighbourhood.[1] In Bombay, when cholera breaks out in a village, the village potter is asked to make an image of the goddess of cholera. When the image is ready, the village people go in procession to the potter's house, and tell him to carry the image to a spot outside the village. When it is taken to the selected place, it is first worshipped by the potter and then by the villagers.[2] Here, as in many instances of similar rites, the priest is a man of low caste, which points to the indigenous character of the worship.

In the western districts of the North-Western Provinces the rite takes a more advanced form. When cholera prevails, Kâli Devî is worshipped, and a magic circle of milk and spirits is drawn round the village, over which the cholera demon does not care to step. They have also a reading of the Scriptures in honour of Durgâ, and worship a Satî shrine, if there be one in the village. The next stage is the actual scapegoat, which is, as we shall see, very generally used for this purpose. A buffalo bull is marked with a red pigment and driven to the next village, where he carries the plague with him. Quite recently, at Meerut, the people purchased a buffalo, painted it red and led the animal through the city in procession. Colonel Tod describes how Zâlim Sinh, the celebrated regent of Kota, drove cholera out of the place. "Having assembled the Brâhmans, astrologers and those versed in incantations, a grand rite was got up, sacrifices made, and a solemn decree of banishment was pronounced against Marî, the cholera goddess. Accordingly an equipage was prepared for her, decorated with funeral emblems, painted black and drawn by a double team of black oxen; bags of grain, also black,

[1] "Allahâbâd Pioneer," 10th March, 1891.
[2] "Bombay Gazetteer," xxii. 155.

were put into the vehicle, that the lady might not go without food, and driven by a man in sable vestments, followed by the yells of the populace, Marî was deported across the Chambal river, with the commands of the priests that she should never again set foot in Kota. No sooner did my deceased friend hear of her expulsion from that capital, and being placed on the road for Bûndi, than the wise men of the city were called on to provide means to keep her from entering therein. Accordingly, all the water of the Ganges at hand was in requisition; an earthen vessel was placed over the southern portal from which the sacred water was continually dripping, and against which no evil could prevail. Whether my friend's supply of the holy water failed, or Marî disregarded such opposition, she reached the palace."[1]

CHOLERA CAUSED BY WITCHCRAFT.

In Gujarât, among the wilder tribes, the belief prevails that cholera is caused by old women who feed on the corpses of the victims of the pestilence. Formerly, when a case occurred their practice was to go to the soothsayer (Bhagat), find out from him who was the guilty witch, and kill her with much torture. Of late years this practice has, to a great extent, ceased. The people now attribute an outbreak to the wrath of the goddess Kâlî, and, to please her, draw her cart through the streets, and lifting it over the village boundaries, offer up goats and buffaloes. Sometimes, to keep off the disease, they make a magic circle with milk or coloured threads round the village. At Nâsik, when cholera breaks out in the city, the leading Brâhmans collect in little doles from each house a small allowance of rice, put the rice in a cart, take it beyond the limits of the town, and there it is thrown away.

A visitation of the plague in Nepâl was attributed to the Râja insisting on celebrating the Dasahra during an intercalary month. On another occasion the arrival of the disease was attributed to the Evil Eye of Saturn and other

[1] "Annals," ii. 744.

[2] "Bombay Gazetteer," xvi. 520; Campbell, "Notes," 96.

planets, which secretly came together in one sign of the zodiac. A third attack was supposed to be caused by the Râja being in his eighteenth year, and the year of the cycle being eighty-eight—eight being a very unlucky number.[1]

So the Gonds try to ward off the anger of the spirits of cholera and small-pox by sacrifices, and by thoroughly cleaning their villages and transferring the sweepings into some road or travelled track. Their idea is that unless the disease is communicated to some person who will take it on to the next village, the plague will not leave them. For this reason they do not throw the sweepings into the jungle, as no one passes that way, and consequently the benefit of sweeping is lost.[2]

An extraordinary case was recently reported from the Dehra Ismâîl Khân District. There had been a good deal of sickness in the village, and the people spread a report that this was due to the fact that a woman, who had died some seven months previously, had been chewing her funeral sheet. The relatives were asked to allow the body to be examined, which was done, and it was found that owing to the subsidence of the ground through rain, some earth had fallen into the mouth of the corpse. A copper coin was placed in the mouth as a viaticum, and a fowl killed and laid on the body, which was again interred. The same result is very often believed to follow from burying persons of the sweeper caste in the usual extended position, instead of a sitting posture or with the face downwards. A sweeper being one of the aboriginal or casteless tribes is believed to have something uncanny about him. Recently in Muzaffarnagar, a corpse buried in the unorthodox way was disinterred by force, and the matter finally came before the courts.

THE DEMON OF CATTLE DISEASE.

In the same way cattle disease is caused by the plague demon. Once upon a time a man, whose descendants live

[1] Wright, "History," 221, 267, 268.
[2] "Central Provinces Gazetteer," 276.

in the Mathura District, was sleeping out in the fields when he saw the cattle disease creeping up to his oxen in an animal shape. He watched his opportunity and got the demon under his shield, which he fixed firmly down. The disease demon entreated to be released, but he would not let it go till it promised that it would never remain where he or his descendants were present. So to this day, when the murrain visits a village, his descendants are summoned and work round the village, calling on the disease to fulfil its contract.[1]

The murrain demon is expelled in the same way as that of the cholera, and removed by the agency of the scapegoat. In the western part of the North-Western Provinces you will often notice wisps of straw tied round the trunks of acacia trees, which, as we shall see, possess mystic powers, as a means to bar disease.

Kâsi Bâba is the tribal deity of the Binds of Bengal. Of him it is reported: "A mysterious epidemic was carrying off the herds on the banks of the Ganges, and the ordinary expiatory sacrifices were ineffectual. One evening a clownish Ahîr, on going to the river, saw a figure rinsing its mouth from time to time, and making an unearthly sound with a conch shell. The lout, concluding that this must be the demon that caused the epidemic, crept up and clubbed the unsuspecting bather. Kâsi Nâth was the name of the murdered Brâhman, and as the cessation of the murrain coincided with his death, the low Hindustâni castes have ever since regarded Kâsi Bâba as the maleficent spirit that sends disease among the cattle. Nowadays he is propitiated by the following curious ceremony. As soon as an infectious disease breaks out, the village cattle are massed together, and cotton seed sprinkled over them. The fattest and sleekest animal being singled out, is severely beaten with rods. The herd, scared by the noise, scamper off to the nearest shelter, followed by the scape bull; and by this means it is thought the murrain is stayed."[2]

[1] "Gurgâon Settlement Report," 37.
[2] Risley, "Tribes and Castes of Bengal," i. 132.

Kâsi Dâs, according to the last census, has 172,000 worshippers in the eastern districts of the North-Western Provinces.

OTHER CHOLERA GODLINGS.

Beside Hardaul Lâla, the great cholera godling, Hulkâ Devî, the impersonation of vomiting, is worshipped in Bengal with the same object. She appears to be the same as Holikâ or Horkâ Maiyyâ, whom we shall meet in connection with the Holî festival. We have already noticed Marî or Marî Mâî, "Mother death," or as she is called when promoted to Brâhmanism, Marî Bhavânî. She and Hatthî, a minor cholera goddess, are worshipped when cholera prevails. By one account she and Sîtalâ are daughters of Râja Vena. About ten thousand people recorded themselves at the last census as worshippers of Hatthî and Marî in the North-Western Provinces. Among the jungle tribes of Mirzapur she is known as Obâ, an Arabic word (*waba*) meaning pestilence. Marî, as we have said, has a special shrine in Sultânpur to commemorate a fatal outbreak of cholera in the army of Safdar Jang. In the Punjâb Marî is honoured with an offering of a pumpkin, a male buffalo, a cock, a ram and a goat. These animals are each decapitated with a single blow before her altar. If more than one blow is required the ceremony is a failure. Formerly, in addition to these five kinds of offering a man and woman were sacrificed, to make up the mystic number seven.[1]

EXORCISM OF DISEASE.

The practice of exorcising these demons of disease has been elaborated into something like a science. Disease, according to the general belief of the rural population, can be removed by a species of magic, usually of the variety known as "sympathetic," and it can be transferred from the sufferer to some one else. The special incantations for

[1] "Panjâb Notes and Queries," i. 1; iv. 51; "Oudh Gazetteer," i. 355, 517; Tod, "Annals," ii. 75.

SHRINES OF GODLINGS OF DISEASE.

disease are in the hands of low-caste sorcerers or magicians. Among the more primitive races, such as those of Drâvidian origin in Central India, this is the business of the Baiga, or aboriginal devil priest. But even here there is a differentiation of function, and though the Baiga is usually considered competent to deal with the cases of persons possessed of evil spirits, it is only special persons who can undertake the regular exorcism. This is among the lower tribes of Hindus the business of the Syâna, "the cunning man," the Sokha (Sanskrit *sukshma*, "the subtile one"), or the Ojha, which is a corruption of the Sanskrit Upâdhyâya or "teacher."

Like Æsculapius, Paieon, and even Apollo himself, the successful magician and healer gradually develops into a god. All over the country there are, as we have seen, the shrines of saints who won the reverence of the people by the cures wrought at their tombs. The great deified healer in Behâr and the eastern Districts of the North-Western Provinces is Sokha Bâba, who, according to the last census, had thirteen thousand special worshippers. He is said to have been a Brâhman who was killed by a snake, and now possesses the power of inflicting snake-bite on those who do not propitiate him.

Exorcisers are both professional and non-professional. "Non-professional exorcisers are generally persons who get naturally improved by a guardian spirit (*deva*), and a few of them learn the art of exorcism from a Guru or teacher. Most of the professional exorcisers learn from a Guru. The first study is begun on a lunar or on a solar eclipse day. On such a day the teacher after bathing, and without wiping his body, or his head or hair, puts on dry clothes, and goes to the village godling's temple. The candidate then spreads a white cloth before the god, and on one side of the cloth makes a heap of rice, and on another a heap of Urad (*phaseolus radiatus*), sprinkles red lead on the heaps, and breaks a cocoanut in front of the idol. The Guru then teaches him the incantation (*mantra*), which he commits to memory. An ochre-coloured flag is then tied to a staff in front of the temple, and the teacher and candidate come home.

"After this, on the first new moon which falls on a Saturday, the teacher and the candidate go together out of the village to a place previously marked out by them on the boundary. A servant accompanies them, who carries a bag of Urad, oil, seven earthen lamps, lemons, cocoanuts, and red powder. After coming to the spot, the teacher and the candidate bathe, and then the teacher goes to the village temple, and sits praying for the safety of the candidate. The candidate, who has been already instructed as to what should be done, then starts for the boundary of the next village, accompanied by the servant. On reaching the village boundary, he picks up seven pebbles, sets them in a line on the road, and after lighting a lamp near them, he worships them with flowers, red powder, and Urad. Incense is then burnt, and a cocoanut is broken near the pebble which represents Vetâla and his lieutenants, and a second cocoanut is broken for the village godling." Here the cocoanut is symbolical of a sacrifice which was probably originally of a human victim.

"When this is over, he goes to a river, well, or other bathing place, and bathes, and without wiping his body or putting on dry clothes, proceeds to the boundary of the next village. There he repeats the same process as he did before, and then goes to the boundary of a third village. In this manner he goes to seven villages and repeats the same process. All this while he keeps on repeating incantations. After finishing his worship at the seventh village, the candidate returns to his village, and going to the temple, sees his teacher and tells him what he has done.

"In this manner, having worshipped and propitiated the Vetâlas of seven villages, he becomes an exorcist. After having been able to exercise these powers, he must observe certain rules. Thus, on every eclipse day he must go to a sea-shore or a river bank, bathe in cold water, and while standing in the water repeat incantations a number of times. After bathing daily he must neither wring his head hair, nor wipe his body dry. While he is taking his meals, he should leave off if he hears a woman in her monthly sickness speak or if a lamp be extinguished.

"The Muhammadan methods of studying exorcism are different from those of the Hindus. One of them is as follows:—The candidate begins his study under the guidance of his teacher on the last day of the lunar month, provided it falls on a Tuesday or Sunday. The initiation takes place in a room, the walls and floor of which have been plastered with mud, and here and there daubed with sandal paste. On the floor a white sheet is spread, and the candidate after washing his hands and feet, and wearing a new waist-cloth or trousers, sits on the sheet. He lights one or two incense sticks and makes offerings of a white cloth and meat to one of the principal Musalmân saints. This process is repeated for from fourteen to forty days."[1]

Few rural exorcisers go through this elaborate ritual, the object of which it is not difficult to understand. The candidate wishes to get the Vetâla or local demon of the village into his power and to make him work his will. So he provides himself with a number of articles which, as we shall see, are known for their influence over the spirits of evil, such as the Urad pulse, lamps, cocoanuts, etc. The careful rule of bathing, the precautions against personal impurity, the worship done at the shrine of the village godling by the teacher, are all intended to guard him in the hour of danger. The common village "wise man" contents himself with learning a few charms of the hocus pocus variety, and a cure in some difficult case of devil possession secures his reputation as a healer.

METHODS OF RURAL EXORCISM.

The number of these charms is legion, and most exorcisers have one of their own in which they place special confidence and which they are unwilling to disclose. As Sir Monier Williams writes[2]:—"No magician, wizard, sorcerer or witch

[1] Campbell, "Notes," 192 sqq.
[2] "Brâhmanism and Hinduism," 201.

whose feats are recorded in history, biography or fable, has ever pretended to be able to accomplish by incantation and enchantment half of what the Mantra-sâstri claims to have power to effect by help of his Mantras. For example, he can prognosticate futurity, work the most startling prodigies, infuse breath into dead bodies, kill or humiliate enemies, afflict any one anywhere with disease or madness, inspire anyone with love, charm weapons and give them unerring efficacy, enchant armour and make it impenetrable, turn milk into wine, plants into meat, or invert all such processes at will. He is even superior to the gods, and can make goddesses, gods, imps and demons carry out his most trifling behests. Hence it is not surprising that the following remarkable saying is everywhere current throughout India: 'The whole universe is subject to the gods; the gods are subject to the Mantras; the Mantras to the Brâhmans; therefore the Brâhmans are our gods.'"

All these devices of Mantras or spells, Kavâchas or amulets, Nyâsas or mentally assigning various parts of the body to the protection of tutelary presiding deities, and Mudras or intertwining of the fingers with a mystic meaning, spring from the corrupt fountain head of the Tantras, the bible of Sâktism. But these are the speciality of the higher class of professional exorciser, who is very generally a Brâhman, and do not concern us here.

A few examples of the formulæ used by the village "cunning man" may be given here. Thus in Mirzapur when a person is known to be under the influence of a witch the Ojha recites a spell, which runs—"Bind the evil eye; bind the fist; bind the spell; bind the curse; bind the ghost and the churel; bind the witch's hands and feet. Who can bind her? The teacher can bind her. I, the disciple of the teacher, can bind her. Go, witch, to wherever thy shrine may be; sit there and leave the afflicted person." In these spells Hanumân, the monkey godling, is often invoked. Thus—"I salute the command of my teacher. Hanumân, the hero, is the hero of heroes. He has in his quiver nine lâkhs of arrows. He is sometimes on the right, sometimes on the left, and sometimes in the front. I serve thee, powerful master. May not this man's body be crippled. I see the cremation ground in the two worlds and outside them. If in my body or in the body of this man any ill arise, then I call on the influence of Hanumân. My piety, the power of the teacher, this charm is true because it comes from the Almighty." In the same way two great witches, Lônâ Chamârin and Ismâîl the Jogi are often invoked. The Musalmân calls on Sulaimân, the lord Solomon, who is a leader of demons and a controller of evil spirits, for which there is ample authority in the Qurân.

But it is in charms for disease that the rural exorciser is most proficient. Accidents, such as the bites of snakes, stings of scorpions, or wasps are in particular treated in this way, and these charms make up most of the folk-medicine of Northern India. Thus, when a man is stung by a scorpion the exorciser says—"Black scorpion of the limestone! Green is thy tail and black thy mouth. God orders thee to go home. Come out! Come out! If thou fail to come out Mahâdeva and Pârvatî will drive thee out!" Another spell for scorpion sting runs thus—"On the hill and mountain is the holy cow. From its dung the scorpions were born, six black and six brown. Help me! O Nara Sinha! (the man lion incarnation of Vishnu). Rub each foot with millet and the poison will depart." So, to cure the bite of a dog, get some clay which has been worked on a potter's wheel, which as we shall see is a noted fetish, make a lump of it and rub it to the wound and say—"The black dog is covered with thick hair." Another plan in cases of hydrophobia is to kill a dog, and after burning it to make the patient imbibe the smoke. Headache is caused by a worm in the head, which comes out if the ear be rubbed with butter. Women of the gipsy tribes are noted for their charms to take out the worm which causes toothache. When a man is bitten by a snake the practitioner says—"True god, true hero, Hanumân! The snake moves in a tortuous way. The male and female weasel come out of their hole to destroy it. Which poison will they devour? First they will eat the black Karait snake, then the snake with the jewel, then the Ghor snake. I pray to thee for help, my true teacher." So, if you desire to be safe from the attacks of the tiger, say—"Tie up the tiger, tie up the tigress, tie up her seven cubs. Tie up the roads and the footpaths and the fields. O Vasudeva, have mercy? Have mercy, O Lonâ Chamârin!" Lastly, if you desire an appointment, say—"O Kâlî, Kankâlî, Mahâkâli! Thy face is beautiful, but at thy heart is a serpent. There are four demon heroes and eighty-four Bhairons. If thou givest the order I will worship them with betel nuts and sweetmeats. Now shout—'Mercy, O Mother Kali!'" It would not be difficult to describe hundreds of such charms, but what has been recorded will be sufficient to exemplify the ordinary methods of rural exorcism.[1]

When the Ojha is called in to identify the demon which has beset a patient, he begins by ascertaining whether it is a local ghost or an outsider which has attacked him on a journey. Then he calls for some cloves, and muttering a charm over them, ties them to the bedstead on which the sick man lies. Then the patient is told to name the ghost which has possessed him, and he generally names one of his dead relations, or the ghost of a hill, a tree or a burial ground. Then the Ojha suggests an appropriate offering, which when bestowed and food given to Brâhmans, the patient ought in all decency to recover. If he does not, the Ojha asserts that the right ghost has not been named, and the whole process is gone through again, if necessary funds are forthcoming.

The Baiga of Mirzapur, who very often combines the function of an Ojha with his own legitimate business of managing the local ghosts, works in very much the same way. He takes some barley in a sieve, which as we shall see is a very powerful fetish, and shakes it until only a few grains are left in the interstices. Then he marks down the intruding ghost by counting the grains, and recommends the sacrifice of a fowl or a goat, or the offering of some liquor,

[1] Numbers of such charms are to be found in vols. i., ii., iii., "North Indian Notes and Queries."

most of which he usually consumes himself. If his patient die, he gets out of the difficulty by saying—"Such and such a powerful Bhût carried him off. What can a poor man, such as I am, do?" If a tiger or a bear kills a man, the Baiga tells his friends that such and such a Bhût was offended because no attention was paid to him, and in revenge entered into the animal which killed the deceased, the obvious moral being that in future more regular offerings should be made through the Baiga.

In Hoshangâbâd the Bhomka sorcerer has a handful of grain waved over the head of the sick man. This is then carried to the Bhomka, who makes a heap of it on the floor, and sitting over it, swings a lighted lamp suspended by four strings from his fingers. He then repeats slowly the names of the patient's ancestors and of the village and local godling, pausing between each, and when the lamp stops spinning the name at which it halts is the name to be propitiated. Then in the same way he asks—"What is the propitiation offering to be? A pig? A cocoanut? A chicken? A goat?" And the same mystic sign indicates the satisfaction of the god.[1]

The Kol diviner drops oil into a vessel of water. The name of the deity is pronounced as the oil is dropped. If it forms one globule in the water, it is considered that the particular god to be appeased has been correctly named; if it splutters and forms several globules, another name is tried. The Orâon Ojha puts the fowls intended as victims before a small mud image, on which he sprinkles a few grains of rice; if they pick at the rice it indicates that the particular devil represented by the image is satisfied with the intentions of his votaries, and the sacrifice proceeds.[2]

The Panjâb diviner adopts a stock method common to such practitioners all over the world. He writes some spells on a piece of paper, and pours on it a large drop of ink. Flowers are then placed in the hands of a young child, who is told to look into the ink and say, "Summon the four

1 "Settlement Report," 256.
2 Dalton, "Descriptive Ethnology," 188, 257.

guardians." He is asked if he sees anything in the ink, and according to the answer a result is arrived at.[1] The *modus operandi* of these exorcisers is, in fact, very much the same in India as in other parts of the world.[2]

EXORCISM BY DANCING.

In all rites of this class religious dancing as a means of scaring the demon of evil holds an important place. Thus of the Bengal Muâsis Col. Dalton writes[3]—"The affection comes on like a fit of ague, lasting sometimes for a quarter of an hour, the patient or possessed person writhing and trembling with intense violence, especially at the commencement of the paroxysm. Then he is seen to spring from the ground into the air, and a succession of leaps follow, all executed as though he were shot at by unseen agency. During this stage of the seizure he is supposed to be quite unconscious, and rolls into the fire, if there be one, or under the feet of the dancers, without sustaining injury from the heat or from the pressure. This lasts for a few minutes only, and is followed by the spasmodic stage. With hands and knees on the ground and hair loosened, the body is convulsed, and the head shakes violently, whilst from the mouth issues a hissing or gurgling noise. The patient next evincing an inclination to stand on his legs, the bystanders assist him, and place a stick in his hand, with the aid of which he hops about, the spasmodic action of the body still continuing, and the head performing by jerks a violently fatiguing circular movement. This may go on for hours, though Captain Samuells says that no one in his senses could continue such exertion for many minutes. When the Baiga is appealed to to cast out the spirit, he must first ascertain whether it is Gansâm or one of his familiars that has possessed the victim. If it be the great Gansâm, the

[1] "North Indian Notes and Queries," i. 85.
[2] Yule, "Marco Polo," i. 71 sq., with note; Tylor, "Primitive Culture," i. 127; Lubbock, "Origin of Civilization," 237; "Farrer, "Primitive Manners," 159 sq.
[3] "Descriptive Ethnology," 232.

Baiga implores him to desist, meanwhile gradually anointing the victim with butter; and if the treatment is successful, the patient gradually and naturally subsides into a state of repose, from which he rises into consciousness, and, restored to his normal state, feels no fatigue or other ill-effects from the attack."

The same religious dance of ecstasy appears in what is known as the Râs Mandala of the modern Vaishnava sects, which is supposed to represent the dance of the Gopîs with Krishna. So in Bombay among the Marâthas the worship of the chief goddess of the Dakkin, Tuljâ Bhavânî, is celebrated by a set of dancing devotees, called Gondhalis, whose leader becomes possessed by the goddess. A high stool is covered with a black cloth. On the cloth thirty-six pinches of rice are dropped in a heap, and with them turmeric and red powder, all scarers of demons, are mixed. On the rice is set a copper vessel filled with milk and water, and in this the goddess is supposed to take her abode. Over it are laid betel leaves and a cocoanut. Five torches are carried round the vessel by five men, each shouting "Ambâ Bhavânî!" The music plays, and dancers dance before her. So at a Brâhman marriage at Pûna the boy and girl are seated on the shoulders of their maternal uncles or other relations, who perform a frantic dance, the object being, as in all these cases, to scare away the spirits of evil.[1]

FLAGELLATION.

So with flagellation, which all over the world is supposed to have the power of scaring demons. Thus in the Central Indian Hills the Baiga with his Gurda, or sacred chain, which being made of iron, possesses additional potency, soundly thrashes patients attacked with epilepsy, hysteria, and similar ailments, which from their nature are obviously due to demoniacal agency. There are numerous instances of the use of the lash for this purpose. In Bombay, among the Lingâyats, the woman who names the child has her

[1] Campbell, "Notes," 72 sq.

back beaten with gentle blows; and some beggar Brâhmans refuse to take alms until the giver beats them.[1] There is a famous shrine at Ghauspur, in the Jaunpur District, where the Ojhas beat their patients to drive out the disease demon.[2] The records of Roman Catholic hagiology and of the special sect of the Flagellants will furnish numerous parallel instances.

TREATMENT OF SORCERERS.

While the sorcerer by virtue of his profession is generally respected and feared, in some places they have been dealt with rather summarily. There is everywhere a struggle between the Brâhman priest of the greater gods and the exorciser, who works by the agency of demons. Sudarsan Sâh rid Garhwâl of them by summoning all the professors of the black art with their books. When they were collected he had them bound hand and foot and thrown with their books and implements into the river. The same monarch also disposed very effectually of a case of possession in his own family. One day he heard a sound of drumming and dancing in one of his courtyards, and learnt that a ghost named Goril had taken possession of one of his female slaves. The Râja was wroth, and taking a thick bamboo, he proceeded to the spot and laid about him so vigorously that the votaries of Goril soon declared that the deity had taken his departure. The Râja then ordered Goril to cease from possessing people, and nowadays if any Garhwâli thinks himself possessed, he has only to call on the name of Sudarsan Sâh and the demon departs.[3]

APPOINTMENT OF OJHAS.

The mode of succession to the dignity of an Ojha varies in different places. In Mirzapur the son is usually educated by his father, and taught the various spells and modes of

[1] Cooper, "Flagellation and the Flagellants," *passim*; Dalton, *loc. cit.*, 256; Campbell, *loc. cit.*, 44 sq.; for restoration to life by beating, Tawney, "Katha Sarit Sâgara," ii. 245.

[2] "Nineteenth Century," 1880.

[3] Atkinson, "Himâlayan Gazetteer," ii. 833, 823.

incantation. But this is not always the case; and here at the present time the institution is in a transition stage. South of the Son we have the Baiga, who usually acts as an Ojha also; and he is invariably drawn from the aboriginal races. Further north he is known as Nâya (Sanskrit *nâyaka*) or "leader." Further north, again, as we leave the hilly country and enter the completely Brâhmanized Gangetic valley, he changes into the regular Ojha, who is always a low-class Brâhman.

In one instance which came under my own notice, the Nâya of the village had been an aboriginal Kol, and he before his death announced that "the god had sat on the head" of a Brâhman candidate for the office, who was duly initiated, and is now the recognized village Ojha. This is a good example of the way in which Brâhmanism annexes and absorbs the demonolatry of the lower races. This, too, enables us to correct a statement which has been made even by such a careful inquirer as Mr. Sherring when he says[1]—"Formerly the Ojha was always a Brâhman; but his profession has become so lucrative that sharp, clever, shrewd men in all the Hindu castes have taken to it." There can be no question that the process has been the very reverse of this, and that the early Ojhas were aboriginal sorcerers, and that their trade was taken over by the Brâhman as the land became Hinduized.

In Hoshangâbâd the son usually succeeds his father, but a Bhomka does not necessarily marry into a Bhomka family, nor does it follow that "once a Bhomka, always a Bhomka." On the contrary, the position seems to be the result of the special favour of the godling of the particular village in which he lives; and if the whole of the residents emigrate in a body, then the godling of the new village site will have to be consulted afresh as to the servant whom he chooses to attend upon him.

"If a Bhomka dies or goes away, or a new village is established, his successor is appointed in the following way.

[1] "Hindu Tribes and Castes," i. 36.

All the villagers assemble at the shrine of Mutua Deo, and offer a black and white chicken to him. A Parihâr, or priest, should be enticed to grace the solemnity and make the sacrifice, but if that cannot be done the oldest man in the assembly does it. Then he sets a wooden grain measure rolling along the line of seated people, and the man before whom it stops is marked out by the intervention of the deity as the new Bhomka."[1]

It marks perhaps some approximation to Hinduism that the priest, when inspired by the god, wears a thread made of the hair of a bullock's tail, unless this is based on the common use of thread or hair as a scarer of demons, or is some token or fetish peculiar to the race. At the same time the non-Brâhmanic character of the worship is proved by the fact that the priest, when in a state of ecstasy, cannot bear the presence of a cow, or Brâhman. "The god," they say, "would leave their heads if either of these came near."

On one occasion, when Sir C. A. Elliott saw the process of exorcism, the men did not actually revolve when "the god came on his head." He covered his head up well in a cloth, leaving space for the god to approach, and in this state he twisted and turned himself rapidly, and soon sat down exhausted. We shall see elsewhere that the head is one of the chief spirit entries, and the top of the head is left uncovered in order to let the spirit make its way through the sutures of the skull. Then from the pit of his stomach he uttered words which the bystanders interpreted to direct a certain line of conduct for the sick man to pursue. "But perhaps the occasion was not a fair test, as the Parihâr strongly objected to the presence of an unbeliever, on the pretence that the god would be afraid to come before so great an official." This has always been the standing difficulty in Europeans obtaining a practical knowledge of the details of rural sorcery, and when a performance of the kind is specially arranged, it will usually be found that the officiant performs the introductory rites with comparative

[1] "Settlement Report," 256 sq.

success, but as it comes to the crucial point he breaks down, just as the ecstatic crisis should have commenced. This is always attributed to the presence of an unbeliever, however interested and sympathetic. The same result usually happens at spiritualistic séances, when anyone with even an elementary knowledge of physics or mechanics happens to be one of the audience.

FRAUD IN EXORCISM.

The question naturally arises—Are all these Ojhas and Baigas conscious hypocrites and swindlers? Dr. Tylor shrewdly remarks that "the sorcerer generally learns his time-honoured profession in good faith, and retains the belief in it more or less from first to last. At once dupe and cheat, he combines the energy of a believer with the cunning of a hypocrite."[1] This coincides with the experience of most competent Indian observers. No one who consults a Syâna and observes the confident way in which he asserts his mystic power, can doubt that he at least believes to a large extent in the sacredness of his mission. Captain Samuells, who repeatedly witnessed these performances, distinctly asserts that it is a mistake to suppose that there is always intentional deception.[2]

DISEASE CHARMS.

Next to the services of the professional exorciser for the purpose of preventing or curing disease, comes the use of special charms for this purpose. There is a large native literature dealing with this branch of science. As a rule most native patients undergo a course of this treatment before they visit our hospitals, and the result of European medical science is hence occasionally disappointing. One favourite talisman of this kind is the magic square, which consists in an arrangement of certain numbers in a special

[1] "Primitive Culture," i. 134; and compare Lubbock, "Origin of Civilization," 251.

[2] Dalton, "Descriptive Ethnology," 232.

way. For instance, in order to cure barrenness, it is a good plan to write a series of numbers which added up make 73 both ways on a piece of bread, and with it feed a black dog, which is the attendant of Bhairon, a giver of off-spring. To cure a tumour a figure in the form of a cross is drawn with three cyphers in the centre and one at each of the four ends. This is prepared on a Sunday and tied round the left arm. Another has a series of numbers aggregating 15 every way. This is engraved on copper and tied round a child's neck to keep off the Evil Eye. In the case of cattle disease, some gibberish, which pretends to be Arabic or Sanskrit, appealing for the aid of Lonâ Chamârin or Ismâîl Jogi, with a series of mystic numbers, is written on a piece of tile. This is hung on a rope over the village cattle path, and a ploughshare is buried at the entrance to make the charm more powerful. When cattle are attacked with worms, the owner fills a clean earthen pot with water drawn from the well with one hand; he then mutters a blessing, and with some sacred Dâbh grass sprinkles a little water seven times along the back of the animal.

The number of these charms is legion. Many of them merge into the special preservatives against the Evil Eye, which will be discussed later on. Thus the bâzâr merchant writes the words *Râm! Râm!* several times near his door, or he makes a representation of the sun and moon, or a rude image of Ganesa, the godling of good luck, or draws the mystical Swâstika. A house of a banker at Kankhal which I recently examined bore a whole gallery of pictures round it. There were Siva and Pârvatî on an ox with their son Mârkandeya; Yamarâja, the deity of death, with a servant waving a fan over his head; Krishna with his spouse Râdhâ: Hanumân, the monkey godling; the Ganges riding on a fish, with Bhâgîratha, who brought her down from heaven; Bhîshma, the hero of the Mahâbhârata; Arjuna representing the Pândavas; the saints Uddalaka and Nârada Muni; Ganesa with his two maidservants; and Brahma and Vishnu riding on Sesha Nâga, the great serpent.

HOUSE PROTECTED AGAINST THE EVIL EYE.

Beneath these was an inscription invoking Râma, Lakshmana, the Ganges and Hanumân.

RAG OFFERINGS.

Next come the arrangements by which disease may be expelled or transferred to someone else. In this connection we may discuss the curious custom of hanging up rags on trees or near sacred wells. Of this custom India supplies numerous examples. At the Balchha pass in Garhwâl there is a small heap of stones at the summit, with sticks and rags attached to them, to which travellers add a stone or two as they pass.[1] In Persia they fix rags on bushes in the name of the Imâm Raza. They explain the custom by saying that the eye of the Imâm being always on the top of the mountain, the shreds which are left there by those who hold him in reverence, remind him of what he ought to do in their behalf with Muhammad, 'Ali and the other holy personages, who are able to propitiate the Almighty in their favour.[2] Moorcroft in his journey to Ladâkh describes how he propitiated the evil spirit of a dangerous pass with the leg of a pair of worn-out nankin trousers.[3] Among the Mirzapur Korwas the Baiga hangs rags on the trees which shade the village shrine, as a charm to bring health and good luck. These rag shrines are to be found all over the country, and are generally known as Chithariyâ or Chithraiyâ Bhavânî, "Our Lady of Tatters." So in the Panjâb the trees on which rags are hung are called Lingrî Pîr or the rag saint.[4] The same custom prevails at various Himâlayan shrines and at the Vastra Harana or sacred tree at Brindaban near Mathura, which is now invested with a special legend, as commemorating the place where Krishna carried off the clothes of the milkmaids when they were bathing, an incident which constantly appears in both European and Indian folk-lore.[5] In Berâr a heap of stones daubed with

[1] "Himâlayan Gazetteer," iii. 38.
[2] Ferrier, "Caravan Journeys," 113.
[3] "Travels in the Himâlayas," i. 428.
[4] O'Brien, "Multân Glossary," 218.
[5] Clouston, "Popular Tales," i. 191.

red and placed under a tree fluttering with rags represents Chindiya Deo or "the Lord of Tatters," where, if you present a rag in due season, you may chance to get new clothes.[1] The practice of putting or tying rags from the person of the sick to a tree, especially a banyan, cocoanut, or some thorny tree, is prevalent in the Konkan, but not to such an extent as that of fixing nails or tying bottles to trees. In the Konkan, when a person is suffering from a spirit disease, the exorcist takes the spirit away from the sick man and fixes it in a tree by thrusting a nail in it. We have already had an example of this treatment of ghosts by the Baiga. Sometimes he catches the spirit of the disease in a bottle and ties the bottle to a tree.[2] In a well-known story of the Arabian Knights the Jinn is shut up in a bottle under the seal of the Lord Solomon.

There have been various explanations of this custom of hanging rags on trees.[3] One is that they are offerings to the local deity of the tree. Mr. Gomme quotes an instance of an Irishman who made a similar offering with the following invocation: "To St. Columbkill—I offer up this button, a bit o' the waistband o' my own breeches, an' a taste o' my wife's petticoat, in remimbrance of us havin' made this holy station; an' may they rise up in glory to prove it for us in the last day."

He "points to the undoubted nature of the offerings and their service, in the identification of their owners—a service which implies their power to bear witness in spirit-land to the pilgrimage of those who deposited them during lifetime at the sacred well." Some of the Indian evidence seems to show that these rags are really offerings to the sacred tree. Thus, Colonel Tod[4] describes the trees in a sacred grove in Râjputâna as decorated with shreds of various coloured cloth, "offerings of the traveller to the forest divinity for protection against evil spirits." This usage often merges

[1] "Gazetteer," 191. [2] Campbell, "Notes," 239.
[3] "Folk-lore," iii. 13, 380; iv. 410; Hartland, "Legend of Perseus," ii. chap. xi.
[4] "Annals," ii. 717.

into actual tree-worship, as among the Mirzapur Patâris, who, when fever prevails, tie a cotton string which has never touched water round the trunk of a Pîpal tree, and hang rags from the branches. So, the Kharwârs have a sacred Mahua tree, known as the Byâhi Mahua or "Mahua of marriage," on which threads are hung at marriages. At almost any holy place women may be seen winding a cotton thread round the trunk of a Pîpal tree.

Another explanation is that the hanging of the rags is done with the object of transferring a disease to some one else. Professor Rhys suggests that a distinction is to be drawn between the rags hung on trees or near a well and the pins, which are so commonly thrown into the water itself. It is noteworthy that in some cases the pins are replaced by buttons, or even by copper coins. The rags, on the other hand, he thinks may be vehicles of the disease. To this Mr. Hartland objects—"If this opinion were correct, one would expect to find both ceremonies performed by the same patient at the same well; he would throw in the pin and also place the rag on the bush, or wherever its proper place might be. The performance of both ceremonies is, however, I think, exceptional. Where the pin or button is dropped into the well, the patient does not trouble about the rag, and *vice versâ.*"

He goes on to say that "the curious detail mentioned by Mrs. Evans in reference to the rags tied on the bushes at St. Elian's well—namely, that they must be tied with wool—points to a still further degradation of the rite in the case we are now examining. Probably at one time rags were used and simply tied to the sacred tree with wool. What may have been the reason for using wool remains to be discovered. But it is easy to see how, if the reason were lost, the wool might be looked on as the essential condition of the due performance of the ceremony, and so continue after the disuse of the rags."

In reference to this it may be noted that there is some reason to believe that the sheep was a sacred animal. In Western India high-caste Hindus wear blankets after bathing. The Kunbis use a mixture of sheep's milk with lime juice and opium as a cure for diarrhœa. The Parheyas of Bengal used to wash their houses with sheep's dung to scare spirits. And the use of woollen clothes in certain rites is prescribed in the current ritual.

Mr. Hartland is inclined to think that the rags represent entire articles of clothing which were at an earlier time deposited, and on the analogy of the habit of the witch of getting hold of some part of the body, such as nail-cuttings and so on, by which she may get the owner into her power, the rags were meant to connect the worshipper with the deity. "In like manner my shirt or stocking, or a rag to represent it, placed upon a sacred bush or thrust into a sacred well, my name written on the walls of a temple, a stone or pellet from my hand cast upon a sacred image or a sacred cairn, is thenceforth in constant contact with divinity; and the effluence of divinity, reaching and involving it, will reach and involve me. In this way I may be permanently united with the god."

It is quite possible that some or all of the ideas thus given may have resulted in the present practice in India.

DISEASE TRANSFERENCE.

Disease is also transferred in an actual physical way. Thus, in Ireland, a charm or curse is left on a gate or stile, and the first healthy person who passes through will, it is believed, have the disease transferred to him. So, in Scotland, if a child is affected with the whooping cough, it is taken into the land of another laird, and there the disease is left.[1] Similarly, in Northern India, one way of transferring disease is to fill a pot with flowers and rice and bury it in a path, with a stone to cover it. Whoever touches this is supposed to contract the disease. This is known as Chalauwa, which means "passing on" the malady. This goes on daily in Upper India. Often when walking in a bâzâr in the early morning, you will see a little pile of earth

[1] Gregor, "Folk-lore of N.E. Scotland," 46, 157.

decorated with flowers in the middle of the road. This usually contains some of the scabs or scales from the body of a small-pox patient, which are placed there in the hope that someone may touch them, contract the malady and thus relieve the sufferer. In 1885 it was officially reported that in Cawnpur small-pox had greatly increased from the practice of placing these scales on the roads. At the instance of Government the matter was investigated, and it was found that in the early stages of the disease, the Diuli ceremony is performed at cross-roads; and that at a later period the crusts from smallpox patients mixed with curdled milk and cocoanut juice are carried to the temple or platform of the small-pox goddess and are dedicated to her.[1]

One morning, in a village near Agra, I came by chance on two old women fiercely quarrelling. On making inquiries, I found that one of them had placed some small-pox crusts from her child on her neighbour's threshold. The people agreed that this was a wicked act, as it displayed special animus against a particular person. If they had been placed on the cross-road, and any one had been unlucky enough to touch them and contract the disease, it would not have mattered much—that was the will of God.

Some time ago an indigo planter, near Benares, was astonished by a respectable native friend asking the loan of one of his geese. On inquiry he ascertained that his friend's son was suffering from bowel complaint, and that he had been advised by a native physician to get a goose, place it in the boy's bed, and that the disease would be communicated to the bird, with the result of curing the patient. This remedy was known in Italy. One of the prescriptions of Marcellus runs:[2] "To those who are suffering from a colic. Let them fasten a live duck to their stomachs, thus the disease will pass from the man to the duck, and the duck will die." In the same way when any one wants to set their neighbour's household at variance, a quill of a porcupine, which is supposed to be a quarrelsome animal,

[1] "Panjâb Notes and Queries," ii. 42.
[2] Leland, "Etruscan Roman Remains," 293.

is thrown over the wall. On this principle in Italy a short and simple method of setting people by the ears is to buy some of the herb Discordia and throw it into a house, when the result is sure to be a vendetta.[1] In the Indian Hills, in case of illness a stake is driven down into the earth where four roads meet, and certain drugs and grains are buried close by, which are speedily disinterred and eaten by crows. This gives immediate relief to the sufferer.[2] Here the idea apparently is, that the disease is transferred to the crow, a sacred bird, and in close communication with the spirits of the sainted dead. So in cases of cattle disease, a buffalo's skull, a small lamb, fire in a pan, vessels of butter and milk, wisps of grass and branches of the Siras tree (*Acacia speciosa*) are thrown over the boundary of another village and are supposed to carry the disease demon with them. This often causes a riot.[3] In the same way, killing buffaloes and putting their heads in the next village removes cholera, and by pouring oil on grain and burning it, the disease flies elsewhere in the smoke. This seems to be one of the principles which underlie the general practice of fire sacrifice.

SCAPEGOATS.

This brings us to the regular scapegoat. At shrines of Sîtalâ, the small-pox goddess, sweepers bring round a small pig. Contributions are called for from the worshippers, and when the value of the animal is made up, it is driven by the people into the jungle, pursued by an excited crowd, who believe that the creature has taken the disease with it.

General Sleeman gives an excellent example of this custom.[4] "More than four-fifths of the city and cantonments of Sâgar had been affected by a violent influenza, which, commencing with a violent cough, was followed by a fever and in some cases terminated in death. I had an application

[1] Leland, "Etruscan Roman Remains," 330; for other instances, see Hartland, "Legend of Perseus," ii. 101.
[2] Madden, "Journal Asiatic Society, Bengal," 1848, p. 583.
[3] "Panjâb Notes and Queries," i. 64.
[4] "Rambles and Recollections," i. 203.

from the old Queen Dowager of Sâgar, to allow of a noisy religious procession for the purpose of imploring deliverance from this great calamity. The women and children in this procession were to do their utmost to add to the noise by raising their voices in psalmody, beating upon their brass pans and pots with all their might, and discharging firearms where they could get them. Before the noisy crowd was to be driven a buffalo, which had been purchased by general subscription, in order that every family might participate in the merit. They were to follow it out eight miles, where it was to be turned out for anyone who would take it. If the animal returned, the disease must return with it, and the ceremony be performed over again. I was requested to intimate the circumstances to the officer commanding the troops in cantonments, in order that the noise they intended to make might not excite any alarm and bring down upon them the visit of the soldiery. It was, however, subsequently determined that the animal should be a goat, and he was driven before the crowd. Accordingly, I have on several occasions been requested to allow of such noisy ceremonies in cases of epidemics, and the confidence the people feel in their efficacy has, no doubt, a good effect."

DEMONS SCARED BY NOISE.

This incidentally leads to the consideration of the principle that evil spirits are scared by noise. In the first place this appears largely to account for the use of bells in religious worship. The tolling of the bells keeps off the evil spirits which throng round any place where the worship of the regular gods is being performed. Milton speaks of—

> "The bellman's drowsy charm;
> To bless the doors from nightly harm." [1]

So, the passing bell protects the departing soul as it flies through the air from demoniacal influence. As Grose writes [2] —"The passsing bell was anciently rung for two purposes;

[1] "Penseroso," 83, 84. [2] Brand, "Observations," 424.

one to bespeak the prayers of all good Christians for a soul just departing; the other, to drive away the evil spirits who stood at the bed's foot, and about the house, ready to seize their prey, or at least to molest and terrify the soul in its passage; but by the ringing of that bell (for Durandus informs us evil spirits are much afraid of bells), they were kept aloof, and the soul, like a hunted hare, gained the start, or had what is by sportsmen called 'law.'" The keening at an Irish wake is probably a survival of the same custom. But Panjâbi Musalmâns have a prejudice against beating a brass tray, as it is believed to disturb the dead, who wake, supposing the Day of Judgment has arrived.[1]

Another fact which adds to the efficacy of bells for this purpose, is that they are made of metal, which, as we shall see elsewhere, is a well-known scarer of demons.

Hence in Indian temples the use of the bell, or resounding shell trumpet, is universal. The intention is to call the divinity and wake him from his sleep, so that he may consume the offerings prepared for him by his votaries, and to scare vagrant ghosts, who would otherwise partake of the meal. On the same principle the drum is, as we have seen, a sacred instrument. The same is the case with bells. The Todas of Madras worship Hiriya Deva, whose representative is the sacred buffalo bell, which hangs from the neck of the finest buffalo in the sacred herd.[2] The Gonds have also elevated the bell into a deity in the form of Ghagarapen, and one special class of their devil priests, the Ojhyâls, always wear bells.[3] So, the Patâri priest in Mirzapur and many classes of ascetics throughout the country carry bells and rattles made of iron, which they move as they walk to scare demons. Iron, it need hardly be said, is most efficacious for this purpose. This also accounts for the music played at weddings, when the young pair are in special danger from the attacks of evil spirits. At many rites it is the rule to clap the hands at a special part of the ritual with the same purpose. The Râêdâsi Chamârs and many other people shout or sing

[1] "North Indian Notes and Queries," i. 16.
[2] Oppert, "Original Inhabitants," 187. [3] Hislop, "Papers," 6, 47.

loudly as they remove a corpse for burial or cremation, and there are few magistrates in India who have not been asked for leave by some happy father to allow guns to be fired from his house-top to drive evil spirits from the mother and her child. Mr. Campbell records that they fire a gun over the back of a sick cow in Scotland with the same intention.[1]

DISEASE SCAPEGOATS.

To return to the use of the scape animal as a means of expelling disease. In Berâr, if cholera is very severe, the people get a scapegoat or young buffalo, but in either case it must be a female and as black as possible, the latter condition being based on the fact that Yamarâja, the lord of death, uses such an animal as his vehicle. They then tie some grain, cloves and red lead (all demon scarers) on its back and turn it out of the village. A man of the gardener caste takes the goat outside the boundary, and it is not allowed to return.[2] So among the Korwas of Mirzapur, when cholera begins, a black cock, and when it is severe, a black goat, is offered by the Baiga at the shrine of the village godling, and he then drives the animal off in the direction of some other village. After it has gone a little distance, the Baiga, who is protected from evil by virtue of his holy office, follows it, kills it and eats it. Among the Patâris in cholera epidemics the elders of the village and the Ojha wizard feed a black fowl with grain and drive it beyond the boundary, ordering it to take the plague with it. If the resident of another village finds such a fowl and eats it, cholera comes with it into his village. Hence, when disease prevails, people are very cautious about meddling with strange fowls. When these animals are sent off, a little oil, red lead, and a woman's forehead spangle are put upon it, a decoration which, perhaps, points to a survival of an actual sacrifice to appease the demon of disease. When such an animal comes into a village, the Baiga takes it to the local shrine, worships it and

[1] "Popular Tales," Introduction, lxviii.; "Calcutta Review," April, 1884.

[2] "Panjâb Notes and Queries," iii. 81.

then passes it on quietly outside the boundary. Among the Kharwârs, when rinderpest attacks the cattle, they take a black cock, put some red lead on its head, some antimony on its eyes, a spangle on its forehead, and fixing a pewter bangle to its leg, let it loose, calling to the disease—" Mount on the fowl and go elsewhere into the ravines and thickets ; destroy the sin ! " This dressing up of the scape animal in a woman's ornaments and trinkets is almost certainly a relic of some grosser form of expiation in which a human being was sacrificed. We have another survival of the same practice in the Panjâb custom, which directs that when cholera prevails, a man of the Chamâr or currier caste, one of the hereditary menials, should be branded on the buttocks and turned out of the village.[1]

A curious modification of the ordinary scape animal, of which it is unnecessary to give any more instances, comes from Kulu.[2] " The people occasionally perform an expiatory ceremony with the object of removing ill-luck or evil influence, which is supposed to be brooding over the hamlet. The godling (Deota) of the place is, as usual, first consulted through his disciple (Chela) and declares himself also under the influence of a charm and advises a feast, which is given in the evening at the temple. Next morning a man goes round from house to house, a creel on his back, into which each family throws all sorts of odds and ends, parings of nails, pinches of salt, bits of old iron, handfuls of grain, etc. The whole community then turns out and perambulates the village, at the same time stretching an unbroken thread round it, fastened to pegs at the four corners. This done, the man with the creel carries it down to the river bank and empties the contents therein, and a sheep, fowl, and some small animals are sacrificed on the spot. Half the sheep is the property of the man who dares to carry the creel, and he is also entertained from house to house on the following night."

It is obvious that this exactly corresponds with the old English custom of sin-eating. Thus we read :[3]—" Within

[1] " Panjâb Notes and Queries," i. 27. [2] " Settlement Report," 155.
[3] Brand, " Observations," 447.

the memory of our fathers, in Shropshire, when a person died, there was a notice given to an old sire (for so they called him), who presently repaired to the place where the deceased lay, and stood before the door of the house, when some of the family came out and furnished him with a cricket on which he sat down facing the door. Then they gave him a groat, which he put in his pocket; a crust of bread, which he ate; and a full bowl of ale, which he drank off at a draught. After this he got out from the cricket and pronounced, with a composed gesture, the ease and rest of the soul departed, for which he would pawn his own soul."

There are other Indian customs based on the same principle.[1] Thus, in the Ambâla District a Brâhman named Nathu stated "that he had eaten food out of the hand of the Râja of Bilâspur, after his death, and that in consequence he had for the space of one year been placed on the throne at Bilâspur. At the end of the year he had been given presents, including a village, and had then been turned out of Bilâspur territory and forbidden apparently to return. Now he is an outcast among his co-religionists, as he has eaten food out of the dead man's hand." So at the funeral ceremonies of the late Rânî of Chamba, it is said that rice and ghi were placed in the hands of the corpse, which a Brâhman consumed on payment of a fee. The custom has given rise to a class of outcast Brahmans in the Hill States about Kângra. In another account of the funeral rites of the Rânî of Chamba, it is added that after the feeding of the Brâhman, as already described, "a stranger, who had been caught beyond Chamba territory, was given the costly wrappings round the corpse, a new bed and a change of raiment, and then told to depart, and never to show his face in Chamba again." At the death of a respectable Hindu the clothes and other belongings of the dead man are, in the same way, given to the Mahâbrâhman or funeral priest. This seems to be partly based on the principle that he, by using these articles, passes them on for the use of the deceased in the land of death; but the detestation and con-

[1] "Panjâb Notes and Queries," i. 86, ii 93.

tempt felt for this class of priest may be, to some extent, based on the idea that by the use of these articles he takes upon his head the sins of the dead man.[1]

Again, writing of the customs prevailing among the Râjput tribes of Oudh which practise female infanticide, Gen. Sleeman writes:[2]—"The infant is destroyed in the room where it was born, and there buried. The room is then plastered over with cow-dung, and on the thirteenth day after, the village or family priest must cook and eat his food in this room. He is provided with wood, ghi, barley, rice, and sesamum. He boils the rice, barley, and sesamum in a brass vessel, throws the ghi over them when they are dressed, and eats the whole. This is considered as a Homa or burnt offering, and by eating it in that place, the priest is supposed to take the whole Hatya or sin upon himself, and to cleanse the family from it."

So, in Central India the Gonds in November assemble at the shrine of Gansyâm Deo to worship him. Sacrifices of fowls and spirits, or a pig, occasionally, according to the size of the village, are offered, and Gansyâm Deo is said to descend on the head of one of the worshippers, who is suddenly seized with a kind of fit, and after staggering about for a while, rushes off into the wildest jungles, where the popular theory is that, if not pursued and brought back, he would inevitably die of starvation, and become a raving lunatic. As it is, after being brought back by one or two men, he does not recover his senses for one or two days. The idea is that one man is thus singled out as a scapegoat for the sins of the rest of the village.

In the final stage we find the scape animal merging into a regular expiatory sacrifice. Other examples will be given in another connection of the curious customs, like that of the Irish and Manxland rites of hunting the wren, which are almost certainly based on the principle of a sacrifice. Here it may be noted that at one of their festivals, the Bhûmij

[1] With this compare the Karnigor of Sindh—Hartland, "Legend of Perseus," ii. 295.

[2] "Journey through Oudh," ii. 39.

used to drive two male buffaloes into a small enclosure, while the Râja and his suite used to witness the proceedings. They first discharged arrows at the animals, and the tormented and enraged beasts fell to and gored each other, while arrow after arrow was discharged. When the animals were past doing very much mischief, the people rushed in and hacked them to pieces with axes. This custom is now discontinued.[1]

Similarly in the Hills, at the Nand Ashtamî, or feast in honour of Nanda, the foster father of Krishna, a buffalo is specially fed with sweetmeats, and, after being decked with a garland round the neck, is worshipped. The headman of the village then lays a sword across its neck and the beast is let loose, when all proceed to chase it, pelt it with stones, and hack it with knives until it dies. It is curious that this savage rite is carried out in connection with the worship of the Krishna Cultus, in which blood sacrifice finds no place.[2]

In the same part of the country the same rite is performed after a death, on the analogy of the other instances, which have been already quoted. When a man dies, his relations assemble at the end of the year in which the death occurred, and the nearest male relative dances naked (another instance of the nudity charm, to which reference has been already made) with a drawn sword in his hand, to the music of a drum, in which he is assisted by others for a whole day and night. The following day a buffalo is brought and made intoxicated with Bhang or Indian hemp, and spirits, and beaten to death with sticks, stones and weapons.

So, the Hill Bhotiyas have a feast in honour of the village god, and towards evening they take a dog, make him drunk with spirits and hemp, and kill him with sticks and stones, in the belief that no disease or misfortune will visit the village during the year.[3] At the periodical feast in honour of the mountain goddess of the Himâlaya, Nandâ Devî, it is said that a four-horned goat is invariably born and accompanies the pilgrims. When unloosed on the mountain, the

[1] Dalton, "Descriptive Ethnology," 170.
[2] "Himâlayan Gazetteer," ii. 851 sq.
[3] Ibid. ii. 871.

sacred goat suddenly disappears and as suddenly reappears without its head, and then furnishes food for the party. The head is supposed to be consumed by the goddess herself, who by accepting it with its load of sin, washes away the transgressions of her votaries.

CHAPTER IV.

THE WORSHIP OF THE SAINTED DEAD.

> Αἶψα δ' ἵκοντο κατ' ἀσφοδελὸν λειμῶνα
> Ἔνθα τε ναίουσι ψυχαί, εἴδωλα καμόντων.
>
> *Odyssey*, xxiv. 12, 14.

ANCESTOR-WORSHIP: ITS ORIGIN.

THE worship of ancestors is one of the main branches of the religion of the Indian races. "Its principles are not difficult to understand, for they plainly keep up the arrangements of the living world. The dead ancestor, now passed into a deity, simply goes on protecting his own family, and receiving suit and service from them as of old; the dead chief still watches over his own tribe, still holds his authority by helping friends and harming enemies; still rewards the right and sharply punishes the wrong."[1] It is in fact the earliest attempt of the savage to realize the problems of human existence, as the theology of the Vedas or Olympus is the explanation which the youth of the world offers of physical phenomena. The latter is primitive physics, the former primitive biology, and it marks a stage in the growth of anthropomorphism when the worship of unseen spirits in general passes to that of unseen spirits in particular.

AMONG THE ARYANS AND DRÂVIDIANS.

It is admitted on all sides that this form of worship was general among the Aryan nations;[2] but it is a mistake to

[1] Tylor, "Primitive Culture," ii. 113.

[2] Hearn, "Aryan Household," 18; Spencer, "Principles of Sociology," i. 270 sq.; Whitney, "Oriental and Linguistic Studies," 1st Ser. 59; Mommsen, "History of Rome," i. 73.

suppose, as is too often done, that the worship was peculiar to them. That such was not the case can be proved by numerous examples drawn from the practices of aboriginal tribes in India, who have lived hitherto in such complete isolation, that the worship can hardly be due to imitation of the customs of their more civilized neighbours.

Thus, on the tenth day after a death in the family, the Ghasiyas of Mirzapur, about the most degraded of the Drâvidian tribes, feed the brotherhood, and at the door of the cook-house spread flour or ashes a cubit square on the ground. They light a lamp there and cover both the square and the light with a basket. Then the son of the dead man goes a little distance in the direction in which the corpse had been carried out, and calls out his name loudly two or three times. He invites him to come and sit on the shrine which his descendants have prepared for him, and to consume the offerings which they are ready to present. It is said that if the deceased died in any ordinary way and not by the attack of a Bhût, he often calls from the burying ground and says, "I am coming!" After calling his father's spirit two or three times, the son returns to the house and examines the flour or ashes, and if the deceased did not die by the attack of a Bhût, the mark of his spirit is found on the flour or ashes in the shape of the footprint of a rat or a weasel. When this is observed, the son takes a white fowl and sacrifices it with a knife near the cook-house, calling to the spirit of his father—"Come and accept the offering which is ready for you!" Some of them strangle the fowl with their hands, and before killing it sprinkle a little grain before it, saying—"If you are really the spirit of my father, you will accept the grain!" Then he goes on to his father's spirit—"Accept the offering, sit in the corner and bless your offspring!" If the fowl eats the grain, there is great rejoicing, as it implies that the spirit has quietly taken up its residence in the house. If the fowl does not eat, it is supposed that some sorcerer or enemy has detained the spirit with the ultimate object of releasing it some time or other on its own family, with whom it is presumably displeased because they have taken no care to propitiate it. If the soul does not answer from the burial ground, or if there is no mark on the square of ashes, it is assumed that he has fallen into the hands of some Bhût or Pret, who has shut him up in the hollow stalk of a bamboo, or buried him in the earth; in any case there is a risk that he may return, and the rite is still performed as a precautionary measure.

Among the Kharwârs the holiest part of the house is the south room, where it is supposed that the Devatâ pitri or sainted dead reside. They worship the spirits of the dead in the month of Sâwan (August) near the house-fire. The house-master offers up one or two black fowls and some cakes and makes a burnt offering with butter and molasses. Then he calls out—"Whatever ghosts of the holy dead or evil spirits may be in my family, accept this offering and keep the field and house free from trouble!" Many of the Kharwârs are now coming more completely under Brâhmanical influence, and these worship the Pitri at weddings in the courtyard. The house-master offers some balls of rice boiled in milk, and a Brâhman standing by mutters some texts. They are now so advanced as to do the annual service for the repose of the sainted spirits at the Pitripaksha or fortnight of the dead in the month of Kuâr (August).

The other Drâvidian tribes follow similar customs. Thus, the Korwas worship their dead relations in February with an offering of goats, which is done by the eldest son of the dead man in the family cook-house. Their ancestors are said not to appear in the flesh after death, but to show themselves in dreams if they are dissatisfied with the arrangements made for their comfort. On the day on which they are expected to appear the householder makes an offering of cakes to them in the family kitchen. The Patâris think that the dead occasionally attend when worship is being done to them. At other times they remain in the sky or wander about the mountains. Sometimes they call in the night to their descendants and say—"Worship us! Give us food and drink!" If they are not propitiated they give trouble and cause sickness. The Kisâns and Bhuiyârs of Chota Nâgpur adore their ancestors, "but they have no notion that the latter are now spirits, or that there are spirits and ghosts, or a future state, or anything." The Bhuiyas revere their ancestors under the name of Bîr or Vîra, "hero," a term which is elsewhere applied to ghosts of a specially malignant character. The Khariyas put the ashes of their dead into an earthen pot and throw it into a river. They afterwards set up in the vicinity slabs of stone as a resting-place for them, and to these they make daily oblations. The only worship performed by the Korwas of Chota Nâgpur is to their dead relatives, and the same is the case with other allied races, such as the Bhîls and Santâls.[1]

SPIRITS MORTAL.

Most of these Drâvidian tribes believe that like themselves the spirits of the dead are mortal. What becomes of them after a couple of generations no one can say. But when this period has elapsed they are supposed to be finally disposed of some way or other, and being no longer objects of fear to the survivors, their worship is neglected, and attention is paid only to the more recent dead, whose powers of mischief still continue. The Gonds go further and propitiate for only one year the spirits of their departed friends, and this is done even if they have been persons of no note during their lifetime; but with worthies of the tribe the case is different, and if one of them, for example, has founded a village or been its headman or priest, then he is treated as a god for years, and a small shrine of earth is erected to his memory, at which sacrifices are annually offered.[2] It is said that the Juângs, who until quite recently used to dress in garments of leaves, are the only one of these tribes who do not practise this form of

[1] Dalton, "Descriptive Ethnology," 132, 133, 139, 160, 229; Campbell, "Notes," 2 sqq.; Tylor, "Primitive Culture," ii. 117.

[2] Hislop, "Papers," 16 sq.

worship.[1] But these races are particularly reticent about their beliefs and usages, and it is more than probable that further inquiry will show that they are not peculiar in this respect.

ANCESTORS RE-BORN IN CHILDREN.

Among many races, again, there is a common belief that the father or grandfather is re-born in one of his descendants. The modern reader is familiar with examples of such beliefs in Mr. Du Maurier's "Peter Ibbetson," and Mr. Rider Haggard's "She." Manu expresses this belief when he writes—"The husband after conception by his wife, becomes an embryo and is born again of her; for that is the wifehood of a wife, that he is born again by her." The feeling that children are really the ancestors re-born is obviously based on the principle of hereditary resemblance. Hence the general feeling in favour of calling a child by the name of the grandfather or grandmother, which is about as far as the rustic goes in recognizing the ascending line. The Konkan Kunbis, and even Brâhmans, believe that the dead ancestors sometimes appear in children. Among Gujarât Musalmâns the nurse, if a child is peevish, says, "Its kind has come upon its head." The same idea is found among the Khândhs. Among the Laplanders of Europe an ancestral spirit tells the mother that he has come into the child, and directs her to call it after his name.[2] Another variant of the same belief is that common among some of the Drâvidian races that the ancestor is revived in a calf, which is in consequence well fed and treated with particular respect.

THE SRÂDDHA.

The ordinary worship of ancestors among Brâhmanized Hindu races has been so often described in well-known books as to need little further illustration.[3] The

[1] Dalton, *loc. cit.*, 158.
[2] Campbell, "Notes," 5; Tylor, *loc. cit.*, ii. 116.
[3] E.g. Monier-Williams, "Brâhmanism and Hinduism," 278 sqq.

spirits of departed ancestors attend upon the Brâhmans invited to the ceremony of the Srâddha, "hovering round them like pure spirits, and sitting by them when they are seated." "An offering to the gods is to be made at the beginning and end of the Srâddha; it must not begin and end with an offering to ancestors, for he who begins and ends it with an offering to the Pitri quickly perishes with his progeny." The belief is common to many races that the spirits of the dead assemble to partake of the food provided by the piety of their relations on earth. Alcinous addressing the Phæacians tells them—"For ever heretofore the gods appear manifest among us, whensoever we offer glorious hecatombs, and they feast at our side sitting by the same board." And the old Prussians used to prepare a meal, to which, standing at the door, they invited the soul of the deceased. "When the meal was over the priest took a broom and swept the souls out of the house, saying—'Dear souls! ye have eaten and drunk. Go forth! go forth!'"[1]

The place where the oblation is to be made is to be sequestered, facing the south, the land of departed spirits, and smeared with cow-dung. The use of this substance is easily to be accounted for, without following the remarkable explanation of a modern writer, who connects it with the dropping of the Aurora.[2] "The divine manes are always pleased with an oblation in empty glades, naturally clean, on the banks of rivers, and in solitary spots." The ceremony is to be performed by the eldest son, which furnishes the Hindu with the well-known argument for marriage and the procreation of male issue. We have seen that the Drâvidians also regard the rite as merely domestic and to be performed by the house-master.

The orthodox Hindu, besides the usual Srâddha, in connection with his daily worship, offers the Tarpana or water oblation to the sainted dead. The object of the annual Srâddha is, as is well known, to accelerate the

[1] See Frazer, "Golden Bough," i. 177.
[2] Gubernatis, "Zoological Mythology," i. 279.

progress (*gati*) of the soul through the various stages of bliss, known as Sâlokya, Sâmîpya and Sârûpya, and by its performance at Gaya the wearied soul passes into Vaikuntha, or the paradise of Vishnu.

Hindus do not allow their sons to bathe during the fortnight sacred to the manes, as they believe that the dirt produced by bathing, shaving, and washing the apparel will reach and annoy the sainted dead. The story goes that Râja Karana made a vow that he would not touch food until he had given a maund and a quarter (about one hundred pounds) of gold daily to Brâhmans. When he died he went to heaven, and was there given a palace of gold to dwell in, and gold for his food and drink, as this was all he had given away in charity during his mortal life. So in his distress he asked to be allowed to return to earth for fifteen days. His prayer was granted, and warned by sad experience he occupied himself during his time of grace in giving nothing but food in charity, being so busy that he neglected to bathe, shave, or wash his clothes, and thus he became an example to succeeding generations.[1]

DEGRADATION OF ANCESTOR-WORSHIP.

The worship which has been thus described easily passes into other and grosser forms. Thus, in the family of the Gâikwârs of Baroda, when they worship Mahâdeva they think of the greatest of this line of princes. The temple contains a rudely-executed portrait of Khândê Râo, the shrine to the left the bed, garments, and phial of Ganges water, which commemorate his mother, Chimnâbâî. Govind Râo has an image dressed up, and Fateh Sinh a stone face.[2]

In Central India Râjputs wear the figure of a distinguished ancestor or relation engraved in gold or silver. This image, usually that of a warrior on horseback, is sometimes worshipped, but its chief utility is as a charm to keep off ghosts and evil spirits.[3]

1 "North Indian Notes and Queries," i. 95.
2 "Bombay Gazetteer," vii. 16 sq.
3 Malcolm, "Central India," i. 144.

The aboriginal Bhuiyas of Chota Nâgpur, "after disposing of their dead, perform a ceremony which is supposed to bring back to the house the spirit of the deceased, henceforth an object of household worship. A vessel filled with rice and flour is placed for the time on the tomb, and when brought back the mark of a fowl's foot is found at the bottom of the vessel, and this indicates that the spirit of the deceased has returned."[1] This is, as we have seen, common to many of the Drâvidian tribes, and we shall meet instances of similar practices when we consider the malignant variety of ghosts.

A curious example of the popular form of ancestor-worship is given by General Sleeman :—" Râma Chandra, the Pandit, said that villages which had been held by old Gond proprietors were more liable than others to visitation from local ghosts, that it was easy to say what village was or was not haunted, but often exceedingly difficult to say to whom the ghost belonged. This once discovered, the nearest surviving relation was, of course, expected to take steps to put him to rest. But," said he, "it is wrong to suppose that the ghost of an old proprietor must be always doing mischief. He is often the best friend of the cultivators, and of the present proprietor too, if he treats him with proper respect; for he will not allow the people of any other village to encroach upon the boundaries with impunity, and they will be saved all expense and annoyance of a reference to the judicial tribunals for the settlement of boundary disputes. It will not cost much to conciliate these spirits, and the money is generally well laid out."

He instances a case of a family of village proprietors, "who had for several generations insisted at every new settlement upon having the name of the spirit of the old proprietor inserted in the lease instead of their own, and thereby secured his good graces on all occasions." "A cultivator who trespassed on land believed to be in charge of such a spirit had his son bitten by a snake, and his two oxen were seized with the murrain. In terror he went off to the village temple, confessed his sin, and vowed to restore not

[1] Dalton, "Descriptive Ethnology," 148.

only the half-acre of land, but to build a very handsome temple on the spot as a perpetual sign of his repentance. The boy and the bullocks all then recovered, the shrine was built, and is, I believe, still to be seen as a boundary mark."[1]

WORSHIP OF WORTHIES.

From this family worship of deceased relations, the transition to the special worship of persons of high local reputation in life, or who have died in some remarkable way, is easy. The intermediate links are the Sâdhu and the Satî, and the worship finally culminates in a creed like that of the Jainas, who worship a pantheon of deified saints, that of the Lingâyat worship of Siva incarnated as Chambasâpa, or the godlike weaver Kabîr of the Kabîrpanthis. The lowest phase of all is the worship by the Halbas of Central India of a pantheon of glorified distillers.[2]

THE SÂDHU.

The Sâdhu is a saint who is regarded as "the great power of God," the name meaning "he that is eminent in virtue." He is a visible manifestation of the divine energy acquired by his piety and self-devotion. We shall meet later on instances of deified holy men of this class. Meanwhile, it may be noted, we see around us the constant development of the cultus in all its successive stages. Thus, in Berâr at Askot the saint is still alive; at Wadnera he died nearly a century ago, and his descendants live on the offerings made by the pious; at Jalgânw a crazy vagabond was canonized on grounds which strict people consider quite insufficient. There is, of course, among the disciples and descendants of these local saints a constant competition going on for the honour of canonization, which once secured, the shrine may become a very valuable source of income and reputation. But the indiscriminate and ill-regulated deification of mortals

[1] "Rambles and Recollections," i. 269 sqq.
[2] "Central Provinces Gazetteer," Introduction, cxxi.

is one of the main causes of the weakness of modern Hinduism, because, by a process of abscission, the formation of multitudinous sects, which take their titles and special forms of belief from the saint whose disciples they profess to be, is promoted and encouraged. Thus, as has been well remarked, Hinduism lies in urgent need of a Pope or acknowledged orthodox head, "to control its wonderful elasticity and receptivity, to keep up the standard of deities and saints, and generally to prevent superstitions running wild into a tangled jungle of polytheism."[1]

It would be out of place to give here any of the details of the numerous sects which have been founded in this way to commemorate the life and teaching of some eminent saint. The remarkable point about this movement is that the leaders of these sects are not always or even constantly drawn from the priestly classes. Thus the Charandâsis, who are Krishna worshippers, take their name from Charan Dâs, a Dhûsar, who are usually classed as Banyas, but claim to be Brâhmans; Jhambajî, the founder of the Bishnois, was a Râjput; Kabîr, whoever he may have been, was brought up by a family of Muhammadan weavers at Benares; Nâmdeo was a cotton carder; Râê Dâs is said to have been a Chamâr; Dâdu was a cotton cleaner; many of them are half Muhammadans, as the Chhaju-panthis and Shamsis. It is difficult to estimate highly enough the result of this feeling of toleration and catholicism on the progress of modern Hinduism.

MIRACLE-WORKING TOMBS.

These saints have wrested from the reluctant gods by sheer piety and relentless austerities, a portion of the divine thaumaturgic power, which exudes after their death from the places where their bodies are laid. This is the case with the shrines of both Hindu and Musalmân saints. Many instances of this will be found in succeeding pages. Thus at Chunâr there is a famous shrine in honour of Shâh Qâsim

[1] "Berâr Gazetteer," 191.

Sulaimâni,[1] a local saint whose opinions were so displeasing to Akbar that he imprisoned him here till his death in 1614 A.D. His cap and turban are still shown at his tomb, and these, when gently rubbed by one of his disciples, pour out a divine influence through the assembled multitude of votaries, many of whom are Hindus. This holy influence extends even to the animal kingdom. Thus the tomb of the saint Nirgan Shâh at Sarauli in the Bareilly District abounds in scorpions, which bite no one through the virtue of the saint.

Hindu saints of the same class are so directly imbued with the divine afflatus that they need not the purifying influence of fire, and are buried, not cremated. Their Samâdhi or final resting-place is usually represented by a pile of earth, or a tomb or tumulus of a conical or circular form. Others, again, like some of the Gusâîns, are after death enclosed in a box of stone and consigned to the waters of the Ganges. These shrines are generally occupied by a disciple or actual descendant of the saint, and there vows and prayers are made and offerings presented.

THE SATÎ.

The next link between ancestor-worship and that of special deceased worthies is seen in the Satî, or "faithful wife," who, before the practice was prohibited by our Government, was bound to bear her deceased lord company to the world of spirits for his consolation and service. The rite seems to have at one time prevailed throughout the Aryan world.[2] It undoubtedly prevailed in Slavonic lands,[3] and there are even traces of it in Greece. Evadne is said to have burnt herself with the body of her husband, Capaneus, and Oenone, according to one account, leaped into the pyre on which the body of Paris was being cremated. There are indications that

[1] For an account of this worthy see "North Indian Notes and Queries," i. 163.

[2] Spencer, "Principles of Sociology," i. 187; Lubbock, "Origin of Civilization," 284; Tylor, "Primitive Culture," i. 458 sq.

[3] Ralston, "Songs of the Russian People," 327.

the rite prevailed among the Drâvidian races, and it has been suggested that the Hindus may have adopted it from them. Even to the present day among some of the Bhîl tribes the wife of the dead man is carried along with him on the bier to the burning ground, where she is laid down. There she breaks her marriage necklace, and her ornaments are consumed with the corpse of her husband, obviously a survival of the time when she was actually burnt with him.[1]

It is unnecessary here to enter into the controversy whether or not the rite was based on a misinterpretation or perversion of one of the sacred texts. That in old times the Satî was treated with exceptional honour is certain. In some places she went to the burning ground richly dressed, scattering money and flowers, and calling out the names of the deities, with music sounding and drums beating. In some places she used to mark with her hands the gateways and walls of the chief temple, and she sometimes marked in the same way a stone for her descendants to worship, a practice to which reference will be made later on. On such stones it was the custom to carve a representation of her, and in many places a Chhatri, or ornamental cenotaph pavilion, was erected in her honour. The small shrines in honour of the village Satî are found often in considerable numbers on the banks of tanks all over Upper India. They are visited by women at marriages and other festivals, and are periodically repaired and kept in order. According to Mr. Ibbetson,[2] in the Delhi territory, these shrines take the place of those dedicated to the Pitri, or sainted dead. They often contain a representation in stone of the lord and his faithful spouse, and one of his arms rests affectionately on her neck. Sometimes, if he died in battle, he is mounted on his war steed and she walks beside him; but her worshippers are not always careful in identifying her shrine, and I have seen at least one undoubted Revenue Survey pillar doing duty as a monument to some unnamed local divinity of this class.

Among the warrior tribes of Râjputâna, the Satî shrine

[1] Hislop, "Papers," 19; Appendix, iii. [2] "Panjâb Ethnography," 115.

SATI SHRINES.

I. 187.

usually takes the form of a monument, on which is carved the warrior on his charger, with his wife standing beside him, and the images of the sun and the moon on either side, emblematical of never-dying fame. Such places are the scene of many a ghostly legend. As Col. Tod writes in his sentimental way[1]—"Among the altars on which have burnt the beautiful and brave, the harpy or Dâkinî takes up her abode, and stalks forth to devour the heart of her victims." The Râjput never enters these places of silence, but to perform stated rites or anniversary offerings of flowers and water to the manes of his ancestors. There is a peculiarly beautiful Satî necropolis at Udaypur, and the Satî Burj, or tower at Mathura, erected in honour of the queen of Râja Bihâr Mal of Jaypur in 1570 A.D., is one of the chief ornaments of the city.[2]

THE SATÎ AND THE PITRI.

The connection between the special worship of the Satî and that of the Pitri or sainted dead will have been remarked. In many places the Satî represents the company of the venerated ancestors and is regarded as the guardian mother of the village, and in many of the rustic shrines of this class the same connection with the Pitri is shown in another interesting way. The snake is, as we shall see, regarded as a type of the household deity, which is often one of the deified ancestors, and so, in the Satî shrine we often see a snake delineated in the act of rising out of the masonry, as if it were the guardian mother snake arising to receive the devotion of her descendants.

The Satî having thus secured the honour of deification by her sacrifice, is able to protect her worshippers and gratify their desires. Some are even the subject of special honour, such as Sakhû Bâî, who is worshipped at Akola.[3] Even the Drâvidian Kaurs of Sarguja worship a deified Satî, another

[1] "Annals," i. 79.
[2] Ferguson, "History of Indian Architecture," 470; "Râjputâna Gazetteer," iii. 46; Growse, "Mathura," 138.
[3] "Berâr Gazetteer," 191.

link connecting the cultus with the aboriginal races. She has a sacred grove, and every year a fowl is sacrificed to her, and every third year a goat. Col. Dalton [1] observes that the Hindus who accompanied him were intensely amused at the idea of offering fowls to a Satî, who is accustomed to the simpler bloodless tribute of milk, cakes, fruit and flowers. This is the form of the offering at Jilmili, the Satî shrines belonging to the local Râja. The curses of a dying Satî were greatly feared. Numerous instances of families ruined in this way are told both in Râjputâna and in Nepâl, the last places where the rite is occasionally performed.[2]

The arrangements for the cremation varied in different places. In Western India she sat in a specially built grass hut, and keeping her husband's head in her lap, supported it with her right hand, while she kindled the hut with a torch held in her left hand. Nowadays in Nepâl the husband and the Satî are made to lie side by side on the pyre. The woman's right hand is put under the husband's neck, and round her face are placed all kinds of inflammable substances. Three long poles of undried wood are laid over the bodies—one over the legs, the second over the chest, and the third over the neck. Three men on either side press down the poles till the woman is burnt to death. There have been cases in which the wretched victim tried to escape, and was dragged back by force to her death.

A curious modification of the practice of Satî, which so far has been traced only in Râjputâna, is what is known as Mâ Satî, or mother Satî, where the mother immolates herself with her dead child. Colonel Powlett [3] remarks that in inquiring about it one is often told that it is really Mahâ Satî, or "the great Satî." He adds that there can be no doubt that mother Satî really prevails, but was confined to the sandy and desert tract, where domestic affection is said

[1] "Descriptive Ethnology," 138.

[2] Tod, "Annals," ii. 544, 546, 676; Wright, "History of Nepâl," 159, 212.

[3] "North Indian Notes and Queries," ii. 199; "Panjâb Notes and Queries," iv. 44 sq. In the "Katha Sarit Sâgara" (Tawney, ii. 254), a mother proposes to go into the fire with her dead children.

to be stronger than elsewhere. "In one large remote village I found five monuments to Mother Satîs, one a Chhatri or pavilion of some pretensions. A Râjput lady from Jaysalmer was on a visit to her father's family with her youngest son. The boy was thrown when exercising his pony, dragged in the stirrup and killed. His mother became Satî with her son's body, and probably her example, for she was a person of some rank, led to the subsequent practice of Mâ Satî in the same district."

MODERN SAINTS.

We have already noticed some instances of the canonization in modern times of saints and holy men. Of worthies of this kind, who have received divine honours, the number is legion. This deification of human beings is found in the very early Brâhmanical literature. One of the most noteworthy ideas to be found in the Brâhmanas is that the gods were merely mortal till they conquered Death by their sacrifices. Death, alarmed, protested to the gods, and it was then arranged that no one should become immortal by the force of his piety without first offering his body to Death. Manu declares that "from his birth alone a Brâhman is regarded as a divinity, even by the gods."[1] Modern practice supports this by calling him Mahâ-râja or "Great king," and he rises to heaven as a deity, like many of the famous kings of old.[2] In the same way the Etruscans had certain rites through which the souls of men could become gods and were called Dii Animales, because they had once been human souls. Quite in consonance with Indian practice they first became Penates and Lares before they rose to the rank of the superior deities.[3]

DEIFICATION IN MODERN TIMES.

A few examples of modern deification may be given to illustrate this phase of the popular faith. Thus, one Gauhar

[1] "Institutes," xi. 84. [2] Frazer, "Golden Bough," i. 8.
[3] Leland, "Etruscan Roman Remains," 202.

Shâh was quite recently canonized at Meerut because he delivered a prophecy that a windmill belonging to a certain Mr. Smith would soon cease to work. The fulfilment of his prediction was considered ample evidence of his sanctity, and the question was put beyond the possibility of doubt when, just before his death, the holy man directed his disciples to remove him from an inn, which immediately fell down. Another saint of the same place is said to have given five years of his life to the notorious Begam Samru, who died in 1836, in all the odour of sanctity.

SHAIKH BÛRHAN.

Shaikh Bûrhan, a saint of Amber, was offered a drink of milk by Mokul, one of the Shaikhâwat chiefs, and immediately performed the miracle of drawing a copious stream of milk from the udder of an exhausted female buffalo. "This was sufficient to convince the old chief that he could work other miracles, and he prayed that through his means he might no longer be childless. In due time he had an heir, who, according to the injunction of Bûrhan, was styled, after his own tribe, Shaikh, whence the title of the clan. He directed that the child should wear the cross strings (*baddiya*) worn by Muhammadan children, which, when laid aside, were to be deposited at the saint's shrine, and further that he should assume the blue tunic and cap, abstain from hog's flesh, and eat no meat in which the blood remained. He also ordained that at the birth of every Shaikhâwat a goat should be sacrificed, the Islâmite creed or Kalima recited, and the child sprinkled with the blood." These customs are still observed, and the Shaikh's shrine is still a sanctuary, while his descendants enjoy lands specially assigned to them.[1]

SALÎM CHISHTI.

The power of conferring male offspring has made the reputation of many saints of this class, like the famous

[1] Tod, "Annals," ii. 430 sq.

Salîm Chishti of Fatehpur Sîkri, whose prayers were efficacious in procuring an heir for the Emperor Akbar. Up to the present day childless women visit his shrine and hang rags on the delicate marble traceries of his tomb to mark their vows.

DEIFICATION OF NOTED PERSONS.

Besides this sainthood which is based on sanctity of life and approved thaumaturgic powers, the right of deification is conferred on persons who have been eminent or notorious in their lives, or who have died in some extraordinary or notorious way. All or nearly all the deified saints of Northern India may be grouped under one or other of these categories.

HARSHU PÂNRÊ.

We have already given an instance of the second class in Hardaul Lâla, the cholera godling. Another example of the same kind is that of Harshu Pânrê or Harshu Bâba, the local god of Chayanpur, near Sahsarâm in Bengal, whose worship is now rapidly spreading over Northern India, and promises to become as widely diffused as that of Hardaul himself. He was, according to the current account, a Kanaujiya Brâhman, the family priest of Râja Sâlivâhana of Chayanpur. The Râja had two queens, one of whom was jealous of the priest's influence. About this time the priest built a fine house close to the palace, and one night the Râja and the Rânî saw a light from its upper story gleaming aloft in the sky. The Rânî hinted to the Râja that the priest had designs of ousting his master from the kingdom; so the Râja had his house demolished and resumed the lands which had been conferred upon him. The enraged Brâhman did *dharnâ*, in other words fasted till he died at the palace gate. This tragical event occurred in 1427 A.D., and when they took his body for cremation at Benares, they found Harshu standing in his wooden sandals on the steps of the burning Ghât. He then informed them that he had become a Brahm, or malignant Brâhman ghost. The Râja's daughter had been kind to the Brâhman in his misfortunes and he blessed her, so that her family exists in prosperity to this day. But the rest of his house was destroyed, and now only the gateway at which the Brâhman died remains to commemorate the tragedy.[1]

Harshu is now worshipped as a Brahm with the fire sacrifice and offerings of Brâhmanical cords and sweetmeats. If any one obtains his desires through his intercession, he makes an offering of a golden sacred cord and a silken waist-string, and feeds Brâhmans in his honour. Harshu's speciality is exorcising evil spirits which attack people and cause disease. Such spirits are usually of low caste and cannot withstand the influence of this deified Brâhman.

RATAN PÂNRÊ.

Another worthy, whose legend much resembles that of Harshu, is Ratan Pânrê, who is venerated by the Kalhans Râjputs of Oudh. The last of the race, Râja Achal Nârâyan Sinh, ravished the daughter of Ratan Pânrê. He pleaded in vain to the wicked Râja for reparation, and at last he and his wife starved themselves to death at the gate of the fort. He too, like Harshu, spared a princess of the Râja's house, but he cursed the rest of his family with ruin. After he died his ghost went to the river Sarjû and claimed her assistance in revenging himself on the Râja. She at last consented to help him, provided he could get the Râja into his power by inducing him to accept some present from him. So he went to the Râja's family priest and induced him to take from him a sacred cord with which he was to invest the Râja. When Achal Nârâyan Sinh heard to whom he was indebted for the gift he flung it away in terror. But soon after an angry wave rushed from the Sarjû, and on its crest sat the wraith of Ratan Pânrê. It swept away his palace and left not a soul of his household alive.[2]

[1] Cunningham, "Archæological Reports," xvii. 160 sqq.; Buchanan, "Eastern India," i. 488; "North Indian Notes and Queries," ii. 38.

[2] "Oudh Gazetteer," i. 540 sq.

MAHENÎ.

There is a similar case among the Hayobans Râjputs of Ghâzipur. In 1528 A.D. their Râja Bhopat Deva, or perhaps one of his sons, seduced Mahenî, a Brâhman girl, a relation of their family priest. She burned herself to death, and in dying, imprecated the most fearful curses on the Hayobans sept. In consequence of a succession of disasters which followed, the tribe completely abandoned their family settlement at Baliya, where the woman's tomb is worshipped to this day. Even now none of the sept dares to enter the precincts of their former home. In the same way, in the case of Harshu Pânrê no pilgrim will eat or drink near his tomb, as the place is accursed through the murder of a Brâhman.[1]

There are numerous other cases of this deification of suicide Brâhmans in Northern India. The forms in which they sought vengeance by their death on their persecutors are diversified in the extreme. There is a case of a Brâhman in the Partâbgarh District who, when turned out of his land, to avenge himself, gathered a heap of cow-dung in the centre of one of the fields and lay down on it till he was devoured by worms. This happened sixty years ago, but his fields still stand a waste of jungle grass in the midst of rich cultivation, and neither Hindu nor Muhammadan dares to plough them.[2]

At the last census of the North-Western Provinces over four hundred thousand people recorded themselves as worshippers of various forms of the Brahm or malignant Brâhman ghost. Most of these are Râjputs, who were probably the most violent oppressors of Brâhmans in the olden days.

NÂHAR KHÂN.

Another instance of the same type may be given from Râjputâna. Jaswant Sinh of Mârwâr had an intrigue with

[1] Oldham, "Memoir of Ghazipur," i. 55 sq.
[2] Baillie, "N.-W.P. Census Report," 214.

the daughter of one of his chief officers. "But the avenging ghost of the Brâhman interposed between him and his wishes; a dreadful struggle ensued, in which Jaswant lost his senses, and no effort could banish the impression from his mind. The ghost persecuted his fancy, and he was generally believed to be possessed of a wicked spirit, which when exorcised was made to say he would depart only on the sacrifice of a chief equal in dignity to Jaswant. Nâhar Khân, 'the tiger lord,' chief of the Kumpâwat clan, who led the van in all his battles, immediately offered his head in expiation for his prince; and he had no sooner expressed his loyal determination, than the holy man who exorcised the spirit, caused it to descend into a vessel of water, and having waved it round his head, they presented it to Nâhar Khân, who drank it off, and Jaswant's senses were instantly restored. This miraculous transfer of the ghost is implicitly believed by every chief of Râjasthân, by whom Nâhar Khan is called 'the faithful of the faithful,' and worshipped as a local god."[1]

GANGÂNÂTH AND BHOLANÂTH.

Two other godlings of the Hills owe their promotion to the tragic circumstances of their deaths. Gangânâth was a Râja's son, who quarrelled with his father and became a religious mendicant. He subsequently fell into an intrigue with the wife of an astrologer, who murdered him and his paramour. They both became malignant ghosts, to whom numerous temples were erected. When anyone is injured by the wicked or powerful, he has recourse to Gangânâth, who punishes the evil-doer. Of the same type is Bholanâth, whose brother, Gyân Chand, was one of the Almora princes. He had him assassinated with his pregnant mistress, both of whom became malignant ghosts, and are especially obnoxious to gardeners, one of whom murdered them. This caste now specially worships them, and a small iron trident is sometimes placed in the corner of a cottage and resorted

[1] Tod, "Annals," ii. 40.

to in their names when any sudden or unexpected calamity attacks the occupants.[1]

BHAIRWANAND.

Similar is the case of Bhairwanand, the tribal deity of the Râikwâr Râjputs of Oudh. He was pushed into a well in order to fulfil a prophecy, and has since been deified.[2]

So with the queen of Ganor, who killed herself by means of a poisoned robe when she was obliged to surrender her honour to her Mughal conqueror. He died in extreme torture, and was buried on the road to Bhopâl. A visit to his grave is believed to cure tertian ague.[3]

VYÂSA.

Next come those mortals who have been deified on account of the glory of their lives. Vyâsa, the compiler of the Vedas, has been canonized, and there is a temple in his honour both at Benares and Râmnagar. In the latter place he has been promoted to the dignity of an incarnation of Siva, whereas in Benares he has a temple of his own. His worship extends as far as Kulu, where he has an image near a stream. Pilgrims offer flowers in his name and set up a stone on end in commemoration of their visit.[4]

VÂLMÎKI.

Vâlmîki, the author of the Râmâyana, is worshipped in the same way. He has shrines at Bâlu in the Karnâl District and at Baleni of Meerut. Baliya, the headquarters of the district of that name, is said to be called after him. The Aheriyas and Baheliyas, both hunting tribes of the North-Western Provinces, claim descent from him, and he has now,

1 Atkinson, "Himâlayan Gazetteer," ii. 817; "North Indian Notes and Queries," iii. 5.

2 "Oudh Gazetteer," i. 284.

3 Tod, "Annals," i. 659 sq.

4 Sherring, "Sacred City," 118, 174; Moorcroft, "Journey to Ladakh," i. 190.

by an extraordinary feat in hagiolatry, become identified with Lâl Beg, the low caste godling of the sweepers.[1]

VARIOUS SAINTS.

Many other worthies of the olden time are worshipped in the same way. From the Himâlaya to Bombay, Dattâtreya, a saint in whom a part of Brahma, Vishnu, and Siva was incarnate, is worshipped by Vaishnavas as a partial manifestation of the deity, and by Saivas as a distinguished authority on the Yoga philosophy. He has temples both in Garhwâl and in the Konkan, like Parâsara Rishi, the reputed author of the Vishnu Purâna, who wished to make a sacrifice to destroy the Râkshasas, but was dissuaded by the saints, and then scattered the fire over the slope of the Himâlaya, where it blazes forth at the phases of the moon.[2] In like fashion the records of the last census have shown worshippers of the poets Kâlidâsa and Tulasi Dâs, as in Bombay their great writers Dnyânadeva and Tûkarâm are deified by the Marâthas. Nearly seven thousand people in the North-Western Provinces adore Vasishtha, the famous Rishi, and many others Nârada Muni, who is a well-known personage and generally acts as a sort of *Deus ex machinâ* in the folk-tales. On the whole in the North-Western Provinces over a quarter million people recorded themselves as votaries of these deified saints, devotees and teachers.

The same form of worship largely prevails in the Panjâb. Among other worthies we find Syâmji, a Chauhân Râja who is said to have given his head to Krishna and Arjuna on condition that he should be allowed to witness the fight between the Kauravas and Pândavas; Dhanwantari, the physician of the gods; Drona Achârya, the teacher of military science to the heroes of the great war. The Kumhârs or potters worship Prajapati, the active creator of the universe; and the Kâyasth scribes adore Chitragupta, who keeps the register

[1] "Panjâb Notes and Queries," i. 1; "Indian Antiquary," xi. 290; "Gazetteer, N.-W.P.," vi. 634; "Dâbistân," ii. 24 sq.

[2] Atkinson, *loc cit.*, ii. 805; "Bombay Gazetteer," xi. 300, 302.

of the deeds of men, which will be opened at the last day. This is quite irrespective of a horde of tutelary saints, who are adored by various tribes of handicraftsmen.

DEIFIED ROBBERS.

Even the thieving and nomadic tribes have as their godlings deified bandits. Such is Gandak, the patron of the Magahiya Doms, and Salhes, who is worshipped by the Doms and Dusâdhs of Behâr. He was a great hero and the first watchman. He fought a famous battle with Chûhar Mal of Mohâma, and is the subject of a popular epic in Tirhût. With his worship is associated that of his brother Motirâm, another worthy of the same kind.[1] At Sherpur near Patna is the shrine of Goraiya or Gauraiya, a Dusâdh bandit chief, to which members of all castes resort, the higher castes making offerings of meal, the outcastes sacrificing a hog or several young pigs and pouring out libations of spirits on the ground. But even here the primitive local cultus is in a state of transition, as in the case of Salhes, who, according to some, was the porter of Bhîm Sen.[2] Doubtless he and his comrades will some day blossom forth as manifestations of one or other of the higher gods.

Another bandit godling is Mitthu Bhûkhiya, a freebooter, worshipped by the Banjâras or wandering carriers. He has a special hut, in which no one may drink or sleep, and which is marked with a white flag. The tribe always worship him before committing a crime. They assemble together and an image of the famous tribal Satî is produced. Butter is put into a saucer, and in this a light is placed, very broad at the bottom and tapering upwards. The wick, standing erect, is lit, an appeal is made to the Satî for an omen, and those worshipping mention in a low tone to the godling where they are going, and what they propose to do. The wick is then carefully watched, and should it drop at all, the omen

[1] Cunningham, "Archæological Reports," xvi. 28; Grierson, "Behâr Peasant Life," 407; "Maithili Chrestomathy," 3 sqq.
[2] Risley, "Tribes and Castes," i. 256.

is propitious. All then salute the flag and start on their marauding expedition.[1]

Vindhya-bâsinî Devî, the personification of the Vindhyan range, is, as we have seen, the goddess of the Thags, and the Dhânuks, a thieving tribe in Behâr, worship one of their chiefs who was killed in a skirmish with the Muhammadans six hundred years ago, and whose ghost has since been troublesome. He is worshipped in a shrine of brick, and one of the members of the tribe acts as his priest.[2]

RÂJA LÂKHAN.

We have already spoken of Gansâm, one of the tribal deities of the Kols. Another famous Kol deity in Mirzapur is Râja Lâkhan. One story of him is that he came from Lucknow, a legend based, of course, on the similarity of the name. But there can be no reasonable doubt that he was really Lakhana Deva, the son of the famous Râja Jaychand of Kanauj, who is known in the popular ballads as the Kanaujiya Râê. There is an inscribed pillar erected by him near Bhuili in the Mirzapur District, and he was perhaps locally connected with that part of the country in some way.[3] Some say that he was taken to Delhi, where he became a Musalmân, and the popularity of his name in the local legends points to the theory that he was possibly one of the leaders of the Hindus against the Muhammadan invaders. All this being granted, it is remarkable that he, a Râjput, and almost as much a stranger to those primitive jungle dwellers as his Muhammadan rival, should have found a place in the Drâvidian pantheon.

RÂJA CHANDOL.

Another deity of the same race is Râja Chandol, who is said to have been a jungle Râja of the Bhuiyâr tribe. He was attacked by his neighbour the Râja of Nagar, who

1 "Berâr Gazetteer," 199 sq.
2 Buchanan, "Eastern India," i. 83.
3 Cunningham, "Archæological Reports," xi. 129.

overcame him and cut off his head. Meanwhile the conqueror forgot his patron deity, and his temple was overturned and the image buried in the earth. One day a goldsmith who was passing by the place heard a voice from beneath the ground saying that if he dug there he would find the idol. He did so, and, digging up the image, which was of gold, cut it up and sold it. But his whole household came to ruin, and then the Râja of Nagar restored the temple, and the Kols remembered Râja Chandol and have venerated him ever since.

BELÂ.

The goddess Belâ was the sister of Lakhana Deva, whose story has been already told. Once, the story goes, Siva went to pay a visit to Hastinapura, and the bell of his bull Nandi disturbed the brothers Arjuna and Bhîma, who, thinking the god a wandering beggar, drove him out of the palace. Then he cursed the Râjput race that among them should be born two fatal women, who should work the ruin of their power. So first was born Draupadî, who caused the war of the Mahâbhârata, and after her Belâ, to whom was due the unhappy warfare which paved the way to the Musalmân invasion. Belâ now has a famous temple at Belaun on the banks of the Ganges in Bulandshahr.

We shall come elsewhere on instances of the belief that human beings were sacrificed under the foundations of important buildings. Nathu Kahâr, the godling of the Oudh boatmen, is said to have been buried alive under the foundations of the fort of Akbarpur in the Faizâbâd District, where a fair is held in his honour.[1] At the last census one hundred and twenty-four thousand persons recorded themselves as his votaries.

JOKHAIYA.

Jokhaiya, who had by the same enumeration eighty-seven thousand worshippers, was a Bhangi or sweeper, who is said

[1] "Oudh Gazetteer," i. 517.

to have been killed in the war between Prithivi Râja of Delhi and Jaychand of Kanauj. He has a noted shrine at Paindhat in the Mainpuri District, where a sweeper for a small fee will kill a pig and let its blood drop on his shrine.

RAMÂSA PÎR.

So, the godling invoked by the Pindhâri women when their husbands went on marauding expeditions, was Ramâsa Pîr. He was a well-known warrior killed in a battle at Ranuja, near Pushkar. Saturday is his day for prayer, on which occasions small images of horses in clay or stone are offered at his shrine. The figure of a man on horseback, stamped in gold or silver, representing the godling, was found on the necks of many of the Pindhâris killed in the great campaign of 1817-18. It was worn by them as an amulet. He is now known as Deva Dharma Râja, which is one of the titles of Yama, the god of death, and Yudhisthira, his putative son.

RÂÊ SINH.

Another local godling of the same class is Râê Sinh, whose legend is thus told by General Sleeman: "At Sanoda there is a very beautiful little fortress or castle, now occupied, but still entire. It was built by an officer of Râja Chhattar Sâl of Bundelkhand about 1725 A.D. His son, by name Râê Sinh, was, soon after the castle had been completed, killed in an attack upon a town near Chhatarkot, and having in the estimation of the people become a god, he had a temple and a tank raised to him. I asked the people how he became a god, and was told that some one who had been long suffering from quartan ague went to the tomb one night and promised Râê Sinh, whose ashes lay under it, that if he could contrive to cure his ague for him, he would during the rest of his life make offerings at his shrine. After this he never had an attack and was very punctual in his offerings. Others followed his example and with like success, till Râê Sinh was recognized universally among them as a god, and had a temple raised to his name." "This is the way," remarks General Sleeman, "gods were made all over the world and are now made in India."[1]

THE PÎRS AND SAYYIDS.

We now come to a more miscellaneous class—the Pîrs and Sayyids. Some of these we have encountered already. We have also seen instances of some holy men who, like Paul and Silas at Lystra, have been raised to the rank of deities. These saints are usually of Muhammadan origin, but most of them are worshipped indiscriminately both by Musalmâns and low class Hindus. The word Pîr properly means "an elder," but according to Sûfi belief is the equivalent of Murshid, or "religious leader." Sayyid, an Arabic word meaning "lord" or "prince," is probably in many cases a corruption of Shahîd, "a martyr of the faith," because many of these worthies owe their reputation to having lost their lives in the early struggles between Islâm and Hinduism. Mr. Ibbetson notes that he has seen a shrine of some Sayyids in the Jâlandhar District, who were said to have been Sikhs, who died in the front of the battle. It took the form of a Muhammadan tomb, lying east and west, surmounted by two small domes of Hindu shape with their openings to the south. Under each, in the face of the tomb, was a niche to receive a lamp.[2]

This and many other instances of the same kind illustrate in an admirable way the extreme receptivity of the popular belief. We have here a body of saints, many of whom were deadly enemies of the Hindu faith, who are now worshipped by Hindus. This is well put by Sir A. Lyall—"The 'Urs, or annual ceremony of these saints, like the martyr's day of St. Edmund or St. Thomas of Canterbury, has degenerated into much that is mere carnal traffic and pagan idolatry, a scandal to the rigid Islâmite. Yet, if he uplifts his voice against such soul-destroying abuses, he may be hooted by

[1] "Rambles and Recollections," i. 116.
[2] "North Indian Notes and Queries," iii. 200.

loose-living Musalmâns as a Wahhâbi who denies the power of intercession, while the shopkeepers are no better than Ephesian goldsmiths in crying down an inconvenient religious reformer."[1] And the same writer illustrates the fusion of the two creeds in their lower forms by the fact that the holy Hindu now in the flesh at Askot has only recently taken over the business, as it were, from a Muhammadan Faqîr, whose disciple he was during his life, and now that the Faqîr is dead, Narsinh Bâwa presides over the annual veneration of his slippers. Similarly at the Muharram celebration and at pilgrimages to tombs, like those of Ghâzi Miyân, a large number of the votaries are Hindus. In many towns the maintenance of these Muhammadan festivals mainly depends on the assistance of the Hindus, and it is only recently that the unfortunate concurrence of these exhibitions with special Hindu holidays has, it may be hoped only temporarily, interrupted the tolerant and kindly intercourse between the followers of the rival creeds.

In many of these shrines the actual or pretended relics of the deceased worthy are exhibited. Under the shadow of the Fort of Chunâr is the shrine of Shâh Qâsim Sulaimâni, of whom mention has been already made. The guardian of the shrine shows to pilgrims the turban of the saint, who was deified about three hundred years ago, and the conical cap of his supposed preceptor, the eminent Pîr Jahâniya Jahângasht; but, as in many such cases, the chronology is hopeless.

THE PANJ PÎR.

The most eminent of the Pîrs are, of course, the Panj Pîr, or five original saints of Islâm. They were—the Prophet Muhammad, 'Ali, his cousin-german and adopted son, Fâtima, the daughter of the Prophet and wife of 'Ali, and their sons, Hasan and Husain, whose tragical fate is commemorated with such ardent sympathy at the annual celebration of the Muharram.[2] But by modern Indian

[1] "Berâr Gazetteer," 195.

[2] The Persian version of the play has been translated by Sir Lewis Pelly. See Hughes' "Dictionary of Islâm," 185 sq.

Muhammadans the name is usually applied to five leading saints—Bahâ-ud-dîn Zikariya of Multân, Shâh Ruqa-i-Âlam Hazrat of Lucknow, Shâh Shams Tabrîz of Multân, Shaikh Jalâl Makhdûm Jahâniyân Jahângasht of Uchcha in Multân, and Bâba Shaikh Farîd-ud-dîn Shakkarganj of Pâk Patan. Another enumeration gives the Châr Pîr or four great saints as 'Ali and his successors in saintship—Khwâja Hasan Basri, Khwâja Habîb 'Ajmi, 'Abdul Wâhid. Another list of Pîrs of Upper India gives their names as Ghâzi Miyân, Pîr Hathîlê, sister's son of Ghâzi Miyân, Pîr Jalîl of Lucknow, and Pîr Muhammad of Jaunpur. It is, in fact, impossible to find a generally recognized catalogue of these worthies, and modern Islâm is no less subject to periodical change than other religions organized on a less rigid system.[1]

CASTE SAINTS.

The worship of the original saints of Islâm has, however, undergone a grievous degradation. We are familiar in Western hagiology with the specialization of saints for certain purposes. St. Agatha is invoked to cure sore breasts, St. Anthony against inflammation, St. Blaise against bones sticking in the throat, St. Martin for the itch, St. Valentine against epilepsy, and so on. So St. Agatha presides over nurses, St. Catherine and St. Gregory over learned men, St. Cecilia over musicians, St. Valentine over lovers, St. Nicholas over thieves, while St. Thomas à Becket looks after blind men, eunuchs, and sinners.[2] So almost all the artizan classes have each their special patron saint. The dyers venerate Pîr 'Ali Rangrez, the Lohârs or blacksmiths, Hazrat Dâûd, or the Lord David, because the Qurân says—"We taught him the art of making coats of mail that they might defend you from your suffering in warring with your enemies." The Mehtars or sweepers have Lâl Pîr or Lâl

[1] The five Pîrs give their name to the Pîr Panjâl pass in Kashmîr (Jarrett, "Aîn-i-Akbari," ii. 372, note). For another list of the Pîrs see Temple's "Legends of the Panjâb," ii. 372, note.

[2] See Brand, "Observations," 197.

Beg, of whom something more will be said later on. In the Panjâb Sadhua Bhagat is the saint of butchers, because once when he was about to kill a goat, the animal threatened that he would revenge himself in another life, and so he joined the sect of Sâdhs, who refrain from destroying animal life. The barbers revere Sain Bhagat or Husain Bhagat. He is said to have been a resident of Pratâppura in the Jâlandhar District, and his descendants were for some time family Gurus or preceptors of the Râja of Bandhogarh. One day he was so engaged in his devotions that he forgot to shave the Râja's head, but when he came in fear and trembling to apologize, he found the Râja shaved and in his right mind. Then it was found that the deity himself had come and officiated for him. So, Nâmdeo, the Chhîpi or cotton-printer, became a follower of Râmanand, and is regarded as the tribal saint.

DOMESTIC WORSHIP OF THE PÎR.

Muhammadan domestic worship is largely concerned with the propitiation of the household Pîr. In almost every house is a dreaded spot where, as the Russian peasant keeps his holy image, is the abode or corner of the Pîr, and the owner erects a little shelf, lights a lamp every Thursday night, and hangs up garlands of flowers. Shaikh Saddu, of whom we shall see more later on, is the women's favourite Pîr, especially with those who wish to gain an undue ascendency over their husbands. When a woman wishes to have a private entertainment of her own, she pretends to be "shadow smitten," that is that the shadow of some Pîr, usually Shaikh Saddu, has fallen upon her, and her husband is bound to give an entertainment, known as a Baithak or "session," for the purpose of exorcising him, to which no male is allowed admittance. At these rites of the Bona Dea, it is believed that the Pîr enters the woman's head and that she becomes possessed, and in that state of frenzy can answer any question put to her. All her female neighbours, accordingly, assemble to have their fortunes told by the Pîr, and when they are satisfied they exorcise him with music and singing.

THE PACHPIRIYAS.

But it is in the eastern districts of the North-Western Provinces and Behâr that the worship has reached its most degraded form. No less than one million seven hundred thousand persons at the last census, almost entirely in the Gorakhpur and Benares Divisions, recorded themselves as Pachpiriyas or worshippers of the Pânch Pîr. It is impossible to get any consistent account of these worthies, and the whole cultus has become imbedded in a mass of the wildest legend and mythology.[1] According to the census lists these five saints are, in the order of their popularity—Ghâzi Miyân, Buahna Pîr, Palihâr, Aminâ Satî and Hathîlê or Hathîla. In Benares, according to Mr. Greeven, there are no less than five enumerations of the sacred quintette. One gives—Ghâzi Miyân, Aminâ Satî, Suthân, 'Ajab Sâlâr and Palihâr; a second—Ghâzi Miyân, Aminâ Satî, Suthân, 'Ajab Sâlâr and Buahna; a third—Ghâzi Miyân, Aminâ Satî, Buahna, Bhairon and Bandê; a fourth—Ghâzi Miyân, Aminâ Satî, Palihâr, Kâlikâ and Shahzâ; a fifth—Ghâzi Miyân, Suthân, 'Ajab Sâlâr, Buahna and Bahlâno. Among these we have the names of well-known Hindu gods, like Bhairon and Kâlikâ, a form of Kâlî. Among the actual companions of Ghâzi Miyân are, it is believed, Hathîlê Pîr, who is said to have been his sister's son, Miyân Rajjab or Rajjab Sâlâr, and Sikandar Diwâna, the Buahna Pîr, who are all buried at Bahrâich, and Sâhu Sâlâr, father of the martyr prince, whose tomb is near Bârabanki.

In Behâr, again, the five saints are Ghâzi Miyân, Hathîla, Parihâr, Sahjâ Mâî and 'Ajab Sâlâr, and with them are associated Aminâ Satî, Langra Târ, who is represented by a piece of crooked wire, and Sobarna Tîr, the bank of the Sobarna river. Here we reach an atmosphere of the crudest fetishism. A little further west Sânwar or Kunwar Dhîr, of

[1] For a very complete account of the cultus, see Mr. R. Greeven's articles in Vol. I. "North Indian Notes and Queries," afterwards republished as "Heroes Five."

whom nothing certain is known, is joined with them, and has numerous worshippers in the Gorakhpur and Benares Divisions.

THE PÂNCH PÎR AND THE PÂNDAVAS.

It has often been remarked that the five Pândavas have strangely passed out of the national worship. At the last census in the North-Western Provinces only four thousand people gave them as their personal deities, and in the Panjâb only one hundred acknowledged them. Now in the west the title of Pânch Pîr is sometimes given to five Râjput heroes, Râmdeo, Pâbu, Harbu, Mallinâth and Gûga,[1] and it is at least a plausible theory that the five Pîrs may have originally been the five Pându brothers, whose worship has, in course of time, become degraded, been annexed by the lower Musalmâns, and again taken over by their menial Hindu brethren.

As a matter of fact, the system of worship does not materially differ from the cultus of the degraded indigenous godlings, such as Kârê Gôrê Deo, Bûrhê Bâba, Jokhaiya, and their kindred. The priests of the faith are drawn from the Dafâli or Musalmân drummer caste, who go about from house to house reciting the tale of Ghâzi Miyân and his martyrdom, with a number of wild legends which have in course of time been adopted in connection with him. An iron bar wrapped in red cloth and adorned with flowers represents Ghâzi Miyân, which is taken from door to door, drums are beaten and petty offerings of grain collected from the villagers. Low caste Hindus, like Pâsis and Chamârs, worship them in the form of five wooden pegs fixed in the courtyard of the house. The Barwârs, a degraded criminal tribe in Oudh, build in their houses an altar in the shape of a tomb, at which yearly in August the head of the family sacrifices in the name of the Pîrs a fowl and offers some thin cakes, which he makes over to a Muhammadan beggar who goes about from house to house beating a drum.

[1] "Panjâb Notes and Queries," iv. 64.

GHÂZI MIYÂN.

The whole worship centres round Ghâzi Miyân. His real name was Sayyid Sâlâr Masaud, and he was nephew of Sultân Mahmûd of Ghazni. He was born in 1015 A.D., was leader of one of the early invasions of Oudh, and is claimed as one of the first martyrs of Islâm in India. He was killed in battle with the Hindus of Bahrâich in 1034 A.D. Close to the battle-field was a tank with an image of the sun on its banks, a shrine sacred in the eyes of all Hindus. Masaud, whenever he passed it, was wont to say that he wished to have this spot for a dwelling-place, and would, if it so pleased God, through the power of the spiritual sun, destroy the worship of the material. He was, it is said, buried by some of his followers in the place which he had chosen for his resting-place, and tradition avers that his head rests on the image of the sun, the worship of which he had given his life to destroy.

There is some reason to believe that this cultus of Masaud may have merely succeeded to some local worship, such as that of the sun, and in this connection it is significant that the great rite in honour of the martyr is called the Byâh or marriage of the saint, and this would associate it with other emblematical marriages of the earth and sun or sky which were intended to promote fertility.[1] Masaud, again, is the type of youth and valour in military Islâm, and to the Hindu mind assumes the form of one of those godlike youths, such as Krishna or Dûlha Deo, snatched away by an untimely and tragical fate in the prime of boyish beauty. So, though he was a fanatical devotee of Islâm, his tomb is visited as much by Hindus as by Muhammadans. Besides his regular shrine at Bahrâich, he has cenotaphs at various places, as at Gorakhpur and Bhadohi in the Mirzapur District, where annual fairs are held in his honour. The worship of Masaud, which is now discouraged by Muhammadan purists, embodied, even in early times, so much idolatry and fetishism as to be obnoxious to the puritanic party; it fell under the

[1] For instances see Frazer, "Golden Bough," i. 279.

censure of the authorities, and Sikandar Lodi interdicted the procession of his spear.[1] Nowadays at his festivals a long spear or pole is paraded about, crowned at the top with bushy hair, representing the head of the martyr, which, it is said, kept rolling on the ground long after it was severed from the trunk.[2]

SAKHI SARWAR.

Sakhi Sarwar, or "generous leader," the title of a saint whose real name was Sayyid Ahmad, is hardly popular beyond the Panjâb, where his followers are known as Sultânis, and are more than four hundred thousand in number.[3] No one knows exactly when he lived; some place him in the twelfth and others in the thirteenth century; but there are other traditions which would bring him down to the sixteenth. Whatever be the exact time of his birth and death, he was one of the class of Muhammadan saints, like Bahâ-ud-dîn and Shams Tabrîz, who settled and practised austerities in the country about Multân. Other names for him are Lâkhdâta or "the giver of lâkhs," Lâlanwâla, "he of the rubies," and Rohiânwâla, or "he of the Hills." His life, as we have it, is but a mass of legends. He once cured a camel of a broken leg by riveting it together. Miraculously, as so many of these saints do, he gave two sons to one Gannu of Multân and married his daughter. The hill that overlooks his tomb at Nigâha in the Dera Ghâzi Khân District, at the edge of the Sulaimân mountains, is said to have been infested by a fearful giant. This monster used at night to stand on the hill-top and with a torch lure unwary travellers to their destruction. Against him Sakhi Sarwar and his four companions waged war, but

[1] Briggs, "Farishta," i. 587.

[2] For the history of Masaud, see "Oudh Gazetteer," i. 111 sqq.; Sleeman, "Journey through Oudh," i. 48; Elliot, "Supplementary Glossary," 51.

[3] Maclagan, "Panjâb Census Report," 132; "North Indian Notes and Queries," ii. 182; "Calcutta Review," lx. 78 sqq.; Ibbetson, "Panjâb Ethnography," 115; Oldham, "Contemporary Review," xlvii. 412; "Panjâb Notes and Queries," ii. 181 sq.; Temple, "Legends of the Panjâb," i. 66 sqq.

all except the saint were killed; and such was the fall of the monster that the hill trembled to its base. Within an enclosure are seen the tombs of the saint, his lady, Bîbî Râê, and a Jinn who fell before the onset of the hero. To the east is the apartment containing the stool and spinning-wheel of Mâî 'Aeshan, Sakhi Sarwar's mother. It is a curious instance of the combination of the two rival faiths, so constantly observable in this phase of the popular worship, that close to the shrine of Sakhi Sarwar is a temple of Vishnu, a shrine of Bâba Nânak, the founder of Sikhism, and an image of Bhairon, who appears in the legends as the servant or messenger of the saint. The tomb presents a curious mixture of Musalmân and Hindu architecture. It was recently destroyed by fire, and two rubies presented by Nâdir Shâh, and some valuable jewels, the gift of Sultân Zamân Shâh, were destroyed or lost.

The Sultâni sect, in large numbers, under the guidance of conductors known as Bharai, make pilgrimages to the tomb. Near it are two dead trees, said to have sprung from the pegs which were used to tether Kakkî, the saint's mare. The walls are hung with small pillows of various degrees of ornamentation. Persons who suffer from ophthalmia vow gold or silver eyes for their recovery. They vow to shave the hair of an expected child at the temple, and its weight in gold or silver is presented to the saint. Some childless parents vow to him their first child, and on its birth take it to the temple with a cord round its neck. There are numbers of sacred pigeons attached to the shrine, which are supported by an allowance realized from certain dedicated villages. The marks of 'Ali's fingers and the print of his foot are still shown to the devout in consideration of a fee to the guardians, and a visit is considered peculiarly efficacious for the cure of demoniacal possession, exhibiting itself in the form of epilepsy or hysteria.

Besides the shrine at Nigâha, there are numerous other shrines of the saint, of which the most celebrated are those connected with the annual fair at Dhonkal in Gujrânwâla, the Jhanda fair at Peshâwar, and the Kadmon fair at

Anârkali, near Lahore. At Dhonkal there is a magic well which was produced by the saint, the water of which is much in request. At Anârkali a class of musicians, called Dholis, take young children, who are presented at the tomb, and dance about with them. In the neighbourhood of Delhi he is not held in so much respect, but shrines in his honour are common, vows and pilgrimages to him are frequent, and Brâhmans tie threads on the wrists of their clients on a fixed day in his name. Under the name of Lâkhdâta he has become the patron deity of athletes, and especially of wrestlers.

In the central districts of the Panjâb, his shrine, an unpretending little edifice, is to be seen outside nearly every hamlet. "The shrine is a hollow plastered brick cube, eight or ten feet in each direction, covered with a dome some ten or twelve feet high and with low minarets or pillars at the four corners, and a doorway in front, opening out generally on a plastered brick platform. Facing the doorway inside are two or three niches for lamps, but otherwise the shrine is perfectly empty. The saint is especially worshipped on Thursdays, when the shrine is swept, and at night lamps are lit inside it. The guardians of the shrine are Musalmâns of the Bharai clan, who go round on Thursdays beating drums and collecting offerings. These offerings, which are generally in small change or small handfuls of grain or cotton, are mainly presented by women. Another method of pleasing the saint is by vowing a Rôt; the Rôt is made by placing dough to the extent vowed on a hot piece of earth, where a fire has been burning, and distributing it when it is baked. He is also worshipped by sleeping on the ground instead of on a bed. Wrestling matches are also held in his honour, and the offerings made to the performers go towards keeping up the shrine at Nigâha. A true worshipper of Sultân will not sell milk on Thursday; he will consume it himself or give it away."

Sarwar is essentially a saint of the Jâts, and he is also revered by Gûjars and Jhînwars, and women even of the Khatri and Brâhman castes adore him. He has, according to the last returns, over four hundred thousand worshippers in the Panjâb, and eight thousand in the North-Western Provinces.

GÛGA PÎR.

Another noted local saint is Gûga Pîr, also known as *Zâhir* Pîr, "the saint apparent," or *Zâhir* Dîwân, "the minister apparent," or in the Panjâb as Bâgarwâla, as his grave is near Dadrewa in Bikâner, and he is said to have reigned over the Bâgar or great prairies of Northern Râjputâna. Nothing is known for certain about him, and the tales told of him are merely a mass of wild legends. According to some he flourished somewhere about the middle of the twelfth century, when Indian hagiolatry was at its zenith. Others say that he was a Chauhân Râjput, a contemporary of Prithivi Râja of Delhi, while by another story he died with his forty-five sons and sixty nephews opposing Mahmûd of Ghazni. He is said to have been a Hindu with the title of Gûga Bîr, or "the hero"; and one account represents him to have become a convert to Islâm. "He is said to have killed his two nephews and to have been condemned by their mother to follow them below. He attempted to do so, but the earth objected that he being a Hindu, she was quite unable to receive him till he should be properly burnt. As he was anxious to revisit his wife nightly, this did not suit him, and so he became a Musalmân, and her scruples being thus removed, the earth swallowed him and his horse alive."[1] In another and more degraded form of the legend current in Muzaffarnagar, he is said to have jumped into a pile of cow-dung, where he disappeared, a series of stories which remind us of the Curtius myth.[2]

Another elaborate legend represents Gûga to be the son of the Rânî Bâchhal, and fixes his birthplace at Sirsâwa in the Sahâranpur District. About the time of the invasion of Mahmûd of Ghazni, she married Vatsa, the Râja of Bâgardesa, or the Râjputâna desert. By the influence of that ubiquitous

[1] Ibbetson, *loc. cit.* 115 sq.

[2] Temple, "Legends of the Panjâb," i. 121 sqq.; iii. 261 sqq.; Tod, "Annals," ii. 492.

saint, Gorakhnâth, she conceived in spite of the intrigues of her sister, and her child was called Gûga, because the saint gave to his mother, as a preservative, a piece of gum resin known as Gûgal. His cousins attacked him and tried to rob him of his kingdom, but Gûga defeated them and cut off their heads, which he presented to his mother. She, in her anger, ordered him to go to the place where he had sent her nephews; so he requested the earth to receive him into her bosom, which she refused to do until he became a convert to Islâm. He then went to Mecca, and became a disciple of one Ratan Hâji, and on his return the earth opened and received him, with his famous black mare Javâdiyâ.[1]

The mare has, of course, a story of her own. Gûga had no children, and lamenting this to his guardian deity, he received from him two barley-corns, one of which he gave to his wife and the other to his famous mare, which gave birth to his charger, hence called Javâdiyâ or "barley-born." We find this wonderful mare through the whole range of folk-lore, but the best parallel to her is the famous mare of Gwri of the golden hair, and Setanta in the Celtic tale.[2]

From Scotland, too, we get a parallel to the magic birth: "Here are three grains for thee that thou shalt give thy wife this very night, and three others to the dog, and these three to the mare; and these three thou shalt plant behind thy house; and in their own time thy wife will have three sons, the mare three foals, and the dog three puppies, and there will grow three trees behind thy house; and the trees will be a sign, when one of thy sons dies one of the trees will wither."[3] It is needless to say that this is a stock incident in folk-lore.

GÛGA AND SNAKE-WORSHIP.

But it is in his function as one of the Snake kings that Gûga is specially worshipped. When he is duly propitiated

[1] "Indian Antiquary," xi. 33 sq.; Cunningham, "Archæological Reports," xvii. 159; "Panjâb Notes and Queries," ii. 1.

[2] Rhys, "Lectures," 502.

[3] Campbell, "Popular Tales," i. 72.

he can save from snake-bite, and cause those who neglect him to be bitten. His shrine is often found in association with that of Nara Sinha, the man-lion incarnation of Vishnu, and of Gorakhnâth, the famous ascetic, whose disciple he is said to have been. He is adored by Hindus and Muhammadans alike, and by all castes, by Râjputs and Jâts, as well as by Chamârs and Chûhras. Even the Brâhman looks on him with respect. "Which is greater," says the proverb, "Râma or Gûga?" and the reply is, "Be who may the greater, shall I get myself bitten by a snake?" in other words, "Though Râma may be the greater, between ourselves, I dare not say so for fear of offending Gûga."

He is represented on horseback, with his mother trying to detain him as he descends to the infernal regions. He holds as a mark of dignity a long staff in his hands, and over him two snakes meet, one being coiled round his staff. Both the Hindu and Muhammadan Faqîrs take the offerings devoted to him, and carry his Chharî or standard, covered with peacocks' feathers, from house to house in the month of August. As is the case with godlings of this class all over India, it is significant of the association of his worship with some early non-Aryan beliefs that the village scavenger is considered to be entitled to a share of the offerings presented at his shrine.

According to the last census Gûga had thirty-five thousand worshippers in the Panjâb and one hundred and twenty-three thousand in the North-Western Provinces.

WORSHIP OF TEJAJÎ.

Another godling of the same kind is Tejajî, the Jât snake godling of Mârwâr. He is said to have lived about 900 years ago. One day he noticed that a Brâhman's cow was in the habit of going to a certain place in the jungle, where milk fell from her udder into the hole of a snake. Teja agreed to supply the snake daily with milk, and thus save the Brâhman from loss. Once when he was preparing to visit his father-in-law, he forgot the compact, and the snake appearing, declared that it was necessary that he should bite Teja. He stipulated for permission first to visit his father-in-law, to which the snake agreed. Teja proceeded on his journey, and on the way rescued the village cattle from a gang of robbers, but was desperately wounded in the encounter. Mindful of his promise, he with difficulty presented himself to the snake, who, however, could find no spot to bite, as Teja had been so grievously wounded by the robbers. Teja therefore put out his tongue, which the snake bit, and so he died. He is now a protector against snake-bite, and is represented as a man on horseback, while a snake is biting his tongue.[1] Tejajî and Gûga, as snake godlings, thus rank with Bhajang, the snake godling of Kâthiawâr, who is a brother of Sesha Nâga, and with Mânasâ, the goddess of Bengal, who is the sister of Vâsuki, the wife of Jaratkâru, and mother of Astikâ, whose intervention saved the snake race from destruction by Janamejaya.[2]

WORSHIP OF BÂBA FARÎD SHAKKARGANJ.

Bâba Farîd Shakkarganj, or "fountain of sweets," so called because he was able miraculously to transmute dust or salt into sugar, was born in 1173 A.D., and died in 1265. His tomb is at PâkPatan, and he enjoys high consideration in Northern India. He was a disciple of Qutb-ud-dîn Bakhtyâr Kâki, who again sat at the feet of Muîn-ud-dîn Chishti of Ajmer, also a great name to swear by. Farîd's most distinguished disciple was Nizâm-ud-dîn Auliya, who has a lovely tomb at Ghayâspur, near Delhi. Farîd was very closely associated with Bâba Nânak, and much of the doctrine of early Sikhism seems to have been based on his teaching. He is said to have possessed the Dast-i-ghaib, or "hidden hand," a sort of magic bag which gave him anything he wished, which is like the wishing hat and inex-

[1] "Râjputâna Gazetteer," ii. 37.
[2] "Bombay Gazetteer," v. 218; Risley, "Tribes and Castes of Bengal," i. 41.

haustible pot or purse, which is a stock element in Indian and European folk-lore.[1]

The Emperor, it is said, tried to humble him when he came to Delhi, but he answered in the famous proverb—*Delhî dûr ast*—"Delhi is far away," the Oriental equivalent to Rob Roy's "It is a far cry to Lochow."

The Musalmân Thags looked on him as the founder of their system, and used to make pilgrimages to his tomb. He is believed to have been connected with the Assassins or disciples of the Old Man of the Mountain.[2] Every devotee who contrives to get through the door of his mausoleum at the prescribed time of his feast is assured of a free entrance into Paradise hereafter. The crowd is therefore immense, and the pressure so great that two or three layers of men, pushed closely over each other, generally attempt the passage at the same time, and serious accidents, notwithstanding every precaution taken by the police, are not uncommon.[3]

He comes in direct succession to some of the worthies to whom reference has been already made. To Khwâja Muîn-ud-dîn Chishti succeeded Khwâja Qutb-ud-dîn Bakhtyâr Kâki, and Bâba Farîd followed him. They were the founders of the Chishtiya order of Faqîrs.

Besides his shrine at Pâkpatan he has another famous Dargâh at Shaikhsir in Bikâner, which is called after him, and the Jâts used to esteem him highly until, as Col. Tod[4] says, "The Bona Dea assumed the shape of a Jâtnî, to whom in the name of Kiranî Mâtâ, 'Our Mother of the ray,' all bend the head." Another legend fixes his tomb at Girâr, in the Wârdha District of the Central Provinces.

The zeolitic concretions of the Girâr hill are accounted for as the petrified cocoanuts and other articles of merchandise belonging to two travelling dealers who mocked the saint, on which he turned their whole stock-in-trade into stones as a punishment. They implored his pardon, and he created a

[1] Miss Roalfe Cox, "Cinderella," 484; Temple, "Wideawake Stories," 423; Knowles, "Folk-tales of Kashmîr," 21; Clouston, "Popular Tales," i. 117; Tawney, "Katha Sarit Sâgara," i. 14, note, 571.

[2] Yule, "Marco Polo," i. 132 sq.

[3] Ibbetson, "Panjâb Ethnography," 115.

[4] "Annals," ii. 199, note.

fresh supply for them from dry leaves, on which they were so struck by his power that they attached themselves to his service till they died.[1]

In the Western districts of the North-Western Provinces the first-fruits of the sugar-cane crop are dedicated to him.

He was a thrifty saint, and for the last thirty years of his life he supported himself by holding to his stomach wooden cakes and fruits whenever he felt hungry. In this he resembled Qutb-ud-Dîn Ushi, who was able by a miracle to produce cakes for the support of his family and himself.[2]

MINOR SAINTS.

Of the minor saints the number is legion, and only a few instances can be given. At Makanpur in the Cawnpur District is the tomb of Zinda Shâh Madâr, who gives his name to the class of Musalmân Faqîrs, known as Madâri. He is said to have been a native of Halab or Aleppo, and to have come to this place in 1415 A.D., when he expelled a famous demon named Makan Deo, after whom the place was named. Low class Hindus and Musalmâns worship him because he is supposed to save them from snakes and scorpions, and the Kahâr bearers, as they go through jungle at night, call out *Dam Madâr!* The saint is said to have had the power of restraining his breath, whence his name. In the holy of holies of his shrine no woman is allowed to enter, no lights are lighted, no hymns are chanted and no food is cooked.

'Abdul Qâdir Jilâni, who is said to take his name from Jil, a village near Bâghdâd, is another noted saint. He is also known as Pîr-i-Dastgîr, Pîr-i-'Azam, Ghaus-ul-'Azam, and was born in 1078 A.D., and died at Bâghdâd. Some say that he is identical with Mîrân Sâhib, who is worshipped all over Northern India. He is said to have been a magician, and to have subdued to his service a Jinn named Zain Khân,

[1] "Central Provinces Gazetteer," 197 sq., 515.

[2] For the History of Farîd, see "Indian Antiquary," xi. 33 sq.; Thomas, "Chronicles of the Pathân Kings," 205; Ibbetson, "Panjâb Ethnography," 115; Sleeman, "Rambles and Recollections," ii. 165; Maclagan, "Panjâb Census Report," 193.

whom he treated with great cruelty. One day the Jinn surprised his master in a state of uncleanness and slew him, but even then he was unable to escape from the influence of this arch-magician, who rules him in the world of spirits. Mîrân Sâhib is said to be buried at Ajmer, but he has Dargâhs at Amroha, in the Morâdâbâd District, at Benares and at Bûndi. By another account the tomb at Amroha is that of Shaikh Saddu or Sadr-ud-dîn, who was once a crier of the mosque, and near his are pointed out the tombs of his mother Ghâziyâ or Asê and of Zain Khân, the Jinn. The saint of Jalesar, Hazrat Pîr Zari, is also known as Mîrân Sâhib, and he is by some identified with the Amroha worthy. In Karnâl he is said to have led the Sayyid army against the Râja of Tharwa, and had his head carried off by a cannon ball during the battle. He did not mind this, and went on fighting. Then a woman in one of the Râja's villages said—"Who is fighting without his head?" upon which the body said—"*Haq! Haq!*" "The Lord! the Lord!" and fell down dead, calling out—"What? Are not these villages upside down yet?" upon which every village in the Râja's territory was turned upside down and everyone killed except a Brâhman girl, the paramour of the Râja. Their ruins remain to authenticate the story. Now the saint and his sister's son, Sayyid Kabîr, are jointly worshipped. We shall meet this headless hero again in the case of the Dûnd, and it will be remembered that a similar legend is told of Ghâzi Miyân.

VILLAGES OVERTURNED.

Of these villages which were overturned by a curse we have many examples all over the country. The ruins at Bakhira Dih in Basti are said to have been a great city which was overthrown because a Râja seduced a Brâhman girl. At Batesar in Agra is the Aundha Khera, which records a similar catastrophe. So Bângarmau in Unâo is called the Lauta Shahr or "overthrown city," because Mîrân Sâhib destroyed it to punish the curiosity of the Râja who wanted to know why the robes of the saint which a washerman was washing gave forth a divine perfume. So the town of Kâko was overwhelmed by the saint Bîbî Kamâlo because the Buddhist Râja gave her a dish cooked of the flesh of rats, which came to life when she touched them. At Besnagar in Bhopâl the king and his subjects clung to a heavenly chariot and were carried to the skies and their city was overthrown, and the saint Qutb Shâh overturned the city of Sunit because the Râja used to kill a child daily to cure an ulcer with which he was afflicted.[1]

Abû 'Ali Qalandar is hardly known beyond the Panjâb. He came from Persia and died at Pânipat in 1324 A.D. He is usually known as Bû 'Ali Qalandar, and it is said that he used to ride about on a wall. He prayed so constantly that it was laborious to get water for his ablutions each time; so he stood in the Jumnâ, which then ran past the town. After standing there seven years the fishes had gnawed his legs and he was so stiff that he could hardly move, so he asked the Jumnâ to step back seven paces. She, in her hurry to oblige the saint, went back seven Kos or ten miles, and there she is now.[2]

Many other saints are said to have had similar power over rivers. So recently as 1865 A.D., a miraculous bridge of sand was built over the Jumnâ at Karnâl by the prayer of a Faqîr, of such rare virtue that lepers passing over and bathing at both ends were cured; but the people say that the bridge had got lost when they came there.[3] It was only the prayers of the saint Farîd-ud-din Shakkarganj which stopped the westward movement of the Satlaj, and the intercession of a holy Rishi changed the course of the river at Bâgheswar.[4]

Bû 'Ali gave the Pânipat people a charm which dispelled all the flies from the town, but they grumbled and said that they rather liked flies; so he brought them back a thousand-fold. He was buried first at Karnâl, but the Pânipat people

[1] Führer, "Monumental Antiquities," 69, 270; "North Indian Notes and Queries," ii. 21, 56, 155, 189.
[2] "Karnâl Settlement Report," 153. [3] "Karnâl Gazetteer," 103.
[4] "North Indian Notes and Queries," iii. 17.

claimed his body, and opened his grave, whereupon he sat up and looked at them till they became ashamed. They then took away some bricks for the foundation of a shrine; but when they got to Pânipat and opened the box, they found his body in it; so he is now buried in both places, and there is a shrine erected over the place where he used to ride on the wall.

MALÂMAT SHÂH.

Malâmat Shâh is treated with much respect in Bârabanki. The disciple in charge of his tomb calls the jackals with a peculiar cry at dusk. They devour what is left of the offerings, but will only touch such things as are given with a sincere mind and not to be seen of men. A religious tiger is also said to come over from Bahrâich and pay an annual visit to the shrine.[1]

MIYÂN AHMAD.

At Qasûr is the tomb of the saint Miyân Ahmad Khân Darvesh, on which the attendants place a number of small pebbles. These are called "Ahmad Khân's lions," and are sold to people who tie them round the necks of children troubled in their sleep.[2]

SHAIKH SADDÛ.

Shaikh Saddû has been mentioned in another connection. His visitations cause melancholy and hypochondria. He is exorcised by the distribution of sweets to the poor and the sacrifice of a black goat. He once found a magic lamp, like that of Alâuddin, the powers of which he abused, and was torn to pieces by the Jinn.[3]

The list of these worthies is immense. We can only mention in passing Shâh Abdul Ghafûr, commonly known as Bâba Kapûr, a disciple of Shâh Madâr, whose shrine is

[1] "Oudh Gazetteer," i. 92. [2] "Panjâb Notes and Queries," iii. 81.
[3] Mrs. Mîr Hasan 'Ali, "Observations on the Muhammadans of India," ii. 324.

in Gwâlyâr; Mîr Abdul 'Ala, the Nakhshbandi who is buried at Agra; Sultân Bayazîd, who kindled a lamp which lighted the world for one hundred and twenty miles, and thus drove the Jinn from Chatgânw in Bengal, where he is worshipped; Shaikh Kabîr, known as Bâla Pîr, the son of Shâh Qâsim Sulaimâni of Chunâr, whose shrine is at Kanauj; Shaikh Muhammad Ghaus of Gwâliyâr; and Sidi Maula, who possessed the power of transmuting metals into gold. Lastly comes Shâh Daula, whose shrine is at Gujarât in the Panjâb. His priest is able to confer offspring on childless people on condition that they dedicate the first child to the saint, and this child is then born with the head of a rat. Some wretched imbeciles with rat-like features are found at his tomb.[1]

These wonder-working shrines belong to Hindu as well as Musalmân saints. In the Etah District is the tomb of Kalyân Bhârati, a Hindu ascetic. He was buried alive at his own request about four hundred years ago. Before his death he announced that exactly six months after he was dead the arch of his tomb would crack, and so it happened. Now a mound of earth in the centre is supposed to mark the head of the saint. The virtue of his shrine is such that if any one take a false oath within its precincts he will die at once. The tomb is hence largely used for the settlement of disputes, and many a wearied district officer longs that there were more such places throughout the land.

SHRINES WHICH CURE DISEASE.

Many of these local shrines owe their reputation to notorious cures, which have been performed by the intervention of the local saint. At Chhattarpur is the shrine of Rûkhar Bâba, an ascetic of the Gusâîn class, who has the power of removing fever and ague, and hence among the many tombs of his brethren his is kept clean and whitewashed, while the others are neglected.[2] A shrine in Berâr

[1] Maclagan, "Panjâb Census Report," 198.
[2] "North Indian Notes and Queries," iii. 18.

is noted for its power in cases of snake-bite and scrofula. A large two-storied gate of its enclosure owes its erection to the gratitude of a wealthy tailor, who was cured of sore disease of the loins.[1] Recently at the shrine of the saint of Fatehpur in the Sahâranpur District, the Faqîr in charge informed me that when the people bring sick children to him, he pulls off a leaf from the tree overhanging the tomb, blows upon it, and says to the disease, "Begone, you rascal!" and the child is cured. At the tomb of Pîr Jahâniyân in the Muzaffargarh District, people suffering from leprosy and boils get the incumbent to prepare baths of heated sand, in which the diseased part, or the whole body is placed. The efficacy of the remedy is ascribed to the thaumaturgic power of the saint.[2] The tomb of Makhdûm Sâhib in the Faizâbâd District is famous for the exorcism of evil spirits, a reputation which it shares with the shrine of Bairâm at Bidauli in Muzaffarnagar, and that of Bîbî Kamâlo at Kâko, half-way between Gaya and Patna.[3]

So, in Bengal, the chief disease shrines are those of Tarakeswara in Hughli, sacred to Mahâdeva, of Vaidyanâtha in the Santâl Parganas, and Gondalpâra in Hughli, famous in cases of hydrophobia. "The device followed at the last place is for the bitten person, after fasting, to defray the expense of a special service, and to receive a piece of broad cloth impregnated with the snuff of a lamp-wick, and secreted in the heart of a plantain. As long as this charm is preserved and the patient abstains from eating of this variety of plantain, the effects of the bite are warded off. Another plan is for the patient to take a secret medicine, probably cantharides, pounded with twenty-one pepper-corns, before the twenty-first day. This causes the patient to throw off some mucus, known as 'the dog's whelp,' and this leads to cure."[4]

In the Partâbgarh District are to be seen here and there strange-looking brick-built erections called Kûkar Deora or

[1] "Berâr Gazetteer," 192. [2] O'Brien, "Multâni Glossary," 146.
[3] "Oudh Gazetteer," i. 334; Cunningham, "Archæological Reports," xvi. 5. For the Chanod shrine, "Bombay Gazetteer," vi. 160.
[4] Risley, "Tribes and Castes," i. 367.

"dogs' house," in the shape of cupolas or pyramids. Some of them are supposed to be the treasure houses of the ancient races. If a man walks round one of these seven times and then looks in at the door, he will be cured from the bite of a mad dog.[1]

SAYYID YÛSUF.

Dr. Buchanan gives a case at Patna of a certain Sayyid Yûsuf, who manifested himself to a poor blind weaver and told him that he would recover his sight next day. At the same time the saint ordered his patient to search for his tomb and proclaim its virtues. The weaver, on recovering his sight, did not fail to obey the orders of his benefactor, and he and his descendants have since then lived on the contributions of the faithful, though the tomb is a mere heap of clay and has no endowment.[2]

The tomb at Faizâbâd known as Fazl-ul-haqq, or "Grace of God," brings good luck if sweetmeats are offered every Thursday, and another, called 'Ilm Bakhsh, or "Wisdom-giver," causes boys who are taken there to learn their lessons quickly.[3] The same result may be secured by a charm which is found in the Samavidhana Brâhmana—"After a fast of three nights, take a plant of Soma, recite a certain formula and eat of the plant a thousand times, you will be able to repeat anything after hearing it once."

WONDER-WORKING TOMBS.

There are other tombs which present special peculiarities. Thus, not long since crowds of people assembled at Khetwadi, in Bombay, to see a shrine erected by some sweepers to *Zâhir Pîr*, which at intervals seemed to oscillate from its foundations. At Anjar in Sindh are the tombs of a noted outlaw named Jaisar Pîr and his wife Turî Khatrânî, who were originally buried apart, but their tombs are gradually approaching, and it is believed that at their meet-

[1] "North Indian Notes and Queries," iii. 144.
[2] "Eastern India," i. 82 sq.
[3] "Panjâb Notes and Queries," iii. 143.

ing the world will be destroyed. So there is a wall at Gurdâspur which a Faqîr saw being built, and asked the master-mason if he considered it to be firm. The mason said that he believed it to be substantial, whereupon the holy man touched it and made it shake, and it has gone on shaking ever since. At Faizâbâd is the tomb of a saint, and some time ago the metal top of one of the pinnacles took to shaking, and the weaver population were so impressed that they levied a tax on the community for its repair. At Jhanjhâna is the tomb of Sayyid Mahmûd, who was buried next to one of his disciples. But the latter is too modest to place himself on an equality with his master, so his tomb, however much it is repaired, always sinks to a lower level than that of his preceptor. At Bârabanki is the tomb of the saint Shaikh Ahmad Abdul-haq, who thought he could acquire some useful information by keeping company with the dead. So he got himself buried alive, and after six months his grave opened of its own accord and he was taken out half dead.

THE NINE-YARD TOMBS.

There is another class of tombs which are known as the Naugaza or Naugaja, that is to say tombs nine yards long. In these rest the giants of the older world. There is one of these tombs at Nâgaur in Râjputâna, and several others have been discovered in the course of the Archæological Survey.[1] Five of them at Vijhi measure respectively 29, 31, 30 and 38 feet. Mr. W. Simpson calls these tombs Buddhistic, but this is very doubtful.[2] The belief largely prevails among Muhammadans that there were giants in the early times. Adam himself is said to have been sixty yards in height, and there was a monster called 'Uj in the days of Adam, and the flood of Noah reached only to his waist. There is a tomb of Noah at Faizâbâd which is said to have been built by Alexander the Great, and not far off are those

[1] "Reports," i. 98, 130; xiv. 41; xxiii. 63.

[2] "Journal, Asiatic Society of Bengal," xiii. 205; "Panjâb Notes and Queries," i. 109.

of Seth and Job. The latter, curiously enough, are gradually growing in size. They are now 17 and 12 feet long respectively, but when Abul Fazl wrote they were only 10½ and 9 feet long.[1]

SHRINES WITH IMAGES OR RELICS.

The reputation, again, of many shrines rests on the assumed discovery, generally by means of a dream, that an ancient image or the bones of a martyr were buried on the spot, and in their honour a shrine was established. Thus, the great temple at Bandakpur in the Damoh District owes its origin to the fact that a Pandit in 1781 A.D. dreamed a dream, that in a certain spot lay buried in the earth an image of Jagîswar Mahâdeva, and that if he built a suitable temple over the place indicated, the image would make its appearance. On the strength of this dream the Pandit built a temple, and it is asserted that in due course of time the image developed itself without the aid of man.[2] So, the Bhairava temple on the Langûr peak owes its establishment to a cowherd having found on the spot a yellow-coloured stick, which on his attempting to cut it with an axe, poured out drops of blood. Frightened at the sight, the cowherd fled, only to be visited at night by the god in his terrible form, who commanded him to set up his shrine here. A similar legend is attached to the Nârâyana image in Nepâl.[3] The celebrated shrine of Hanumân at Beguthiya was discovered by a wandering ascetic,[4] and a Gûjar cowboy is said not very long ago to have found in one of the Sahâranpur jungles the image of the goddess Sâkambarî Devî, which now attracts large numbers of worshippers. The Mahârâja of Balrâmpur some time ago noticed a rude shrine of Bijleswarî Devî, the goddess of lightning, and remarked that he would build a handsome temple in honour of her, were it not for the sacred banyan tree which shaded it and prevented

[1] "Oudh Gazetteer," i. 11 sq. [2] "Central Provinces Gazetteer," 175.
[3] Atkinson, "Himâlayan Gazetteer," ii. 777; Wright, "History," 114, 124.
[4] "Oudh Gazetteer," i. 38.

the erection of the spire to the proper height. That very night the tree was uprooted by a hurricane, and a handsome temple was erected, this manifestation of her power having made the goddess more popular than ever.[1]

Mistakes are, however, sometimes made. This was the case some time ago at Ajudhya, where certain images were discovered and worshipped, until a learned Pandit ascertained that they were actually the deities of the aboriginal Bhars, who used to sacrifice Brâhmans to them. They were really Jaina images, but it is needless to say that their worship was immediately abandoned.[2]

As is only natural, shrines which have been discovered in this way at the outset rest under a certain degree of suspicion, and have to make their reputation by works of healing and similar miracles. If they fail to do so they sink into disrepute. Such was the case with a very promising shrine, supposed to be that of the saint Ashraf 'Ali, whose bones were found accidentally not long ago at Ahraura in the Mirzapur District. It enjoyed considerable reputation for a time, but failing to maintain its character, was finally discredited and abandoned.

Continuous respect is naturally accorded to ancient saints and local godlings, who have long since established their claim to recognition by a series of exhibitions of their thaumaturgic virtues. But the competition is so keen and the pecuniary value of a successful institution of this kind so considerable, that the claims of any interloper must be well tested and approved before it establishes its position and succeeds in attracting pilgrims.

THE CURING OF BARRENNESS.

Barrenness is in popular belief mainly due to the agency of evil spirits. Sterile women were in Rome beaten with rods by the naked youths who ran through the city at the Lupercalia. The barren, as Shakespeare says, "Touched by this holy chase, shake off their sterile curse." In

[1] "Oudh Gazetteer," i. 210 sq. [2] Ibid., i. 8 sq.

Bombay it is believed that the cause of not getting children is that the man or his wife must have killed a serpent in their former birth, whose spirit haunts them and makes the woman barren. To get rid of the spirit which causes sterility, the serpent's image is burnt and its funeral rites are performed.[1] The desire for male offspring is so intense that some of these shrines do a thriving trade in providing nostrums for this purpose.

One extraordinary method of procuring children, which long troubled our magistrates in Upper India, was for the would-be mother to burn down the hut of some neighbour. The Panjâbi woman, who under the reign of British law is prevented from burning the house of her neighbour, now takes a little grass from seven thatches and burns it.[2]

In another form of the charm the Khândh priest takes the woman to the confluence of two streams, sprinkles water over her to purify her from the dangerous influence of the spirit and makes an offering to the god of births.

Some special influence has been in many lands considered to attach to a person who has been publicly executed, and to the appliances used by the hangman.

Recently at an execution in Bombay, the hangman was observed to carefully secure the rope, and particularly that part of it which had encircled the neck of the culprit. He stated that he could sell every quarter inch of it, as it averted evil spirits and ghosts, and even prevented death from hanging. This idea accounts for the respect paid throughout Europe to the mandrake, which is supposed to be generated from the droppings of the brain of a thief on the gallows. In Cornwall a wen or strumous swelling can be cured by touching it with the hand of a man who has been publicly hanged.[3] According to the same principle, barren women in India bathe underneath a person who has been hanged, and women of the middle classes try to obtain a piece of the wood of the gallows for the same object.

[1] Campbell, "Notes," 366.
[2] "North Indian Notes and Queries," i. 50.
[3] Hunt, "Popular Romances," 378.

Another practice depends upon the principle that creeping under a bent tree or through a perforated stone expels the demon. Other instances of this will be given in another place. Hence in Gujarât, when an ascetic of the Dûndiya sect dies, women who seek the blessing of a son try to secure it by creeping under the litter on which his corpse is removed.[1]

A rite carried out with the same object rests on a sort of symbolic magic indicating fertility. Along the roads may often be seen trees almost destroyed by a noxious creeper known as the Akâsh Bel. Women in hope of offspring often transplant this from one tree to another, and are thus a decided nuisance to a district officer with a taste for arboriculture.

But the most approved plan is to visit a shrine with a reputation for healing this class of malady. There the patient is given a cocoanut, which is a magic substance, a fruit, or even a barley-corn from the holy of holies. Mr. Hartland has recently made an elaborate study of this subject, and he points out the principle on which the eating of such substances produced the desired effect. "Whether from an analogy between the normal act of impregnation and that of eating and drinking, or because savages had learnt that at least one mode of operating effectively on the organism, for purposes alike of injury and healing, was by drugs taken through the mouth, this was the favourite method of supernatural impregnation."

And again—"Flowers, fruit and other vegetables, eggs, fishes, spiders, worms, and even stones, are all capable of becoming human beings. They only await absorption in the shape of food, or in some other appropriate manner, into the body of a woman, to enable the metamorphosis to be accomplished."[2]

The same idea constantly occurs in Indian folk-lore. The barren queen is given the juice of a pomegranate by a Faqîr, or the king plucks one of the seven mangoes which grow on

[1] Forbes, "Râs Mâla," ii. 332, quoted by Campbell, "Notes," 15.
[2] "Legend of Perseus," i. 72, 207.

a special tree, or a beggar gives the princess the drug which causes her to give birth to twins.[1] Even in the Râmâyana we read that Râja Dasaratha divides the oblation among his wives and they conceive. Even nowadays in Florence, if a woman wishes to be with child, she goes to a priest and gets from him an enchanted apple, with which she repairs to Saint Anna, who was the Lucina of Roman times, and repeats a prayer or a spell.[2]

Some holy men, it must be admitted, do not escape the tongue of slander for their doings in this department of their business.

HARMLESS SAINTS AND GODLINGS.

Most of these saints and godlings whom we have been considering, are comparatively harmless, and even benevolent. Such is nearly always the case with the ghosts of the European dead, who are constantly deified. Perhaps because the Sâhib is such a curiously incomprehensible personage to the rustic, he is believed to retain his powers in the other world. But it is a remarkable and unconscious tribute to the foreign ruler that his ghost should be beneficent.

The gardener in charge of the station cemetery in Mirzapur some time ago informed me that he constantly sees the ghosts of the ladies and gentlemen buried there coming out for a walk in the hot summer nights, and that they never harm him.

But with ordinary graves it is necessary to be cautious. As appears in the cycle of tales which turn on the magic ointment which enables the possessor to see the beings of the other world, spirits hate being watched. The spirit, for instance, often announces its wishes. When the Emperor Tughlaq began to build the tomb of the Saint Bahâwal Haq, a voice was heard from below, saying, "You are treading on my body." Another site was chosen at a short

[1] Lâl Bihâri Dê, "Folk-tales of Bengal," 1, 117, 187; Tawney, "Katha Sarit Sâgara," i. 52, 172, 355, 382; ii. 216; Knowles, "Folk-tales of Kashmîr," 131, 416.

[2] Leland, "Etruscan Roman Remains," 246.

distance, and the voice said, "You are treading on my knees." He went a little further, and the voice said, "You are treading on my toes." So he had to go to the other end of the fort, and as the voice was not heard there, the tomb was built. If you visit an old tomb, it is well to clap your hands, as the ghost sometimes revisits its resting-place, and if discovered in *déshabille*, is likely to resent the intrusion in a very disagreeable manner. So it is very dangerous to pollute a tomb or insult its occupant in any way, and instances have occurred of cases of epilepsy and hysteria, which were attributed to the neglect of these precautions.

Thus, there is nothing permanent, no established rule of faith in the popular belief of the rustic. Discredited saints and shrines are always passing into contempt and oblivion; new worthies are being constantly canonized. The worst part of the matter is that there is no official controller of the right to deification, no Advocatus Diaboli to dispute the claims of the candidate to celestial honours. At the same time the system, though often discredited by fraud, admirably illustrates the elastic character of the popular creed. Hinduism would hardly be so congenial to the minds of the masses, if some rigid supervising agency disputed the right of any tribe to worship its hero, of any village to canonize its local worthy. The steady popularity of the system, for the present at least, shows that it satisfactorily provides for the religious wants of the people.

CHAPTER V.

WORSHIP OF THE MALEVOLENT DEAD.

Πρώτη δὲ ψυχὴ Ἐλπήνορος ἦλθεν ἑταίρου,
Οὐ γάρ πω ἐτέθαπτο ὑπὸ χθονὸς εὐρυοδείης.

Odyssey, xi. 51, 52.

THESE deified ghosts and saints whom we have been discussing, though occasionally touchy and sensitive to insult or disrespect, are, as a rule, benevolent. But there is another class of beings at whose feet the rustic lies in grievous and perpetual bondage. These are the malevolent dead.

SPIRITS OF THE DEAD HOSTILE.

It is not difficult to understand why the spirits of the dead should be regarded as hostile. A stranger is, in the belief of all primitive people, synonymous with an enemy; and the spirit of the departed having abandoned his own and joined some other and invisible tribe, whose domains lie outside the world of sense, is sure to be considered inimical to the survivors left on earth. As we have already seen, even the usually kindly spirit of the departed household dead requires propitiation and resents neglect; much more those of a different tribe or family.

Again, those disembodied souls in particular whose departure from the earth occurred under unexpected or specially tragical circumstances are naturally considered to have been ejected against their will from their tenement of clay, and as for many of them the proper funeral rites have not been performed, they carry with them to the next world an angry longing for revenge. As Brand, writing of British ghosts, says, "The ghosts of murdered persons, whose bodies have been secretly buried, are restless until their bones have been taken up and deposited in consecrated ground with the due rites of Christian burial; this idea being the survival of the old heathen superstition that Charon was not allowed to ferry over the ghosts of the unburied, but that they wandered up and down the banks of the river Styx for a period of a hundred years, at the expiration of which they were admitted to a passage."[1]

This conception of the state of the soul after death may be illustrated by the savage theory of dreams.

SAVAGE THEORY OF DREAMS.

Many savages believe that the evidence of dreams is sufficient to prove that the soul moves about during sleep, and that the dream is the record of its experiences in hunting, dancing, visiting friends, and so on.

THE SEPARABLE SOUL.

Hence arises the possibility that in the temporary absence of a man's soul his body may be occupied by some other person's spirit, or even by a malignant ghost or demon. In the Panchatantra there is a story of a king who lost his own soul, but afterwards recovered it. A Panjâb tale tells how a Hindu was once asleep and his soul went on its travels as usual. During its wanderings it felt thirsty and went into a pitcher of water to drink. While it was in the pitcher some one shut the lid, and it was imprisoned. His friends took the corpse to the cremation ground, but some one happened fortunately to open the pitcher just in time, and the spirit flew into its own body, which awoke on the bier.[2] In the same way, according to Apollonius, the soul of

[1] "Observations," 625; and see Frazer, "Golden Bough," i. 150; Lubbock, "Origin of Civilization," 220; Tylor, "Primitive Culture," ii. 27; Spencer, "Principles of Sociology," i. 215 sq.; Sir W. Scott, "Letters on Demonology," 90.

[2] "Panjâb Notes and Queries," iii. 166.

Hermotimos of Klazomenoe left his body frequently, resided in different places, uttered all sorts of predictions, and used to come back to his body, which remained in his house. At last some spiteful persons burnt his body in the absence of his soul. In another tale of Somadeva the soul of Chandraprabha abandons his own body and enters that of a hero under the influence of Mâyâ or delusion.[1]

On this principle Hindus are very cautious about awaking a sleeping friend, lest his soul may happen to be absent at the time, and in Bombay it is considered most reprehensible to play jokes on a sleeping person, such as painting the face in fantastic colours, or giving moustaches to a sleeping woman. The absent soul may not be able to find its own body, the appearance of which has been thus changed, and may depart altogether, leaving the body a corpse.

It is a common incident of the folk-tales that the soul departs in a dream and falls in love with a girl. We have it in the common tale of the Rival Queens, where the king sees in a dream the most lovely woman in the world, and imposes on his courtiers the task of finding her. The same idea is found more or less in Somadeva, and constantly recurs in European folk-lore.[2] In the same way we have the well-known tale of the instantaneous lapse of time in dreams, as that of the king who plunges his head into water, goes through wondrous adventures, and when he takes his head out of the vessel, finds himself surrounded by his courtiers as before.

The rustic Hindu firmly believes that in the absence of a man's proper soul in a dream his body is occupied by some strange and consequently malignant ghost. Hence come the nightmare and evil dreams. Thus the Korwas of Mirzapur believe that a Bhûtin or dangerous female ghost named Reiyâ besets them at night under the orders of some witch, and attacks people's joints with the rheumatism.

[1] Tawney, "Katha Sarit Sâgara," i. 21, 420; Miss Cox, "Cinderella," 489; Clouston, "Popular Tales," i. 437.

[2] "North Indian Notes and Queries," iii. 31; Clouston, *loc. cit.*, ii 228; Tawney, "Katha Sarit Sâgara," ii. 588.

The Majhwârs believe that the Râkshasa attacks them in dreams. He comes in the shape of an old man with enormous teeth, brown of colour, with black, entangled hair, and sometimes swallows his victims. It is fear of him that brings the fever, and he can be exorcised only by the Baiga with an offering of rice and pulse. The Dâno also comes in dreams, squeezes a man's throat, and stops his breath. The Bhuiyârs have adopted from the Hindu mythology Jam or Yama as one of their dream ghosts. He sits on his victim's breast in sleep, and it is impossible to shake him off or make an alarm. Sometimes these night ghosts come as tigers, wolves, or bears, and hunt a man down in his sleep.

On the same principle the shadow of a man is believed to be part of a man's soul, and may be separated from him, injured or wounded by an enemy. Hence it is considered dangerous to tread on the shadow of a man in the sunshine. Buddha is said to have left his shadow in the cave at Pabhosa, where he killed the Nâga.[1]

The same is the case with looking into other people's mirrors, because you may chance leave behind your reflection, which is part of your soul. As we have seen, this is the basis of much of the theory of water spirits, which lurk in water holes and seize the reflection of anyone who looks into them. The Sunni Muhammadans in Bombay cover up all the looking-glasses in a house when a person is sick, as the soul, which is just then on the prowl, may be absorbed, and leave its owner a corpse.

Lastly, the same theory accounts for the disinclination which rustics have to being painted or photographed. Some of the soul goes out in the image and does not return. There is a rest-house on the Asthbhuja Hill at Mirzapur which was many years ago presented to the Europeans of the station by a wealthy banker. He was overpersuaded to allow his picture to be painted, and fell into a lingering consumption, of which he soon after died.

[1] Führer, "Monumental Antiquities," 144.

THE BHÛT.

The general term for these spirits is Bhût, in Sanskrit Bhûta, which means "formed" or "created." In the earlier Hindu writings the word is applied to the powers of Nature, and even to deities. Siva himself is called Bhûtîsvara, or "Lord of spirits," and, under the name of Bhûtîsvara Mahâdeva, has a shrine at Mathura. But as the Greek Dæmon acquired a less respectable meaning in the later ages of the history of the nation, so Bhût has now come to imply a malignant evil spirit.

But Bhût is a general term which includes many grades of evil spirits which it is necessary to distinguish. We shall first, however, deal with certain characters common to Bhûts in general.

The proper Bhût is the spirit emanating from a man who has died a violent death, either by accident, suicide, or capital punishment. Such a soul reaches an additional grade of malignancy if he has been denied proper funeral ceremonies after death. This is one of his special wants which deprive the spirit of his longed-for rest. Thus, we read in Childe Harold, "Unsepulchred they roamed and shrieked, each wandering ghost." The shade of Patroclus appeared to Achilles in his sleep and demanded the performance of his funeral, and the younger Pliny tells of a haunted house in Athens, in which a ghost played all kinds of pranks owing to his funeral rites having been neglected. This idea is at the base of the Hindu funeral ceremonies, and of the periodical Srâddha. Hence arose the conception of the Gayâl, or sonless ghost. He is the spirit of a man who has died without any issue competent to perform the customary rites; hence he is spiteful, and he is especially obnoxious to the lives of the young sons of other people. Accordingly in every Panjâb village will be seen small platforms, with rows of little hemispherical depressions into which milk and Ganges water are poured, and by which lamps are lit and Brâhmans fed to conciliate the Gayâl; "while the careful mother will always dedicate a rupee to him, and hang it round her child's neck till he grows up." Mr. Ibbetson [1] suggests that this may have been the origin of the mysterious so-called "cup-marks," described by Mr. Rivett-Carnac. But this is far from certain; they may equally well have been used for sacrifices to Mother Earth, or in any other primeval form of worship.

SHRINES TO PERSONS ACCIDENTALLY KILLED.

Many of these shrines to persons who have died by an untimely death are known by special names, which indicate the character of the accident. We shall meet again with the Baghaut, or shrine, to a man killed by a tiger. We have also Bijaliya Bîr, the man who was killed by lightning, Târ Bîr, a man who fell from a Târ or toddy tree, and Nâgiya Bîr, a person killed by a snake. General Cunningham mentions shrines of this kind; one to an elephant driver who was killed by a fall from a tree, another to a Brâhman who was killed by a cow, a third to a Kashmîri lady who had only one leg and died in her flight from Delhi to Oudh of exhaustion on the journey.

Bhûts are most to be feared by women and children, and by people at any serious crisis of their lives, such as marriage or child-birth. They also attack people after eating sweets, "so that if you treat a school to sweetmeats, the sweetmeat seller will also bring salt, of which he will give a pinch to each boy to take the sweet taste out of his mouth." [2] Salt is, as we shall see later on, particularly offensive to evil spirits.[3]

SECOND MARRIAGE AND BHÛTS.

Women who have married a second time are specially liable to the envious attacks of the first husband. If in Bombay "a Mahâdeo Koli widow bride or her husband sicken, it is considered the work of the former husband. Among the Somavansi Kshatriyas, there is a strong belief

[1] "Panjâb Ethnography," 116. [2] Ibbetson, *loc. cit.*, 117.
[3] Aubrey, "Remaines," 121; Lady Wilde, "Legends," 44, 233.

that when a woman marries another husband, her first husband becomes a ghost and troubles her. This fear is so strongly rooted in their minds, that whenever a woman of this caste sickens, she attributes her sickness to the ghost of her former husband, and consults an exorcist as to how she can get rid of him. The exorcist gives her some charmed rice, flowers, and basil leaves, and tells her to enclose them in a small copper box and wear it round her neck. Sometimes the exorcist gives her a charmed cocoa-nut, which he tells her to worship daily, and in some cases he advises the woman to make a copper or silver image of the dead and worship it every day."[1]

So in Northern India, people who marry again after the death of the first wife wear what is known as the Saŭkan Maura, or second wife's crown. This is a little silver amulet, generally with an image of Devî engraved on it. This is hung round the husband's neck, and all presents made to the second wife are first dedicated to it. The idea is that the new wife recognizes the superiority of her predecessor, and thus appeases her malignity. The illness or death of the second wife or of her husband soon after marriage is attributed to the jealousy of the ghost of the first wife, which has not been suitably propitiated.

In the Panjâb, on the same principle, if a man has lost two or three wives in succession, he gets a woman to catch a bird and adopt it as her daughter. He then pays the dower, marries his bird bride, and immediately divorces her. By this means the malignant influence is diverted to the bird, and the real wife is safe.[2] We shall meet again with the same principle in dealing with the curious custom of tree marriage.

FOOD OF BHÛTS.

Like evil spirits all the world over, Bhûts will eat filthy food, and as they are always thirsty, they are glad to secure

[1] Campbell, "Notes," 171.
[2] "Panjâb Notes and Queries," i. 13; "North Indian Notes and Queries," i. 4.

even a drop of water, no matter how impure the purpose may have been for which it has been used. On the other hand, they are very fond of milk, and no Panjâbi woman likes her child to leave the house after drinking fresh milk. If she cannot prevent it from going, she puts some salt or ashes into its mouth to scare the Bhût.[1]

POSTURE OF BHÛTS.

Bhûts can never sit on the ground, apparently, because, as has been shown already, the earth, personified as a goddess, scares away all evil influence. Hence, near the low-caste shrines a couple of pegs or bricks are set up for the Bhût to rest on, or a bamboo is hung over it, on which the Bhût perches when he visits the place.[2] On the same principle the Orâons hang up the cinerary urn containing the bones of a dead man on a post in front of the house,[3] and the person who is going on a pilgrimage, or conveying the bones of a relative to the Ganges, sleeps on the ground; but the bones must not rest on the ground; they are hung on the branch of a tree, so that their late owner may revisit them if so disposed. Near shrines where Bhûts are always about on the chance of appropriating the offerings, it is expedient to sleep on the ground. So the bride and bridegroom rest, and the dying man is laid at the moment of dissolution.

TESTS OF BHÛTS.

There are at least three infallible tests by which you may recognize a Bhût. In the first place he casts no shadow. In the third Canto of the Purgatorio, Dante is much distressed because Virgil, being a disembodied spirit, casts no shadow. In the second place a Bhût can stand almost anything in his neighbourhood but the scent of burning turmeric, which, as we shall see, is a well-known demon-scarer. Thirdly, a genuine Bhût always speaks with a nasal

1 "Panjâb Notes and Queries," iv. 57.
2 See Cunningham, "Archæological Reports," xvii. 147.
3 Dalton, "Descriptive Ethnology," 261.

twang, and it is possibly for this last reason that the term for the gibberish in the mediæval plays and for modern English is Pisâcha Bhâsha, or the language of goblins.[1] Some of them have throats as narrow as a needle, but they can drink gallons of water at a time. Some, like the Churel, whom we shall meet later on, have their feet turned backwards. Some, like Brâhman ghosts, are wheat-coloured or white; others, like the Kâfari, the ghost of a murdered negro, are black, and particularly dreaded. A famous ghost of this class haunts a lane in Calcutta, which takes its name from him.

SPIRIT LOVERS.

Many denizens of the spirit land have connection with mortals. We have the cycle of folk-tales known as that of the Swan maidens.

Urvasî came and lived with Parûravas until he broke the curiosity taboo. We shall see instances where Indra gives one of his fairies to a mortal lover, and spirits like the Incubi and Succubi of European folk-lore can be brought down by incantation.

SPIRIT ENTRIES: THE HEAD.

Spirits enter and leave the body in various ways. They often use the head in this way, and in particular the tenth aperture of the body, one of the skull sutures, known as Brahma-randhra. This is the reason why the skull is broken at cremation to open the "crevice of Brahma," as this orifice is called.

In the case of one of the ascetic orders, who are buried and not cremated, a blow is given on the head with a cocoanut or a conch shell. Thus, when the chief teacher of the Brâhmans in Bombay dies, his successor breaks a cocoanut on his skull and makes an opening, in which the sacred

[1] "Panjâb Notes and Queries," iv. 51; Lal Bihâri Dê, "Folk Tales," 199; "Govinda Sâmanta," i. 109, 152 sq., 157; "North Indian Notes and Queries," i. 83.

Sâlagrâma stone is laid.[1] This rite of skull-breaking, which is done by the next relation, is a recognized part of the Hindu cremation rite, and is known as Kapâlakriya.

The same theory that the head is an entry for spirits accounts for numerous strange practices. Thus, when in Kumaun a man is bitten by a snake they pull three hairs from his scalp-lock and strike him three times on the top of the head with the first joint of the middle finger, a kind of blow which in ordinary cases is regarded with the utmost terror. So when a person has fever, they take a bone and fill it with grain, and, making the patient stand in the sun, dig a hole where the shadow of his head falls, and there bury the bone, saying, "Fever! Begone with the bone!"[2] At a Gond wedding, the old man who officiates knocks the heads of the bride and bridegroom together to scare the evil spirits,[3] and at a Hindu marriage in Northern India the mother of the youth, as he leaves to fetch his bride, and as he returns with her, waves lamps, a brass tray, grain, and a rice pounder, to drive off the Bhûts fluttering round his head. It is on the same principle that the bridegroom wears a marriage crown, and this also accounts for many of the customs of blessing by the laying on of hands and anointing which prevail all over the world. In the same way the hair has always been regarded as a spirit entry. Magistrates in Northern India are often troubled by people who announce their intention of "letting their hair grow" at some one whom they desire to injure. This, if one can judge by the manifest terror exhibited by the person against whom this rite is directed, must be a very stringent form of coercion. For the same reason ascetics wear the hair loose and keep it uncut, as Sampson did, and the same idea probably accounts for the rites of ceremonial shaving of youths, and of the mourners after death.

[1] "Bombay Gazetteer," xv. 150; Campbell, "Notes," 172.
[2] "Panjâb Notes and Queries," iv. 5; "North Indian Notes and Queries," ii. 9; iii. 74.
[3] Hislop, "Notes," i. 3.

THE MOUTH.

As might have been expected, Bhûts are very fond of entering by the mouth. Hence arise much of the mouth-washing which is part of the daily ritual of the Hindu, and many of the elaborate precautions which he takes at meals. This will be referred to again in connection with the Evil Eye.

YAWNING.

Hence it is very dangerous to yawn, as two kinds of danger are to be apprehended—either a Bhût may go down your throat, or part of your soul may escape, and you will be hard set to recover it. So if you chance to yawn, you should put your hand to your mouth and say Nârâyan—"Great God!" afterwards, or you should crack your fingers, which scares the evil spirit. This idea is the common property of folk-lore.[1]

SNEEZING.

So, sneezing is due to demoniacal influence, but opinions differ as to whether it is caused by a Bhût entering or leaving the nose. The latter view is generally taken by Musalmâns, because it is one of the traditions of the Prophet that the nose should be washed out with water, as the devil resides in it during the night. The sneezing superstition in India is at least as old as the Buddhist Jâtakas, where we have a remarkable tale about it, which describes how the future Buddha and his father Gagga went to pass the night in a place haunted by a Yakkha, or Yaksha, and were very near being devoured by him because they did not say the spell "Live!" when they sneezed.[2]

So, in Somadeva's tale of Sulochana and Sushena, the spirit of the air says, "When he enters into his private apartments, he shall sneeze a hundred times; and if some one there does not say to him a hundred times, 'God bless

[1] "Panjâb Notes and Queries," ii. 114, 167; Tylor, "Primitive Culture," i. 102; Aubrey, "Remaines," 177, 194; Campbell, "Notes," 177.

[2] Fausboll, "Jâtaka," ii. 15 sq.; "Ibbetson, "Panjâb Ethnography," 118.

you,' he shall fall into the grasp of death."[1] It is needless to say that the same belief prevails in Europe. As Dr. Tylor says, "Even the Emperor Tiberius, that saddest of men, exacted this observance." According to the Muhammadan rule, if a person sneezes and then says immediately afterwards, *Al-hamdu li'llah*, "God be praised," it is incumbent upon at least one of the party to reply, *Yarhamu-ka 'llah*, just as among the Jews the sneezing formula was *Tobkin Khayim*, "Good life!"

On the whole, sneezing is considered auspicious, because it implies the expulsion of a Bhût. As a general rule, if a person sneezes when another is beginning some work, the latter stops for a while, and then begins afresh; if there be two sneezes in succession, there is no necessity for interruption. If a man sneezes behind the back of another, the back of the latter is slightly pinched. In Bombay, if a man sneeze during a meal, one of the party calls on him to name his birthplace.[2] The threshold in the folk-lore of all nations is regarded as a sacred place. It is here, according to the Scotch and Irish belief, that the house fairies reside. Sitting on the threshold is believed by Indian matrons likely to produce boils in children in that part of the body which touches it, and it is thought most unlucky to sneeze on the threshold. On the whole, one sneeze is ominous, while after two work may be commenced with safety. So it was in the days of Homer—"Even so she spoke, and Telemachus sneezed loudly, and around the roof rang wondrously, and Penelope laughed, and straightway spoke Eumœus winged words, 'Go! call me the stranger, even so into my presence. Dost thou not mark how my son has sneezed a blessing on all my words?'"[3]

THE HANDS AND FEET.

The hands and feet are also means by which Bhûts enter

[1] Tawney, "Katha Sarit Sâgara," i. 254.
[2] Campbell, "Notes," 177.
[3] "Odyssey," xvii. 541 sq.; Yule, "Marco Polo," ii. 351; Aubrey, "Remaines," 177.

the body. Hence much of the ablution at prayers and meals; the hand-clapping which accompanies so many religious and mystical rites; the passing of the hand over the head; the laying of the hands on the eyes to restore sight, of which we have many examples in the Indian folk-tales; the hand-pledging at marriages; the drinking of the Charan-amrita, or water, in which the feet of a holy man have been washed; the ceremonial washing of the feet of the bridegroom at a wedding by the father of the bride. The stock case of the danger of the not washing the feet at night is that of Adilî, whose impurity allowed Indra to form the Maruts out of her embryo. A man with flat feet is considered most un-unlucky, as in North England, where if you meet a flat-soled man on Monday you are advised to go home, eat and drink, or evil will befall you.[1] The chief basis of feet-washing is the idea that a person coming from abroad and not immediately carrying out the required ablution runs the risk of bringing some foreign, and presumably dangerous, spirit with him.

THE EARS.

And so with the ears, which are believed to communicate direct with the brain, and are kept by the rustic carefully muffled up on chilly mornings. Hence the custom of Kanchhedan, or ear-piercing, which is in Northern India about the only survival of the world-wide rite of mutilation when males attain puberty, and of wearing ear-rings and similar ornaments, which is habitual with all classes of Hindus, and specialized among the Kanphata Jogis, who take their name from this practice.

VARIETIES OF BHÛTS.

In Bengal the ordinary Bhût is a member of the Kshatriya, Vaisya, or Sûdra class. The Brâhman Bhût, or Brahmadaitya, is quite another variety. The ordinary Bhûts are as tall as palmyra trees, generally thin and very black. They

[1] Henderson, "Folk-lore of the Northern Counties," 117.

usually live on trees, except those which the Brahmadaitya frequent. At night, and especially at the hour of midnight, they wander about the fields frightening travellers. They prefer dirty places to those which are clean; so when a person goes to worship a Bhût, he does so in some dirty, retired place, and gives him only half-cooked food, so that he may not have time to gobble it up, and perchance rend his worshipper. They are never seen in the temples of the gods, though they often, as we have seen, lurk about in the vicinity in the hope of getting some of the offerings if the priest be not on the alert and scare them with his bell or shell-trumpet. They are always stark naked, and are fond of women, whom they sometimes abduct. They eat rice, and all sorts of human food, but their favourite diet is fish. Hence no Bengâli, except for a considerable bribe, will talk about fish at night. Here they agree with the fairies of Manxland. Professor Rhys [1] tell a story of a Manx fisherman, who was taking a fresh fish home, and was pursued by a pack of fairy dogs, so that it was only with great trouble he reached his own door. He drove the dogs away with a stone, but he was shot by the fairies, and had a narrow escape of his life. On the other hand, the Small People in Cornwall hate the smell of fish as much as the savour of salt or grease.[2] The best chance of escape from these Bengal Bhûts is when they begin to quarrel among themselves. A person beset by them should invoke the gods and goddesses, especially Kâlî, Durgâ, and Siva, the last of whom is, as already noted, the Lord of Bhûts.[3]

Bhûts are of many varieties. Vetâla, or Baitâl, their leader, is familiar to everyone in the tales of the Baitâl Pachîsi. He is not, as a rule, particularly offensive. More usually he is a vagrant Bhût which enters the body of a man when the real spirit is absent. But he often approximates to the Vampire as we meet him in Western folk-lore. "It is as a vitalized corpse that the visitor from the other

[1] "Folk-lore," ii. 289. [2] Hunt, "Popular Romances," 109.
[3] Lâl Bihâri Dê, "Gobinda Sâmanta," i. 115 sqq.

world comes to trouble mankind, often subject to human appetites, constantly endowed with more than human strength and malignity."[1] Thus in one of Somadeva's stories the hero goes at night to a cemetery and summons at the foot of a tree a Vetâla into the body of a man, and after worshipping him, makes an oblation of human flesh to him. In another there is a Vetâla with a body made up of the limbs of many animals, who hurls the king to the earth, and when he sits on the Vetâla's back the demon flies with him through the air like a bird and flings him into the sea.[2] The spirit entering the body of the dead man forms the leading incident in the tale of Fadlallah in the Arabian Nights, and there are many instances of it in Indian folk-lore. This disposes of the assertion which has been sometimes made that among races which bury their dead little is known of regular corpse spectres, or that they are special to lands tenanted or influenced by the Slavonians.[3] Most usually the Vetâla appears as the spirit of some living person dissatisfied with his lodgings on earth, which leaves his own body and occupies a corpse in preference. He, in company with the Vasus, Yakshas, Bhûtas, and Gandharvas, has passed into the degraded Tantrika worship.[4]

THE PRET.

The Hindu notion of the state of the soul between death and the performance of the prescribed funeral rites agrees exactly with that of the older European races. They wandered about in a state of unhappy restlessness, and were not suffered to mix with the other dead. The term Pret or Preta, which simply means "deceased" or "departed," represents the soul during this time. It wanders round its original home, and, like the Bâlakhilyas, who surround the chariot of the sun, is no larger than a man's thumb. The stages of his progress, according to the best authorities, are that up to the performance of the ten Pindas the dead man

[1] Ralston, "Russian Folk-tales," 306.
[2] Tawney, "Katha Sarit Sâgara," i. 231, 543.
[3] Ibid., ii. 208. [4] Wilson, "Essays," i. 26.

remains a Preta, through the Nârâyanabali rite he becomes a Pisâcha, and by the Sapindikarana he reaches the dignity of the Pitri or sainted dead. The term Preta is, however, sometimes applied to the spirit of a deformed or crippled person, or one defective in some limb or organ, or of a child who dies prematurely owing to the omission of the prescribed ceremonies during the formation of the embryo. Here it may be noted that there are indications in India of the belief which is common among savages, that young children, apparently in consequence of their incomplete protection from the birth impurity, are under a taboo. Thus in India a child is regarded as a Bhût until the birth hair is cut. Some of the jungle tribes believe that it is unnecessary to protect a child from evil spirits until it begins to eat grain, because up to that time it is nothing more than a Bhût itself. Under the old ritual a child under two years of age was not burnt, but buried, and no offering of water was made to it. We are familiar with the same idea in England regarding unbaptized children, whose spirits are supposed to be responsible for the noise of Gabriel's Hounds in the sky, really caused by the bean geese in their southern flight.

The Pret is occasionally under provocation malignant, but as it partakes to some degree of the functions of the benign ancestral household spirit, it is not necessarily malicious or evil-disposed towards living persons. The Pret is specially worshipped at Gaya on the Hill, known as Pretsila, or "the rock of the Pret," and a special class of Brâhmans at Patna call themselves Pretiya, because they worship the ghost of some hero or saint.[1]

THE PISÂCHA.

Next comes the Pisâcha, which, as we have seen, is by one account only a stage in the progress of the soul to its final rest. But more properly speaking it is an evil spirit produced by a man's vices, the ghost of a liar, adulterer, or

[1] Buchanan, "Eastern India," i. 65, 166.

criminal of any kind, or of one who has died insane. But his attributes and functions are not very clearly defined, and he merges into the general class of Bhûts. In some cases he seems to have the power to cure disease. Thus we read in Somadeva, "Rise up in the last watch of the night, and with dishevelled hair, and naked, and without rinsing your mouth, take two handfuls of rice as large as you can grasp with the two hands, and, uttering a form of words, go to a place where four roads meet and there place the two handfuls of rice, and return in silence without looking behind you. Do so always until that Pisâcha appears and says, 'I will put an end to your ailment.' Then receive his aid gladly, and he will remove your complaint."[1]

THE RÂKSHASA.

The Râkshasa again, a word that means "the harmer" or "the destroyer," is of the ogre-vampire type. He goes about at night, haunts cemeteries, disturbs sacrifices and devout men, animates dead bodies, even devouring human beings, in which capacity he is known as Kravyâda, or carnivorous, and is generally hostile to the human race. He is emphatically a devourer of human flesh, and eats carrion. He is often represented in the folk-tales as having a pretty daughter, who protects the hero when he ventures perchance into the abode of the monster. Her father comes in, and with the cry of "*Manush gandha*," which is equivalent to the "Fee! fo! fum! I smell the blood of an Englishman!" of the Western tale, searches about, but fails to find him. When Hanumân entered the city of Lanka in the form of a cat, to reconnoitre, he saw that the Râkshasas who slept in the house "were of every shape and form. Some of them disgusted the eye, while some were beautiful to look on. Some had long arms and frightful shapes; some were very fat and some were very lean; some were dwarf and some were prodigiously tall. Some had only one eye, and others had only one ear. Some had monstrous bellies, hanging

[1] Tawney, "Katha Sarit Sâgara," i. 256 sqq.

breasts, long projecting teeth, and crooked thighs; whilst others were exceedingly beautiful to behold and clothed in great splendour. Some had the heads of serpents, some the heads of asses, some of horses, and some of elephants." The leader of them was Râvana, who is said to have been once a Brâhman and to have been turned into a Râkshasa, "with twenty arms, copper-coloured eyes, and bright teeth like the young moon. His form was as a thick cloud or as a mountain, or the god of death with open mouth."

The Râkshasa is the great *Deus ex machinâ* of folk-lore. He can change into almost any form he pleases, his breath is a roaring wind; he can lengthen his arms to eighty miles; he can smell out human beings like Giant Blunderbore. He can carry a man leagues through the air; if his head be cut off, it grows again. He is the Eastern type of the monster dragon which is subdued by St. George, Siegmund, Siegfried, or Beowulf.

His spouse, the Râkshasî, is a creature of much the same kind. In the folk-tales she often takes the form of the ogress queen who marries the king and gets up at night and devours an elephant, or two or three horses, or some sheep or a camel, and then puts the blood and scraps of meat at the doors of her rivals, and gets them banished, until the clever lad discovers her wiles and brings her to condign punishment.[1] Often she besets a city and demands the daily tribute of a human victim. The king takes the place of the victim, and the Râkshasî is so affected by his generosity that she abandons eating the flesh of men. In a case in the folk-tales a boy becomes a Râkshasa by eating the brains of a corpse.[2] Like all other demons, Râkshasas are scared by light, and one of the names of the lamp is Râkshogna, or "the destroyer of the Râkshasas."

The idea of the Râkshasa comes from the earliest times. Some have thought them to be types of the early Drâvidian opponents of the Hindus. Nirritî, the female personification

[1] Knowles, "Kashmîr Folk-tales," 43; Clouston, "Popular Tales," i. 135.

[2] Tawney, "Katha Sarit Sâgara," i. 210; ii. 318.

of death, is a Râkshasa deity in the Vedas, and Dr. Muir has traced the various stages by which the Râkshasa was developed into a godling.[1] Thus, in the Mahâbhârata, Jarâ is called a household goddess; the great King Jarasandha was born in two halves, and Jarâ united them; she is always represented as seeking to requite by benefits the worship which is paid to her. Manu prescribes a special oblation for "the spirits which walk in darkness." The blood in the sacrifice is, according to the old ritual, offered to them, though even here we notice the transition from animal to corn offerings.[2]

Nowadays Râkshasas live in trees and cause vomiting and indigestion to those who trespass on their domains at night. They mislead night travellers like Will-o'-the-Wisp, and they are always greedy and in quest of food. So, if a man is eating by lamp-light and the light goes out, he will cover the dish with his hands, which are, as we have already seen, scarers of demons, to preserve the food from the Râkshasa, and Bengal women go at night with a lamp into every room to expel the evil spirits.[3]

The Râkshasas are said to be always fighting with the gods and their blood remains on many of these ghostly battle-fields. In the Hills this is believed to be the cause of the red ferruginous clay which is occasionally observed, and the Lohû or "blood-red" river has a similar origin.[4] The same idea appears in the folk-lore of Europe. In a Swabian legend the red colour of shoots of rye when they first appear above the surface is attributed to Cain having killed Abel in a rye-field, which thus became reddened with innocent blood.[5] One species of feathered pink has a dark purple spot in it which people in Germany say is a drop of the

[1] "Journal Royal Asiatic Society," N.S. ii. 300; "Ancient Sanskrit Texts," iv. 247; Wilson, "Rig Veda," i. 107.

[2] Manu, "Institutes," iii. 90; Haug, "Aitareya Brâhmanam," ii. 87, 90 sq.

[3] "Panjâb Notes and Queries," ii. 132; Lal Behâri Dê, "Govinda Sâmanta," i. 117; Campbell, "Notes," 24 sqq.

[4] "Journal Asiatic Society Bengal," 1847, p. 582.

[5] "Folk-lore," iii. 323.

blood of the Redeemer which fell from the Cross.[1] In one of the Irish Sagas the blood of a murdered man fell on a white stone and formed the red veins which are still shown to the traveller.[2] In Cornwall a red stain on the rocks marks where giant Bolster died, and the red lichen in a brook commemorates a murder.[3] Every English child knows the legend of Robin Redbreast.

In folk-lore Râkshasas have kingdoms, and possess enormous riches, which they bestow on those whom they favour, like Târâ Bâî in the story of Seventee Bâî. In this they resemble the Irish fairies, who hide away much treasure in their palaces underneath the hills and in the lakes and sea. "All the treasure of wrecked ships is theirs; and all the gold that men have hidden or buried in the earth when danger was on them, and then died and left no sign to their descendants. And all the gold of the mine and the jewels of the rocks belong to them, and in the Sifra or fairy house the walls are silver and the pavement is gold, and the banquet hall is lit by the diamonds that stud the rocks."[4]

The finger nails of the Râkshasas, as those of Europeans in popular belief, are a deadly poison, and the touch of them produces insensibility, or even death. They often take the disguise of old women and have very long hair, which is a potent charm. Their malignity is so great that it would be difficult to avoid them, but fortunately, like the Devil in the European tales, and evil spirits all the world over, they are usually fools, and readily disclose the secrets of their enchantment to the distressed heroine who is unlucky enough to fall into their power, and the victim has generally only to address the monster as "Uncle!" to escape from his clutches.[5]

They are, as has been said already, usually cannibals. One

[1] Grimm, "Household Tales," ii. 381.
[2] Hartland, "Legend of Perseus," i. 16.
[3] Hunt, "Popular Romances," 75, 270.
[4] Miss Frere, "Old Deccan Days," 41, 198; Wright, "History of Nepâl," 175; Lady Wilde, "Legends," 257.
[5] Miss Frere, *loc. cit.*, 82, 58, 62, 208, 268 sqq.; Knowles, "Kashmîr Folk-tales," 47.

of these was Vaka in the Mahâbhârata, who lived at Ekachakra and levied a daily toll of food and human victims on the Râja till he was torn to pieces by Bhîma. Bhîma also contrived to kill another monster of the same kind named Hidimba. In the great Panjâb legend of Rasâlu, he conquers the seven Râkshasas, who used to eat a human being every day, and there is a Nepâl story of the Râkshasa Gurung Mâpa, who used to eat corpses. He was propitiated with a grant of land to live on and an annual offering of a buffalo and some rice.[1]

POWER OF LENGTHENING THEMSELVES.

All ghosts, as we shall see later on, have the power of lengthening themselves like the Naugaza, whom we have already mentioned. For this reason demons, as a rule, are of gigantic form, and many of the enormous fossil bones found in the Siwâlik Hills were confidently attributed to the Râkshasas, which reminds us of the story of the smith in Herodotus who found the gigantic coffin seven cubits long containing the bones of Orestes.[2]

NIGHT SPIRITS.

Like the ghost in Hamlet, the angel that visited Jacob, and the destroying angels of Sodom, the Râkshasas always fly before the dawn. They invariably travel through the air and keep their souls in birds or trees—a fertile element in folk-lore which has been called by Major Temple "The Life Index."[3]

RÂKSHASAS AS BUILDERS.

The tales of Western lands abound with instances of buildings, bridges, etc., constructed by the Devil. So the Indian

[1] Atkinson, "Himâlayan Gazetteer," ii. 352, note; Cunningham, "Archæological Reports," ii. 21.

[2] Tylor, "Early History," 316; Herodotus, i. 68.

[3] Campbell, "Popular Tales," ii. 95; "Wideawake Stories," 404 sqq.; Miss Stokes, "Fairy Tales," 261; Tylor, "Primitive Culture," i. 161; Frazer, "Golden Bough," ii. 300; Tawney, "Katha Sarit Sâgara," i. 42, 47; Hartland, "Legend of Perseus," ii. chap. viii.

Râkshasa is commonly regarded as an architect. Thus, at Râmtek in the Central Provinces there is a curious old temple built of hewn stones, well fitted together without mortar. From its shape and structure it is probably of Jaina origin, though local tradition connects it with the name of Hemâdpant, the Râkshasa. He is an example of Râkshasas developed in comparatively recent times from a historical personage. He was probably the Minister of Mahâdeva (1260-1271 A.D.), the fourth of the Yâdava Kings of Deogiri. According to the common story, he was a giant or a physician, who brought the current Marâthi character from Ceylon. The Dakkhin swarms with ancient buildings attributed to him.[1]

Such is also the case with another class of demons, the Asuras, a word which means "spiritual" or "superhuman," who were the rivals of the gods. In Mirzapur the ancient embankment at the Karsota tank is considered to be their work. Once upon a time two of these demons vowed that whoever first succeeded in building a fort should be the conqueror, and that his defeated rival should lose his life. So they set to work in the evening, one on the Bijaygarh Hill, and the other on the opposite peak of Kundakot, about twelve miles distant. The demon of Bijaygarh, having lost his tools in the dark, struck a light to search for them. His adversary seeing the light, and imagining that the sun was rising and his rival's work completed, fled precipitously. The Bijaygarh fort was completed during the night and stands to the present day, while on Kundakot you see only a few enormous blocks of stone which was all the vanquished Asura had time to collect. The tales of demons interfering with the construction of buildings are common in European folk-lore.

Many other buildings are said to have been built in the same way. The Bârahkhamba at Shikârpur in the Buland-

[1] "Central Provinces Gazetteer," 428; Cunningham, "Archæological Reports," ix. 142; xviii. 5; "Indian Antiquary," vi. 360; "Bombay Gazetteer," xii. 449; compare Tylor, "Primitive Culture," i. 394 sq.; Wright, "History of Nepâl," 175; "Folk-lore," i. 524.

shahr District was built by demons; Baliya in Pilibhît was the work of Bali, the Daitya; the demon Loha or Lohajangha built Lohâban in Mathura.[1] In the same way the Cornish giants built chiefly in granite, and the Hack and Cast embankment was constructed by them.[2] In Patna the Asura Jarâsandha is the reputed builder of an enormous embankment which is called Asuren after him, and another demon of the same class is said to be the architect of an ancient fortification in Puraniya.[3]

Many buildings, again, are attributed to personages who succeeded in getting an Asura under their influence, and being obliged to find work for him, compelled him to occupy his time in architecture. In the "Lay of the Last Minstrel" Michael Scott got out of the dilemma by making the demons twist ropes of sand, and the same tale is told of Tregeagle in Cornwall.[4]

MODERN RÂKSHASAS.

Râkshasas are developed even in these prosaic days of ours. In the folk-tales many human beings lie under the well-founded suspicion of being Asuras or Râkshasas.[5] The ghost of some Musalmâns is believed by some Hindus to become a most malignant Râkshasa. Such a ghost is conciliated by being addressed by the euphemistic title of Mamduh, "the praised one." Visaladeva, the famous King of Ajmer, was turned into a Râkshasa on account of his oppression of his subjects, in which condition he resumed the evil work of his earthly existence, "devouring his subjects," until one of his grandchildren offered himself as a victim to appease his hitherto insatiable appetite. "The language of innocent affection," says Col. Tod, "made its way to the heart of the Râkshasa, who recognized his offspring, and winged his flight to the Jumnâ."[6]

[1] Führer, "Monumental Antiquities," 7, 40, 103.
[2] Hunt, "Popular Romances," 43, 75.
[3] Buchanan, "Eastern India," i. 88; iii. 56.
[4] Grimm, "Household Tales," ii. 413; Hunt, *loc. cit.*, 136.
[5] Knowles, "Folk-tales of Kashmîr," 423.
[6] Annals, ii. 382, note; Wright, "History of Nepâl," 86.

Young men who are obliged to travel at night have reason to be cautious of the Râkshasî, as well as of the Churel, with whom she is occasionally identified. She takes the form of a lovely woman and lures her victims to destruction.

BRÂHMAN GHOSTS.

We have already mentioned the Brahm or malignant Brâhman ghost. These often develop into Râkshasas, and are a particularly dangerous species. Thus the sept of Gaur Râjputs are haunted by the Râkshasa or ghost of the Brâhman Mansa Râm, who, on account of the tyranny of the Râja Tej Sinh, committed suicide. He lives in a tree in a fort in the Sîtapur District, and no marriage or any other important business in the family of the Râja is undertaken until he has been duly propitiated.[1] So, at the mound of Bilsar in the Etah District, there lived a Râja whose house overlooked that of a Brâhman named Pûran Mall. The Brâhman asked the Râja to change the position of his sitting-room, as it was inconvenient to the ladies of his family, and when the request was refused, poisoned himself with a dose of opium. His body turned blue like indigo, and he became a most malignant demon or Bîr, known as the Brahm Râkshasa, which caused the death of the Râja and his family, and forced his successors to remove to a distance from their original family residence.

THE DEO.

Closely connected with the Râkshasas are various classes of demons, known as Deo, Dâno, or Bîr. The Deo is a survival of the Devas or "shining ones" of the old mythology. It is another of the terms which have suffered grievous degradation. It was originally applied to the thirty-three great divinities, eleven of which inhabited each of the three worlds. Now the term represents a vague class of the demon-ogre family. The Deo is a cannibal, and were he not

[1] "North Indian Notes and Queries," iii. 71.

exceedingly stupid could do much harm, but in the folk-tales he is always being deceived in the most silly way. He has long lips, one of which sticks up in the air, while the other hangs down pendant. Like many of his kinsfolk all over the world, he is a potent cause of tempests.[1]

The Bîr.

The Bîr, who takes his name from the Sanskrit Vîra, "hero," is a very malignant village demon. In one of the Mirzapur villages is the shrine of Kharbar Bîr, or "the noisy hero." No one can give any satisfactory account of him, but it is quite certain that if he is not propitiated by the Baiga, he brings disease on men and cattle. Gendâ Bîr, a woman who was tired of life, and, instead of burning herself, threw herself down from a tree, is worshipped at Nâgpur.[2] Kerâr Bîr has, according to the last census returns, thirty-one thousand worshippers in the eastern districts of the North-West Provinces. He is said to have been a demon who resided on the spot where the present fort of Jaunpur now stands. He became such a pest to the country about, that the great Râma Chandra warred against him and overcame him. His head and limbs he flung to the four corners of heaven, and his trunk in the form of a shapeless mass of stone remains as a memorial and is worshipped. Some allege that he was really some hero of the aboriginal Bhar race who fell in battle with the Aryan. It is also alleged that when the British engineers attempted to blow down the fort their mines failed to disturb the shrine of Kerâr, whose importance has been much increased by this example of his prowess.[3] In Bombay there are seven Bîrs who go about together and scour the fields and gardens at night.[4]

[1] Lâl Bihâri Dê, "Folk-tales," 257; Miss Stokes, "Fairy Tales," 273, 291; Tylor, "Primitive Culture," ii. 98 sq., 378; Hunt, "Popular Romances," 55.
[2] Cunningham, "Archæological Reports," xvii. 1.
[3] "North Indian Notes and Queries," ii. 1.
[4] "Gazetteer," xi. 308.

THE DÂNO.

The Dâno represents the Dânava of the early mythology. Of these there are seven also, and the leader of them is Vritra, who is the ancestor of the dragons and keeps back and steals the heavenly waters, on which account Indra slays him with his thunderbolt. Vala, the cave in which the rain cows are hidden, is called the brother of Vritra. No trace remains now of this beautiful weather myth. The Dâno nowadays is hardly to be distinguished from the Bîr and his brethren, and at Hazâribâgh he is worshipped in the form of a stone daubed with five streaks of red lead and set up outside the house.[1]

THE DAITYA.

So with the Dait or Daitya, who is connected in nothing but name with the demons of the olden world who warred with the gods. In Mirzapur he lives in a tree; in front he looks like a man, but seen from behind he is quite hollow, only a mere husk without a backbone. In this he resembles the Ellekone of Denmark, who is beautiful in front, but hollow in the back like a kneading trough.[2] So the Hadal or Hedali of Bombay is said to be plump in front and a skeleton behind.[3]

At midnight the Daitya shows himself in his tree in a flash of fire and smoke, and sometimes flies off to another tree a short distance off.

In Mirzapur he is sometimes known as Daitra Bîr and is associated with two others named Akata Bîr and Latora Bîr, all of whom live in trees and go out at night and dance for a while with torches in their hands. They are worshipped with an offering consisting of the Kalsa or holy water-pots and some greens.[4] In one village the Daitya is known as Beohâr Bâba or the "father of merchandise," as

[1] Risley, "Tribes and Castes of Bengal," i. 303.
[2] Grimm, "Teutonic Mythology," ii. 449.
[3] Campbell, "Notes," 150.
[4] "North Indian Notes and Queries," iii. 57, 80, 130.

he is supposed in some way to guard merchants. Col. Tod describes a place in the table-land of Central India known as Daitya kâ har or "the demon's bone," on which those who are in search of ease jump from above. Although most of the leapers perish, some instances of escape are recorded. The hope of obtaining offspring is said to be the most usual motive for the act.[1] Instances of religious suicides are common. One of the most famous places for this is behind the peak of Kedâr, where the Pandavas devoted themselves and were carried off to heaven. The practice seems to have almost completely ceased under British rule.

THE HEADLESS HORSEMAN.

At the present time the most dreaded of these creatures is, perhaps, the Headless Horseman, who is popularly known as Dûnd, or "truncated."

He has many of his kindred in other lands. Sir Francis Drake used to drive a hearse into Plymouth with headless horses and followed by yelling hounds. Coluinn gun Cheann of the Highlands goes about a headless trunk. A coach without horses used to career about the neighbourhood of Listowel when any misfortune was about to take place. A monster in one of the German tales carries about his head under his arm.[2]

By one account the Dûnd took his origin from the wars of the Mahâbhârata. However this may be, he appears periodically in the form of a headless trunk seated on horseback, with his head tied before him on the pommel of the saddle. He makes his rounds at night and calls to the householder from outside; but woe to any one who answers him, for this means death. The belief in these visionary death summonses is very common. The Irish Banshee howls at night and announces death. In Mirzapur, Bâghesar, or the tiger demon, lives on the Churni Hill. He

[1] "Annals," ii. 681.

[2] Hunt, "Popular Romances," 145, 244; Campbell, "Popular Tales," ii. 101; "Folk-lore," iv. 352; Grimm, "Household Tales," i. 346.

sometimes comes down at night in human form, and calls people by name at their doors. If any one answers him he becomes sick. The Bengâli personifies Nisi or Night as the Homeric Greeks did.[1] She often comes at midnight, calls the house-master, who when he opens the door falls senseless and follows her where she will. Sometimes she takes him into a tank and drowns him, or leads him into a dense forest and drops him among thorns or on the top of some high tree. In fact it is always very dangerous to speak to these spirits or ghosts. Falstaff knew this well when he said, "They are fairies; he that speaks to them shall die."

The Dûnd makes occasional incursions throughout the country. He was in the neighbourhood of Agra in 1882, and some twelve years after appeared in Mirzapur. On both occasions the news of his arrival caused considerable alarm. Every one shut up their houses at sunset, and no one on any consideration would answer a call from outside after nightfall. It was shrewdly suspected at the time that this rumour was spread by some professional burglar who made a harvest while the scare lasted.

Somewhat akin to the Dûnd is the spectral Râja of Bûndi who occasionally appears in the neighbourhood of Sahâranpur. Some years ago a Brâhman astrologer heard some one calling him from outside one night. When he answered the summons he was told that the Râja of Bûndi wanted to have his horoscope examined and was then encamped near the town. The Pandit proceeded to the place with the guide and saw a splendid encampment, and the Râja in his royal robes sitting in a tent ornamented with pearls. When he saw him the unfortunate astrologer knew that he was a Râkshasa, and he was the more convinced of this when he examined his horoscope and found that he was fated to live for ever. He told the Râja that his life would be long and prosperous, and after receiving three gold coins as his fee went home more dead than alive. Next morning he went

[1] Lâl Bihâri Dê, "Govinda Sâmanta," i. 9; "North Indian Notes and Queries," iii. 199.

to the place, but could find no sign of the camp, and when he looked in his box the coins were found to have disappeared.

There are numerous other versions of the Headless Horseman story in Northern India. In a fight at Khândesh the Gâoli prince engaged in personal conflict with the saint Sayyid Saadat Pîr, and struck off his head. The headless body continued to fight, and the Hindu army fled in panic. The trunk then snatched up the head and led the victorious troops to a neighbouring hill, where the earth opened and swallowed it.[1] So, in Oudh, Malik Ambar, the companion of Sâlâr Masaud, was, it is said, killed with his master at Bahrâich, but wandering back from Bijnor, a headless trunk on horseback, he at length reached the place where his tomb now stands, when the earth opened and received him and his horse.[2]

The Dûnd is apparently a close relation of the Skandhahâta of Bengal, who goes about with his head cut off from the shoulders. He dwells in low moist lands outside a village, in bogs and fens, and goes about in the dark, rolling about on the ground, with his long arms stretched out. Woe betide the belated peasant who falls within his grasp.[3]

THE GHOSTLY ARMY.

Closely connected with this are the numerous legends of the Ghostly Army. Thus, at Faizâbâd, the country people point out a portion of the Queen's highway along which they will not pass at night. They say that after dark the road is thronged with troops of headless horsemen, the dead of the army of Prince Sayyid Sâlâr. The great host moves on with a noiseless tread; the ghostly horses make no sound; and no words of command are shouted to the headless squadrons. Another version comes from Ajmer. There for some time past a troop of four or five hundred

[1] "Bombay Gazetteer," xxv. 457.
[2] "Oudh Gazetteer," i. 308, 311.
[3] Lal Behâri Dê, "Govinda Sâmanta," i. 158.

horsemen, armed and dressed in green, issue from a valley in the neighbourhood of the city, and after riding about for some time, mysteriously disappear. They are believed to be the escort of the Imâm Husain, whose tragical fate is commemorated at the Muharram.

The same idea prevails all through India, and indeed all the world over. The persons killed at a recent disastrous railway accident haunt the locality, and have caused the breakdown of other trains at the same place.[1] The ghosts of the battle of Chiliânwâla began to appear very shortly after the battle, and Abul Fazl mentions the ghosts of Pânipat in the days of Akbar.[2] In America the anniversaries of the battles of Bunker's Hill, Concord, Saratoga, and even as late as that of Gettysburg, are celebrated by spectral armies, who fight by night the conflict o'er again.[3] If you walk nine times round Neville's Cross, you will hear the noise of the battle and the clash of armour, and the same tale is told of the battle of Marathon, which a recent prosaic authority attributes to the beating of the waves on the shore, while others say that these spectral armies of the sky are nothing more than wild geese or other migratory birds calling in the darkness.[4]

MASÂN.

Masân, the modern form of the Sanskrit Smasâna, "a place of cremation," is the general term for those evil spirits which haunt the place where they were forced to abandon their tenements of clay. So the modern Italian Lemuri are the spirits of the churchyard and represent the Lemures or Larvæ, the unhappy ghosts of those who have died evil deaths or under a ban, to which there are innumerable allusions in the Latin writers.[5] In India Masân is very generally regarded as the ghost of a child, and we have

[1] "North Indian Notes and Queries," iii. 180.
[2] Cunningham, "Archæological Reports," xx. 96.
[3] Leland, "Etruscan Roman Remains," 213.
[4] Henderson, "Folk-lore of the Northern Counties," 308; Grote, "History of Greece," iv. 285; "Folk-lore," i. 167.
[5] Leland, *loc. cit.*, 95.

already seen that some tribes regard an infant as a Bhût. He is occasionally the ghost of a low-caste man, very often that of an oilman, who, possibly from the dirt which accompanies his trade, is considered ill-omened. By another account such ghosts prowl about in villages in the Hills in the form of bears and other wild animals.[1] Others say that Masân is of black and hideous appearance, comes from the ashes of a funeral pyre, and chases people as they pass by. Some die of fright from his attacks, others linger for a few days, and some even go mad. "When a person becomes possessed of Masân, the people invoke the beneficent spirit of the house to come and take possession of some member of the family, and all begin to dance. At length some one works himself up into a state of frenzy, and commences to torture and belabour the body of the person possessed by Masân, until at length a cure is effected, or the patient perishes under this drastic treatment." Khabish resembles Masân in his malignant nature and his fondness for burial grounds. He is also met with in dark glens and forests in various shapes. Sometimes he imitates the bellow of a buffalo, or the cry of a goatherd or neatherd, and sometimes he grunts like a pig. At other times he assumes the disguise of a religious mendicant and joins travellers on their way; but his conversation is, like that of ordinary Bhûts, always unintelligible. Like Masân, he often frightens people and makes them ill, and sometimes possesses unfortunate travellers who get benighted.[2]

Children afflicted by Masân are said to be "under his shadow" (*chhâya*), and waste away by a sort of consumption. Here we have another instance of the principle already referred to, that the shadow represents the actual soul.[3] This malady is believed to be due to some enemy flinging the ashes from a funeral pyre over the child. The remedy in such cases is to weigh the child in salt, a well-known demon scarer, and give it away in charity. The cremation

[1] Traill, "Asiatic Researches," xvi. 137 sq.
[2] Atkinson, "Himâlayan Gazetteer," ii. 820.
[3] Tylor, "Primitive Culture," i. 428 sq.

ground and the bones and ashes which it contains are constantly used in various kinds of magical rites. It is believed when thieves enter a house, that they throw over the inmates some Masân or ashes from a pyre and make them unconscious while the robbery is going on. This resembles the English "Hand of Glory," to which reference will be made in another connection. As to the influence by means of the shadow, it may be noted that a Nepâl legend describes how a Lâma arrested the flight of a Brâhman by piercing his shadow with a spear, and the Râkshasî Sinhikâ used to seize the shadow of the object she desired to devour and so drag the prey into her jaws.[1]

TOLA.

Tola is a sort of "Will-o'-the-Wisp" in the Hills. According to one account, he is, like the Gayâl, of whom we have spoken already, the ghost of a bachelor, and other ghosts refuse to associate with him; so he is seen only in wild and solitary places. Others say that he belongs to the class of children ghosts, who have died too young to undergo the rites of tonsure or cremation. They are, as a rule, harmless, and are not much dreaded. After a child undergoes the specified religious ceremonies, its soul is matured, and fitted either to join the spirits of the sainted dead or to assume a new existence by transmigration. The estate of the Tola is only temporary, and after a time, it, too, enters another form of existence.[2]

AIRI.

Another famous Hill Bhût is Airi. He is the ghost of some one who was killed in hunting. We have many instances of these huntsmen ghosts, of which the most familiar example is the European legend of the Wild Huntsman, who haunts the forest in which he used to hunt,

[1] Wright, "History," 153; Frazer, "Golden Bough," i. 142.
[2] Traill, "Asiatic Researches," xvi. 137 sq.; "North Indian Notes and Queries," ii. 27.

and is sometimes heard hallooing to his dogs. So in Cornwall Dando rides about accompanied with his hounds.[1] The British fairies ride at night on horses which they steal from the stables, and in the morning the poor beasts are found covered with sweat and foam.[2] In Southern India Aiyanâr rides about the land at night on a wild elephant, sword in hand, and surrounded by torch-bearers, to clear the country from all obnoxious spirits.[3]

The companions of Airi are fairies, who, like the Churel, have their feet turned backwards. He is accompanied by two litter-bearers and a pack of hounds with bells round their necks. Whoever hears their bark is certain to meet with calamity. Airi is much given to expectoration, and his saliva is so venomous that it wounds those on whom it falls. Incantations must be used and the affected part rubbed with the branch of a tree. If this be not done at once, the injured man dies, and in any case he must abstain from rich food for several days. We shall meet again with the magical power of spittle. Here it may be noted that in Western folk-lore it confers the power of seeing spirits.

"Those who see Airi face to face are burnt up by the flash of his eye, or are torn to pieces by his dogs, or have their livers extracted and eaten by the fairies who accompany him. But should any one be fortunate enough to survive, the Bhût discloses hidden treasures to him. The treasure-trove thus disclosed varies in value from gold coins to old bones. His temples are always in deserted places. A trident represents the god, and a number of surrounding stones his followers. He is worshipped once a year by lighting a bonfire, round which all the people sit. A kettle-drum is played, and one after another they become possessed, and leap and shout round the fire. Some brand themselves with heated iron spoons, and sit in the flames. Those who escape burning are believed to be truly possessed, while those who are burned are considered mere pretenders

[1] Hunt, "Popular Romances," 223.
[2] Brand, "Observation," 571.
[3] Oppert, "Original Inhabitants," 505.

to divine frenzy."[1] This closely resembles the worship of Râhu already described.

"The revels usually last for about ten nights, and until they are ended, a lamp is kept burning at the shrine of the god. Those possessed dye a yard of cloth in red ochre and bind it round their heads, and carry a wallet in which they place the alms they receive. While in this state they bathe twice, and eat but once in the twenty-four hours. They allow no one to touch them, as they consider other men unclean, and no one but themselves is permitted to touch the trident and stones in Airi's temple, at least as long as the festival lasts. The offerings, goats, milk, etc., are consumed by the worshippers. The kid is marked on the forehead with red, and rice and water are thrown over him. If he shakes himself to get rid of it, the god has accepted the offering, whereupon his head is severed with a knife. If he does not shake himself, or bleats, it is a sign that the offering is not accepted, and the victim escapes."

The same rule of testing the suitability of the sacrifice prevailed among the Greeks. The same practice prevails among other tribes. Thus, the Bâwariyas, when they sacrifice a goat, take a little water in the palm of the hand and pour it on the nose of the victim. If it shiver, its head is cut off with a single blow of a sword. The rule has elsewhere received a further development. Thus when the Râo of Cutch sacrifices a buffalo, "as it stoops to eat, a few drops of water are scattered between its horns. If it shake its head it is led away as displeasing to the goddess; if it nods its head a glittering scimitar descends on its neck."[2]

HILL DEMONS.

Other Bhûts in the Hills are Acheri, the ghosts of little girls, who live on the tops of mountains, but descend at night to hold their revels in more convenient places. To

[1] Atkinson, "Himâlayan Gazetteer," ii. 825 sqq.; Madden, "Journal Asiatic Society Bengal," 1847, p. 599 sqq.

[2] "Panjâb Notes and Queries," i. 120; iii. 171.

fall in with their train is fatal, and they have a particular antipathy to red colour. When little girls fall suddenly ill, the Acheri is supposed to have cast her shadow over them. The Deo are the regular demons already described; some are obnoxious to men, some to cattle. The Rûniya moves about at night and uses a huge rock as his steed, the clattering of which announces his approach. He is the demon of the avalanche and landslip. Should he take a fancy to a woman, she is haunted by his spirit in her dreams, and gradually wasting away, finally falls a victim to her passion. He thus resembles the Faun and the Satyr, the Incubus and Succubus, against whose wiles and fascination the Roman maiden was warned.[1]

BIRTH FIENDS.

Another of these night fiends is the Jilaiya of Bihâr, which takes the shape of a night bird, and is able to suck the blood of any person whose name it hears. Hence women are very careful not to call their children at night. It is believed that if this bird fly over the head of a pregnant woman her child will be born a weakling.[2]

Hence it closely approximates to the birth fiends which beset the mother and child during the period of impurity after parturition. Thus the Orâons of Chota Nâgpur believe that the fiend Chordevan comes in the form of a cat and tears the mother's womb.[3] The Brâhman, Prabhu, and other high-caste women of Bombay believe that on the fifth and sixth night after birth the mother and child are liable to be attacked by the birth spirit Satvâî, who comes in the shape of a cat or a hen. Consequently they keep a watch in the lying-in room during the whole night, passing the time in playing, singing and talking to scare the fiend. The Marâthas of Nâsik believe that on the fifth night, at about twelve o'clock, the spirit Sathî, accompanied by a male fiend,

[1] Traill, "Asiatic Researches," xvi. 137; Atkinson, *loc. cit.*, ii. 831; Leland, "Etruscan Roman Remains," 101.

[2] Grierson, "Behâr Peasant Life," 408.

[3] Dalton, "Descriptive Ethnology," 251.

called Burmiya, comes to the lying-in room, and making the mother insensible, either kills or disfigures the child. The Vadâls of Thâna think that on the fifth night the birth spirit Sathî comes in the form of a cat, hen, or dog, and devours the heart and skull of the child. They therefore surround the bed with strands of a creeper, place an iron knife or scythe on the mother's cot, fire in an iron bickern at the entrance of the lying-in room, and keep a watch for the night. The customs all through Northern India are very much of the same type. It is essential that the fire should be kept constantly burning, lest the spirit of evil, stepping over the cold ashes, should enter and make its fatal mark on the forehead of the child. The whole belief turns on the fear of infantile lockjaw, which is caused by the use of foul implements in cutting the umbilical cord and the neglect of all sanitary precautions. It usually comes between the fifth and twelfth day, and as Satvâî, or the Chhathî of Northern India, has been raised to the dignity of a goddess. All this is akin to the belief in fairy changelings and the malignant influences which surround the European mother and her child.[1]

THE PARÎ AND JINN.

Little reference has yet been made to the Parî or fairies, or the Jinn or genii, because they are, in their present state at least, of exotic origin, though their original basis was possibly laid on Indian soil. Thus we have the Apsaras, who in name at least, "moving in the water," is akin to Aphrodite. They appear only faintly in the Veda as the nymphs of Indra's heaven, and the chief of them is Urvasî, to whom reference has been already made. Two of them, Rambhâ and Menakâ, are shown as luring austere sages from their devotions, as in the Irish legend of Glendalough. They are the wives or mistresses of the Gandharvas, the singers and musicians who attend the banquets of the gods.

[1] Campbell, "Notes," 387; Hartland, "Science of Fairy Tales," 93 sqq.

Indra in the Rig Veda is the giver of women, and he provides one of his aged friends with a young wife.[1] Rambhâ, one of the fairies of his court, appears constantly in the tales of Somadeva, and descends in human form to the arms of her earthly lovers, as Titania with Bottom in the "Midsummer Night's Dream." Their successor in the modern tales is Shâhpasand, "The beloved of the king," who takes the shape of a pigeon and kisses the beautiful hero. In one of the stories which appears in many forms, the youth with the help of a Faqîr finds his way to the dance of Râja Indra, takes the place of his drummer, and wins the fairy, whom he identifies in spite of the many schemes which the jovial god invents to deceive him. These ladies are all of surpassing beauty, skilled in music and the dance, with white skins, and always dressed in red.

With the Jinn we reach a chapter of folk-lore of great extent and complexity. They are probably in origin closely allied to the Râkshasa, Deo and his kindred.[2] They are usually divided into the Jann, who are the least powerful of all the Jinn, the Shaitân or Satan of the Hebrews, the Ifrît and the Mârid, the last of whom rules the rest. The Jann, according to the Prophet, were created out of a smokeless fire. The Jann is sometimes identified with the serpent, and sometimes with Iblîs, who has been imported direct from the Greek Diabolos. The Jinn were the pre-Adamite rulers of the world, and for their sins were overcome by the angels, taken prisoners and driven to distant islands. They appear as serpents, lions, wolves or jackals. One kind rules the land, another the air, a third the sea. There are forty troops of them, each consisting of six hundred thousand. Some have wings and fly, others move like snakes and dogs, others go about like men. They are of gigantic stature, sometimes resplendently handsome, sometimes horridly hideous. They can become invisible and move on earth when they please. Sometimes one of them is shut up in a jar under the seal of the Lord Solomon who rules them.

1 "Rig Veda," iv. 17, 16; i. 51, 13.
2 Burton, "Arabian Nights," i. 9, note.

They ride the whirlwind like Indian demons, and direct the storm. Their chief home is the mountains of Qâf, which encompass the earth.

THE GHOUL.

Besides these there is a host of minor demons, such as the Ghûl, the English Ghoul, who is a kind of Shaitân, eats men, and is variously described as a Jinn or as an enchanter. By one tradition, when the Shaitân attempt by stealth to hear the words of men, they are struck by shooting stars, some are burnt, some fall into the sea and become crocodiles, and some fall upon the land and become Ghûls. The Ghûl is properly a female, and the male is Qutrub. They are the offspring of Iblîs and his wife. The Silât or Silâ lives in forests, and when it captures a man makes him dance and plays with him, as the cat plays with the mouse. Similar to this creature is the Ghaddâr, who tortures and terrifies men, the Dalhâm, who is in the form of a man and rides upon an ostrich, and the Shiqq or Nasnâs, who are ogres and vampires. But these are little known in Indian folk-lore, except that directly imported from Arabic sources.[1]

THE BAGHAUT.

As an instance of the respect paid to the ghosts of those who have perished by an untimely death, we may mention the Baghaut. According to the last census returns some eight thousand persons recorded themselves as worshippers in the North-Western Provinces of Bagahu or Sapaha, the ghosts of people killed by tigers or snakes. The Baghaut is usually erected on the place where a man was killed by a tiger, but it sometimes merges into the common form of shrine, as in a case given by Dr. Buchanan, where a person received the same honour because he had been killed by the aboriginal Kols.[2] The shrine is generally a heap of stones or branches

[1] Hughes, "Dictionary of Islâm," s.v. Genii; Burton, "Arabian Nights," passim.

[2] "Eastern India," i. 106.

near some pathway in the jungle. Every passer-by adds to the pile, which is in charge of the Baiga or aboriginal priest, who offers upon it a pig, or a cock, or some spirits, and lights a little lamp there occasionally. Many such shrines are to be found in the Mirzapur jungles. In the Central Provinces they are known as Pât, a term applied in Chota Nâgpur to holy heights dedicated to various divinities.[1] They are usually erected in a place where a man has been killed by a tiger or by a snake; sometimes no reason whatever is given for their selection. "In connection with these shrines they have a special ceremony for laying the ghost of a tiger. Until it is gone through, neither Gond nor Baiga will go into the jungles if he can help it, as they say not only does the spirit of the dead man walk, but the tiger is also possessed, for the nonce, with an additional spirit of evil (by the soul of the dead man entering into him) which increases his power of intelligence and ferocity, rendering him more formidable than usual, and more eager to pursue his natural enemy, man. Some of the Baigas are supposed to be gifted with great powers of witchcraft, and it is common for a Baiga medicine man to be called in to bewitch the tigers and prevent them carrying off the village cattle. The Gonds thoroughly believe in the powers of these men."[2]

I myself came across a singular instance of this some time ago. I was asking a Baiga of the Chero tribe what he could do in this way, but I found him singularly reticent on the subject. I asked the Superintendent of the Dudhi Estate, who was with me, to explain the reason. "Well," he answered, "when I came here first many years ago, a noted Baiga came to me and proposed to do some witchcraft to protect me from tigers, which were very numerous in the neighbourhood at the time. I told him that I could look after myself, and advised him to do the same. That night a tiger seized the wretched Baiga while he was on his way home, and all that was found of him were some scraps of cloth and

[1] Dalton, "Descriptive Ethnology," 132.
[2] "Central Provinces Gazetteer," 280.

pieces of bone. Since then I notice that the Baigas of these parts do not talk so loudly of their power of managing tigers when I am present."

THE CHUREL.

More dreaded even than the ghost of a man who has been killed by a tiger is the Churel, a name which has been connected with that of the Chûhra or sweeper caste. The ghosts of all low-caste people are notoriously malignant, an idea which possibly arises from their connection with the aboriginal faith, which was treated half with fear and half with contempt by their conquerors. The corpses of such people are either cremated or buried face downwards, in order to prevent the evil spirit from escaping and troubling its neighbours. So, it was the old custom in Great Britain in order to prevent the spirit of a suicide from "walking" and becoming a terror to the neighbourhood, to turn the coffin upside down and thrust a spear through it and the body which it contained so as to fix it to the ground.[1] Riots have taken place and the authority of the magistrates has been invoked to prevent a sweeper from being buried in the ordinary way.[2]

The Churel, who corresponds to the Jakhâî, Jokhâî, Mukâî, or Navalâî of Bombay,[3] is the ghost of a woman dying while pregnant, or on the day of the child's birth, or within the prescribed period of impurity. The superstition is based on the horror felt by all savages at the blood, or even touch of a woman who is ceremonially impure.[4] The idea is, it is needless to say, common in India. The woman in her menses is kept carefully apart, and is not allowed to do cooking or any domestic work until she has undergone the purification by bathing and changing her garments. Some of the Drâvidian tribes refuse to allow a woman in this condition to touch the house-thatch, and she is obliged to creep through

[1] Hunt, "Popular Romances," 253.
[2] Ibbetson, "Panjâb Ethnography," 117. [3] Campbell, "Notes," 149.
[4] Frazer, "Golden Bough," i. 185, 187; ii. 238.

a narrow hole in the back wall whenever she has to leave the house. Hence, too, the objection felt by men to walk under walls or balconies where women may be seated and thus convey the pollution. From Kulu, on the slopes of the Himâlayas, a custom is reported which is probably connected with this principle and with the rules of the Couvade, to which reference will be made later on. When a woman who is pregnant dies, her husband is supposed to have committed some sin, and he is deemed unclean for a time. He turns a Faqîr and goes on pilgrimage for a month or so, and, having bathed in some sacred place, is re-admitted into caste. The woman is buried, the child having been first removed from her body by one of the Dâgi caste, and her death is not considered a natural one under any circumstances.[1]

The Churel is particularly malignant to her own family. She appears in various forms. Sometimes she is fair in front and black behind, but she invariably has her feet turned round, heels in front and toes behind. The same idea prevails in many other places. The Gira, a water-spirit of the Konkan, has his feet turned backwards.[2] In the Teignmouth story of the Devil he leaves his backward footsteps in the snow. Pliny so describes Anthropophagi of Mount Imœus, and Megasthenes speaks of a similar race on Mount Nilo.[3]

She generally, however, assumes the form of a beautiful young woman and seduces youths at night, especially those who are good-looking. She carries them off to some kingdom of her own, and if they venture to eat the food offered to them there, she keeps them till they lose their manly beauty and then sends them back to the world grey-haired old men, who, like Rip Van Winkle, find all their friends dead long ago.

So the Lady of the Lake won Merlin to her arms.[4] The same idea prevails in Italy, but there the absence is only temporary. "Among the wizards and witches are even

[1] "North Indian Notes and Queries," iii. 204.
[2] Campbell, "Notes," 156.
[3] Tylor, "Primitive Culture," i. 307; Pliny, "Natural History," vii. 2.
[4] Rhys, "Lectures," 156.

princes and princesses, who to conceal their debauchery and dishonour take the goat form and carry away partners for the dance, bearing them upon their backs, and so they fly many miles in a few minutes, and go with them to distant cities and other places, where they feast, dance, drink, and make love. But when day approaches they carry their partners home again, and when they wake they think they have had pleasant dreams. But indeed their diversion was more real than they supposed."[1] So, the Manxmen tell of a man who was absent from his people for four years, which he spent with the fairies. He could not tell how he returned, but it seemed as if, having been unconscious, he woke up at last in this world.[2] I had a smart young butler at Etah, who once described to me vividly the narrow escape he had from the fascinations of a Churel, who lived on a Pîpal tree near the cemetery. He saw her sitting on the wall in the dusk and entered into conversation with her; but he fortunately observed her tell-tale feet and escaped. He would never go again by that road without an escort. So, the fairies of England and Ireland look with envy on the beautiful boys and girls, and carry them off to fairyland, where they keep them till youth and beauty have departed.

EATING FOOD IN SPIRIT LAND.

The consequences of rashly eating the food of the underworld are well known. The reason is that eating together implies kinship with the dwellers in the land of spirits, and he who does so never returns to the land of men.[3]

The Churel superstition appears in other forms. Thus, the Korwas of Mirzapur say that if a woman dies in the delivery-room, she becomes a Churel, but they do not know, or do not care to say, what finally becomes of her. The Patâris and Majhwârs think that if a woman dies within the

[1] Leland, "Etruscan Roman Remains," 158.
[2] "Folk-lore," ii. 288; Lady Wilde, "Legends," 7, 39.
[3] Tawney, "Katha Sarit Sâgara," ii. 198; Hartland, "Science of Fairy Tales," 42.

period of pregnancy or uncleanness, she becomes a Churel. She appears in the form of a pretty little girl in white clothes, and seduces them away to the mountains, until the Baiga is called in to sacrifice a goat and release her victim. The Bhuiyârs go further and say that little baby girls who die before they are twenty days old become Churels. They live in stones in the mountains and cause pain to men. The remedy is for the afflicted one to put some rice and barley on his head, turn round two or three times, and shake off the grain in the direction of the jungle, when she releases her victim. The idea seems to be that with these holy grains, which are scarers of demons, the evil influence is dispersed. But she continues to visit him, and requires propitiation. Among these people the Churel has been very generally enrolled among the regular village godlings and resides with them in the common village shrine, where she receives her share of the periodical offerings. Any one who sees a Churel is liable to be attacked by a wasting disease, and, as in the case of the Dûnd, to answer her night summons brings death.

MODES OF REPELLING THE CHUREL.

There are fortunately various remedies which are effective in preventing a woman who dies under these circumstances from becoming a Churel. One way is that practised by the Majhwârs of Mirzapur, which resembles that for laying the evil spirit of a sweeper, to which reference has been made already. They do not cremate the body, but bury it, fill the grave with thorns and pile heavy stones above to keep down the ghost.

Among the Bhandâris of Bengal, when a pregnant woman dies before delivery, her body is cut open and the child taken out, both corpses being buried in the same grave.[1] In Bombay, when a woman dies in pregnancy, her corpse, after being bathed and decked with flowers and ornaments, is carried to the burning ground. There her husband

[1] Risley, "Tribes and Castes," i. 94.

sprinkles water on her body from the points of a wisp of the sacred Darbha grass and repeats holy verses. Then he cuts her right side with a sharp weapon and takes out the child. Should it be alive, it is taken home and cared for; should it be dead, it is then and there buried. The hole in the side of the corpse is filled with curds and butter, covered with cotton threads, and then the usual rite of cremation is carried out.[1] In one of the tales of Somadeva, Saktideva cuts the child out of his pregnant wife.[2]

In the Hills, if a woman dies during the menstrual period or in childbirth, the corpse is anointed with the five products of the cow, and special texts are recited. A small quantity of fire is then placed on the chest of the corpse, which is either buried or thrown into flowing water.[3] Here we have the three great demon-scarers,—fire, earth and water, combined. In another device, iron, which has similar virtue, is used. Small round-headed iron spikes, specially made for the purpose, are driven into the nails of the four fingers of the corpse, while the thumbs and great toes are securely fastened together with iron rings. Most Hindus, it may be remarked, tie the corpse to the bier, whatever may have been the cause of death, and in parts of Ireland a thread is tied round the toe of the corpse, the object apparently being to secure the body and prevent an evil spirit from entering it.[4]

In the Hills the place where a pregnant woman died is carefully scraped and the earth removed. The spot is then sown with mustard, which is sprinkled along the road traversed by the corpse on its way to the burial ground. The reason given for this is twofold. First, the mustard blossoms in the world of the dead, and its sweet smell pleases the spirit and keeps her content, so that she does not long to revisit her earthly home; secondly, the Churel rises from her grave at nightfall and seeks to return to her

[1] Campbell, "Notes," 488.
[2] Tawney, "Katha Sarit Sâgara," i. 227.
[3] Atkinson, "Himâlayan Gazetteer," ii. 932.
[4] "Folk-lore," iv. 363.

friends; she sees the minute grains of the mustard scattered abroad and stoops to pick it up, and while so engaged cock-crow comes, she is unable to visit her home, and must return to her grave. This is another instance of the rule that evil spirits move about only at night.

COUNTING.

This counting of the grains of mustard illustrates another principle which is thus explained by Mr. Leland:[1] "A traveller in Persia has observed that the patterns of carpets are made intricate, so that the Evil Eye, resting upon them and following the design, loses its power. This was the motive of all the interlaces of the Celtic and Norse designs. When the witch sees the Sâlagrâma, her glance is at once bewildered with its holes and veins. As I have elsewhere remarked, the herb Rosaloaccio, not the corn poppy, but a kind of small house leek, otherwise called 'Rice of the Goddess of the four Winds,' derives its name from looking, ere it unfolds, like confused grains of rice, and when a witch sees it she cannot enter till she has counted them, which is impossible; therefore it is used to protect rooms from witchcraft." Sarson or mustard is, it may be noted, used as a scarer of demons. In all the principal Hindu ceremonies in Western India, grains of Sarshapa or Sarson (*Sinapis dichotoma*) and parched rice are scattered about to scare fiends. Akbar used to have Sipand or Sarson burnt on a hot plate to keep off the Evil Eye—*Nazar-i-bad*—from his valuable horses.[2]

Though the Churel is regarded with disgust and terror, curiously enough a family of Chauhân Râjputs in Oudh claim one as their ancestress.[3]

THE COUVADE.

In connection with this subject of parturition impurity, the very remarkable custom of the Couvade may be referred to here. This is the rule by which at the birth of a child

[1] "Etruscan Roman Remains," 337.

[2] Blochmann, "Aîn-i-Akbari, i. 139.

[3] "Oudh Gazetteer," ii. 418.

the father is treated as an invalid, instead of or in addition to the mother:—

When Chineses go to bed,
And lie in in their ladies' stead.

Marco Polo, writing of Zardandan, gives a good example:—"When one of their wives has been delivered of a child, the infant is washed and swathed, and then the woman gets up and goes about her household affairs, whilst the husband takes to bed with the child by his side, and so keeps his bed for forty days; and all the kith and kin come to visit her, and keep up a great festivity. They do this because they say the woman has had a bad time of it, and it is but fair that the man should have a share of suffering."[1] Professor Rhys remarks that the gods of Celtic Ireland used to practise the Couvade.[2]

Professor Max Müller thinks that it is clear that the poor husband was at first tyrannized over by his female relations and afterwards frightened into superstition. He then began to make a martyr of himself, till he made himself really ill, or took to bed in self-defence. The custom appears, however, to rest on a much more primitive set of ideas. It partly implies, perhaps, the transition from that social state in which, owing to the laxity of the connection between the sexes, the only recognized form of descent was through the mother, and partly, the kindred conception that the father has more to do with the production of the child than the mother, and that the father must, at the critical period of the baby's existence, exercise particular caution that through his negligence no demoniacal influence may assail the infant.[3]

[1] Yule, "Marco Polo," ii. 70, with note. [2] "Lectures," 626 sq.

[3] The most recent authority on the subject, Mr. Hartland, sums up the matter thus: "It is founded on the belief that the child is a part of the parent; and, just as after apparent severance of hair and nails from the remainder of the body, the bulk is affected by anything which happens to the severed portion, so as well after as before the infant has been severed from the parent's body, and in our eyes has acquired a distinct existence, he will be affected by whatever operates on the parent. Hence whatever the parent ought for the child's sake to do or avoid before severance it is equally necessary to do or avoid after. Gradually, however, as the infant grows and strengthens he becomes able to digest the same food as his parents, and to take part in the ordinary avocations of their

It is curious that in India itself so few actual instances of the Couvade have been discovered. This, however, as Mr. Hartland shows, is not unusual, and the Couvade is not found in the lowest stage of savagery. But that the custom once generally prevailed is quite certain, and in Northern India, at least, it seems to have been masked by special birth ceremonies of great stringency and elaborate detail, but of distinctly later date than the very primitive usage with which we are now concerned.

One instance of the actual Couvade is given by Professor Sir Monier-Williams.[1] Among a very low caste of basket-makers in Gujarât, it is the usual practice for a wife to go about her work immediately after delivery, as if nothing had occurred. "The presiding Mother (Mâtâ) of the tribe is supposed to transfer the weakness to her husband, who takes to his bed and has to be supported for several days with good nourishing food." Again, among the Kols of Chota Nâgpur, father and mother are considered impure for eight days, during which period the members of the family are sent out of the house, and the husband has to cook for his wife. If it be a difficult case of parturition, the malignancy of some spirit of evil is supposed to be at work, and after divination to ascertain his name, a sacrifice is made to appease him.[2] Among many of the Drâvidian tribes of Mirzapur, when the posset or spiced drink is prepared for the mother after her confinement, the father is obliged to drink the first sup of it. Among all these people, the father does not work or leave the house during the period of parturition impurity, and cooks for his wife. When asked why he refrains from work, they simply say that he is so pleased with the safety of his wife and the birth of his child, that he takes a holiday; but some survival of the Couvade is probably at the root of the custom. The same idea prevails in a modified form in Bombay. The Pomaliyas,

lives. Precaution then may be relaxed, and ultimately remitted altogether."—"Legend of Perseus," ii. 406.

[1] "Brâhmanism and Hinduism, 229.

[2] Dalton, "Descriptive Ethnology," 191; Risley, "Tribes and Castes," i. 323; Tylor, "Primitive Culture," i. 84.

gold-washers of South Gujarât, after a birth, take great care of the husband, give him food, and do not allow him to go out; and "when a child is born to a Deshasth Brâhman, he throws himself into a well with all his clothes on, and, in the presence of his wife's relations, lets a couple of drops of honey and butter fall into the mouth of the child."[1]

VARIOUS BIRTH CEREMONIES.

The same idea that the infant is likely to receive demoniacal influences through its father appears to be the explanation of another class of birth ceremonies. In Northern India, in respectable families, the father does not look on the child until the astrologer selects a favourable moment. If the birth occur in the unlucky lunar asterism of Mûl, the father is often not allowed to see his child for years, and has in addition to undergo an elaborate rite of purification, known as Mûla-sânti. So, in Bombay, "the Belgaum Chitpavans do not allow the father to look on the new-born child, but at its reflection in butter. The Dharwâr Radders do not allow the father to see the lamp being waved round the image of Satvâî, the birth goddess. If the father sees it, it is believed that the mother and child will sicken. The Karnâtak Jainas allow anyone to feed the new-born babe with honey and castor oil, except the father. Among the Beni Isrâels, when the boy is being circumcised, the father sits apart covered with a veil. Among the Pûna Musalmâns, friends are called to eat the goat offered as a sacrifice on the birth of a child. All join in the feast except the parents, who may not eat the sacrifice."[2] Probably on the same principle, among most of the lower castes, the father and mother do not eat on the wedding day of their children until the ceremony is over.

PLACES INFESTED BY BHÛTS: BURIAL PLACES.

There are, of course, certain places which are particularly

[1] Campbell, "Notes," 410. [2] Ibid.

infested by Bhûts. To begin with, they naturally infest the neighbourhood of burial places and cremation grounds. This idea is found all over the world. Virgil says:—

> *Moerim, saepe animas imis excire sepulcris,*
> *Atque satas alio vidi traducere messes;*

and Shakespeare in the "Midsummer Night's Dream,"—

> Now it is the time of night
> That graves all gaping wide,
> Every one lets forth its sprite,
> In the church-way paths to glide.

DESERTS.

All deserts, also, are a resort of Bhûts, as the great desert of Lop, where Marco Polo assures us they are constantly seen at night. In the Western Panjâb deserts, during the prairie fires and in the dead of night, the lonely herdsmen used to hear cries arising from the ground, and shouts of *Mâr! Mâr!* "Strike! Strike!" which were ascribed to the spirits of men who had been killed in former frontier raids. Such supernatural sounds were heard by the early settlers within the last fifty years, and, until quite recently, the people were afraid to travel without forming large parties for fear of encountering the supernatural enemies who frequented these uninhabited tracts.[1] So, among the Mirzapur jungle tribes, the wild forests of Sarguja are supposed to be infested with Bhûts, and if any one goes there rashly he is attacked through their influence with diarrhœa and vomiting. The site of the present British Residency at Kathmându in Nepâl was specially selected by the Nepâlese as it was a barren patch, supposed to be the abode of demons. So, in Scotland, the local spirit lives in a patch of untilled ground, known as the "Gudeman's field" or "Cloutie's Croft."[2]

1 "Sirsa Settlement Report," 32.

2 Wright, "History," 15; Yule, "Marco Polo," i. 203; Spencer, "Principles of Sociology," i. 249 sq.; Henderson, "Folk-lore of the Northern Counties," 278.

OWLS AND BATS.

The goblins of the churchyard type very often take the form of owls and bats, which haunt the abodes of the dead. "Screech owls are held unlucky in our days," says Aubrey.[1]

> *Sedit in adverso nocturnus culmine bubo,*
> *Funereosque graves edidit ore sonos.*

The Strix, or screech owl, in Roman folk-lore was supposed to suck the blood of young children. Another form of the word in Latin is Striga, meaning a hag or witch. The Lilith of the Jews, the "night monster" of our latest version of the Old Testament, becomes in the Rabbinical stories Adam's first wife, "the Queen of demons" and murderess of young children, who is the "night hag" of Milton.[2]

The Kumaun owl legend is that they had originally no plumes of their own, and were forced to borrow those of their neighbours, who pursue them if they find them abroad at daylight. Owl's flesh is a powerful love philter, and the eating of it causes a man to become a fool and to lose his memory; hence, women give it to their husbands, that as a result of the mental weakness which it produces they may be able to carry on their flirtations with impunity. On the other hand, the owl is the type of wisdom, and eating the eyeballs of an owl gives the power of seeing in the dark, an excellent example of sympathetic magic. If you put an owl in a room, go in naked, shut the door and feed the bird with meat all night, you acquire magical powers. I once had a native clerk who was supposed to have gone through this ordeal, and was much feared accordingly. Here we have another instance of the nudity charm. In the same way in Gujarât, if a man takes seven cotton threads, goes to a place where an owl is hooting, strips naked, ties a knot at each hoot, and fastens the thread round the right arm of a fever patient, the fever goes away.[3]

[1] "Remaines," 109 sq.; Spencer, *loc. cit.*, i. 329; Farrer, "Primitive Manners," 24, 225 sq.

[2] Isaiah xxxiv. 14; Mayhew, "Academy," June 14th, 1884; Conway, "Demonology," ii. 91 sqq.; Gubernatis, "Zoological Mythology," ii. 202.

[3] Campbell, "Notes," 59.

GHOSTS AND BURIAL GROUNDS.

To return to the connection of ghosts with burial grounds. At Bishesar in the Hills, the Hindu dead from Almora are burnt. The spirits of the departed are supposed to lurk there and are occasionally seen. Sometimes, under the guidance of their leader Bholanâth, whom we have mentioned already, they come, some in palanquins and some on foot, at night, to the Almora Bâzâr and visit the merchants' shops. Death is supposed to follow soon on a meeting with their processions. These ghosts are supposed to be deficient in some of their members. One has no head, another no feet, and so on; but they can all talk and dance.[1]

MUTILATION.

This illustrates another principle about ghosts, that mutilation during life is avoided, as being likely to turn the spirit into a malignant ghost after death. This is the reason that many savages keep the cuttings of their hair and nails, not only to put them out of the way of witches, who might work evil charms by their means, but also that the body when it rises at the Last Day may not be deficient in any part.[2] This also explains the strong feeling among Hindus against decapitation as a form of execution, and the dread which Musalmâns exhibit towards cremation. It also, in all probability, explains the lame demons, which abound all the world over, like Hephaistos, Wayland Smith, the Persian Æshma, the Asmodeus of the book of Tobit, and the Club-footed Devil of Christianity. The prejudice against amputation, based on this idea, is one of the many difficulties which meet our surgeons in India.

GHOSTS OF OLD RUINS.

Another place where ghosts, as might have been expected,

[1] "Journal Asiatic Society Bengal," 1848, p. 609; Benjamin, "Persia," 192; Tylor, "Primitive Culture," i. 451.

[2] Frazer, "Golden Bough," i. 204; Tylor, *loc. cit.*, ii. 230; "Early History," 358; Cox, "Mythology of the Aryan Nations," ii. 327; Conway, "Demonology," i. 18.

resort is in old ruins. Many old buildings are, as we have seen, attributed to the agency of demons, and in any case interference with them is resented by the *Deus loci* who occupies them. This explains the number of old ruined houses which one sees in an Indian town, and with which no one cares to meddle, as they are occupied by the spirits of their former owners. The same idea extends to the large bricks of the ancient buildings which are occasionally disinterred. Dr. Buchanan describes how on one occasion no one would assist him in digging out an ancient stone image. The people told him that a man who had made an attempt to do so some time before had met with sudden death.[1] The landlord of the village stated that he would gladly use the bricks from these ruins, but that he was afraid of the consequences. So, in Bombay, interference with the bricks of an ancient dam brought Guinea worm and dysentery into a village, and some labourers were cut off who meddled with some ancient tombs at Ahmadnagar.[2] General Cunningham, in one of his Reports, describes how on one occasion, when carrying on some excavations, his elephant escaped, and was recovered with difficulty; the people unanimously attributed the disaster to the vengeance of the local ghosts, who resented his proceedings. The people who live in the neighbourhood of the old city of Sahet Mahet are, for the same reason, very unwilling to meddle with its ruins, or even to enter it at night. When Mr. Benett was there, a storm which occurred was generally believed to be a token of the displeasure of the spirits at his intrusion on their domains.[3] The tomb of Shaikh Mîna Shâh at Lucknow was demolished during the Mutiny, and the workmen suffered so much trouble from the wrath of the saint, that when the disturbances were over they collected and rebuilt it at their own expense.

The same theory exists in other countries. Thus, in the Isle of Man, "a good Manx scholar told me how a relative of his had carted the earth from an old burial ground on his

[1] "Eastern India," i. 414. [2] "Bombay Gazetteer," xii. 13; xvii. 703.
[3] "Oudh Gazetteer," iii. 286.

farm and used it as manure for his fields, and how his beasts died afterwards. It is possible for a similar reason that a house in ruins is seldom pulled down and the materials used for other buildings; where that has been done misfortunes have ensued."[1]

In the Konkan it is believed that all treasures buried underground, all the mines of gold, silver, and precious stones, all old caves and all ruined fortresses, are guarded by underground spirits in the shape of a hairy serpent or frog. These spirits never leave their places, and they attack and injure only those persons who come to remove the things which they are guarding.[2] In short, these places are like the Sith Bhruaith mounds in Scotland, which were respected, and it was deemed unlawful and dangerous to cut wood, dig earth there, or otherwise disturb them. In the same way the sites of ancient villages which abound in Northern India are more or less respected. They were abandoned on account of the ravages of war, famine, or pestilence, and are guarded by the spirits of the original owners, these calamities being self-evident proofs of the malignity and displeasure of the local deities.

MINE AND CAVE SPIRITS.

We have already mentioned incidentally the mine spirits. It is not difficult to see why the spirits of mine and cave should be malignant and resent trespass on their territories, because by the nature of the case they are directly in communication with the under-world. In the folk-tales of Somadeva we have more than one reference to a cave which leads to Pâtâla, "the rifted rock whose entrance leads to hell." Others are the entrance to fairy palaces, where dwell the Asura maidens beneath the earth.[3] Of a mine at Patna, Dr. Buchanan writes: "A stone-cutter who was in my service was going into one of the shafts to break a specimen, when the guide, a Muhammadan trader, acquainted

[1] "Folk-lore," iii. 83. [2] Campbell, "Notes," 150 sq.
[3] Tawney, "Katha Sarit Sâgara," i. 446, 558; ii. 197.

CAVE TEMPLE OF ANNAPÛRNÂ.

I. 283.

with the fears of the workmen, pulled him back in alarm, and said, 'Pull off your shoes! Will you profane the abode of the gods?'" Under the same belief, the Cornish miners will allow no whistling underground.[1]

Mr. Spencer suggests that the respect for caves is based on the early practice of burial in such places.[2] At any rate, the belief is very general that spirits and deities live in caves. There is a whole cycle of fairy legend centring round the belief that some of the heroes of old live in caves surrounded by their faithful followers, and will arise some day to win back their kingdom. Thus, Bruce and his enchanted warriors lie in a cave in Rathlin Island, and one day they will arise and win back the island for Scotland.[3] The same tale is told of Arthur, Karl the Great, Barbarossa, and many other heroes. The same tale appears in Oriental folk-lore in the shape of the Ashâbu-'l-Kahf, "the companions of the cave," the seven sleepers of Ephesus. So the famous Alha of the Bundelkhand epic is said to be still alive. He makes regular visits on the last day of the moon to Devî Sârad's temple on the Mahiyâr Hill, where he has been repeatedly seen and followed. But he sternly warns any one from approaching him, and the main proof of his presence is that some unknown hand puts a fresh garland on the statue of the goddess every day.[4]

CAVE DEITIES.

In India many deities live in caves. There are cave temples of Kâlî, Annapûrnâ, and Sûraj Nârâyan, the Sun god, at Hardwâr. Kumaun abounds in such temples. That at Gaurî Udyâr is where Siva and Pârvatî once halted for the night with their marriage procession. Their attendants overslept themselves and were turned into the stalactites for which the cave is famous. Another is called from its depth Pâtâla Bhuvaneswar, from the roof of which a

[1] Hunt, "Popular Romances," 431.
[2] "Principles of Sociology," i. 201. [3] Lady Wilde, "Legends," 86.
[4] "North Indian Notes and Queries," ii. 27.

white liquid trickles. The attendant of the shrine says that this was milk in the olden days, but a greedy Jogi boiled his rice in it and since then the supply has ceased. Another is called Guptâ Gangâ or "the hidden Ganges," whose waters may be heard rushing below. Hence bathing there is as efficacious as in the sacred river itself.[1] Among the Korwas of Chota Nâgpur, their bloodthirsty deity has a cave for her residence. Mahâdeva, say the Gonds, shut up the founders of their race in a cave in the Himâlayas, but Lingo removed the stone and released sixteen crores of Gonds. Talâo Daitya, a noted demon of Kâthiâwâr, lives in a cave where a lamp is lit which never goes out, however violently the wind may blow or the rain may fall. Saptasrî Devî, a much dreaded spirit in the Konkan, lives in a cave; such is also the case with the eight-armed Devî at Asthbhuja, in the Mirzapur District. Her devotees have to creep through a narrow passage into what is now the shrine of the goddess, but is said to have been, and very probably was, a cave.[2]

When the Korwas of Mirzapur have to enter a cave, they first arm themselves with a rude spear and axe as a protection against Bhûts. There are two haunted caves in the Mircha and Banka Hills in Sarguja. The Mircha cave is inhabited by a demon called Mahâdâni Deo, who is much feared. Not even a Baiga can enter this cave, but many of them have seen his white horse tied up near the entrance, and green grass and horsedung lying there. In the cave on the Banka Hill lives a Dâno, whose name either no one knows or dares to tell. No one ventures to enter his cave, and he worries people in dreams and brings sickness, unless a Baiga periodically offers a cock with black and white feathers below the cave, makes a fire sacrifice and throws some grains of rice in the direction of the mountain. When this Deo is enraged, a noise which sounds like *Gudgud! Gudgud!* comes from the cave. He is also heard shouting

[1] "North Indian Notes and Queries," ii. 106; iii. 147.

[2] Atkinson, "Himâlayan Gazetteer," ii. 321 sq.; "Bombay Gazetteer," viii. 660; xi. 383.

at night, and when cholera is coming he calls out *Khabardâr! Khabardâr!* "Be cautious! Be cautious!" Any one who goes near the cave gets diarrhœa. Captain Younghusband has recently solved the mystery of the famous Lamp Rock cave of Central Asia, which is simply the light coming through a concealed aperture at the rear of the entrance.[1]

Many caves, again, have acquired their sanctity by being occupied by famous Hindu and Muhammadan saints. Such are some of the Buddhistic caves found in many places, which are now occupied by their successors of other faiths. There is a cave at Bhuili, in the Mirzapur District, which has a very narrow entrance, but miraculously expands to accommodate any possible number of pilgrims. They say that when the saint Salîm Chishti came to visit Shâh Vilâyat at Agra, the stone seat in front of the mosque of the latter was large enough to accommodate only one person, but when Salîm Chishti sat on it its length was miraculously doubled.[2]

These cave spirits are common in European folk-lore. Such are the Buccas and Knockers of the Cornwall mines,[3] and the Kobolds of Germany. Falstaff speaks of "learning, a mere hoard of gold kept by a devil." Burton thus sums up the matter: "Subterraneous devils are as common as the rest, and do as much harm. These (saith Munster) are commonly seen among mines of metals, and are some of them noxious; some, again, do no harm. The metal men in many places account it good luck, a sign of treasure and rich ore, when they see them. Georgius Agricola reckons two more notable kinds of them, Getuli and Kobali; both are clothed after the manner of mortal men, and will many times imitate their works. Their office is, as Pictorius and Paracelsus think, to keep treasure in the earth, that it be not all at once revealed."[4]

1 "North Indian Notes and Queries," i. 103 sq.
2 Ibid., ii. 3.
3 Hunt, "Popular Romances," 82.
4 "Anatomy of Melancholy," 126.

BHÛTS TREASURE GUARDIANS.

This leads us to the common idea that Bhûts, like the Cornwall Spriggans,[1] guard treasure. Ill luck very often attaches to treasure-trove. Some years ago a Chamâr dug up some treasure in the ancient fort of Atranji Khera in the Etah District. He did his best to purge himself of the ill luck attaching to it by giving away a large portion in charity. But he died a beggar, and the whole country-side attributes his ruin to the anger of the Bhûts who guarded the treasure. Some time ago an old man came into my court at Mirzapur and gave up two old brass pots, which he had found while ploughing about a year before. Since then he had suffered a succession of troubles, and his son, who was with him when he found the property, died. He then called a conference of sorcerers to consider the matter, and they advised him to appease the Bhût by giving up the treasure. He further remarked that the Sarkâr or Government doubtless knew some Mantra or charm which would prevent any harm to it from taking over such dangerous property. Occasionally, however, the Bhût is worsted, as in a Kumaun tale, where an old man and his daughter-in-law tie up a Bhût and make him give up five jars full of gold.[2]

Treasure is often thus kept guarded in sacred caves. In Jaynagar is said to be the treasury of Indradyumna, sealed with a magic seal. He was king of Avanti, who set up the image of Jagannâtha in Orissa. The spot presents the appearance of a plain smooth rock, which has been perhaps artificially smoothed. It is said that Indradyumna had a great warrior, whom he fully trusted and raised to the highest honours. At last this man began to entertain the idea of asking his master's daughter in marriage. The king, hearing this, was sorely wroth, but his dependent was too powerful to be easily subdued. So he contrived that a cavern should be excavated, and here he removed all his treasure, and when all was secured he invited the warrior to

[1] Hunt, *loc. cit.*, 81.

[2] Ganga Datt Upreti, "Folk-lore," 10.

the place. The man unsuspectingly went in, when Indradyumna let fall the trap-door and sealed it with his magic seal; but he was punished for his wickedness by defeat at the hands of the Muhammadans.[1]

In Ireland the Leprehaun, a little cobbler who sits under the hedge and whose tapping as he mends his shoes may be heard in the soft summer twilight, is a guardian of treasure, and if any one can seize him he will give a pot of gold to secure his escape.[2]

FAIRY GIFTS.

In connection with these treasure guardians, we reach another cycle of folk-lore legends, that of gifts or robberies from fairy-land. Professor Rhys, writing of the Celts, well explains the principle on which these are based.[3] "The Celts, in common with all other peoples of Aryan race, regarded all their domestic comforts as derived by them from their ancestors in the forgotten past, that is to say from the departed. They seem, therefore, to have argued that there must be a land of untold wealth and bliss somewhere in the nether world inhabited by their dead ancestors; and the further inference would be that the things they most valued in life had been procured from the leaders of that nether world through fraud or force by some great benefactor of the human race; for it seldom seems to have entered their minds that the powers below would give up anything for nothing." Hence the many tales which thus account for the bringing of fire and other blessings to man.

Of the same type are the usual tales of the fairy gifts. Thus, in one version from Patna we read that one day a corpse came floating down the river, and a Faqîr announced that this was Chân Hâji. He was duly buried and honoured, and in many places he used to keep silver and gold vessels for the use of travellers. If anyone wanted

[1] Cunningham, "Archæological Reports," x. 117.
[2] Lady Wilde, "Legends," 56; Henderson, "Folk-lore of the Northern Counties," 320 sq.; "Folk-lore," iv. 180.
[3] "Lectures," 265.

a vessel, he had only to say so, and one used to float out of the water. But a covetous man appropriated one, and since then the supply has ceased.[1] The same legend is told of the great Karsota lake in Mirzapur, and of numbers of others all over the country. The culprit is generally a Banya, or corn-chandler, the type of sneaking greediness. The same story appears constantly in European folk-lore, as is shown by Mr. Hartland's admirable summary.[2]

Another version current in India also corresponds with the Western tradition. This is where a person receives a gift from the fairies, which he does not appreciate, and so loses. Thus, in a tale from Râêpur, in the Central Provinces, the goatherd used to watch a strange goat, which joined his flock. One day it walked into the tank and disappeared. While the goatherd was looking on in wonder, a stone was thrown to him from the water, and a voice exclaimed, "This is the reward of your labour." The disappointed goatherd knocked the stone back into the water with his axe. But he found that his axe had been changed by the touch into gold. He searched for the stone, but could never find it again.[3]

In another tale of the same kind, the cowherd tends the cow of the fairy, and, following the animal into a cave, receives some golden wheat. In a third version, the fool throws away a handful of golden barley, and only comes to know of his mistake when his wife finds that some fuel cakes, on which he had laid his blanket, had turned into gold.[4] So, at Pathari, in Bhopâl, there lived a Muni, or a Pîr, in a cave unknown to any one. His goat used to graze with the herdsman's flock. The shepherd, one day, followed the goat into the cave and found an old man sitting intent in meditation. He made a noise to attract the saint's attention, who asked the object of his visit. The herdsman asked for wages, whereupon the saint gave him a handful of barley. He took it home, and, in disgust,

[1] "North Indian Notes and Queries," ii. 58.
[2] "Science of Fairy Tales," chap. vi.
[3] "Archæological Reports," xxiii. 91. [4] Ibid., xvii. 31; x. 72.

threw it on fire, where his wife soon after found it turned into gold. The herdsman went back to thank the old man, but found the cave deserted, and its occupant was never heard of again. The shepherd devoted the wealth, thus miraculously acquired, to building a temple.[1]

UNDERGROUND TREASURE.

This underground kingdom, stored with untold treasure, appears in other tales. Thus, Kâfir Kot, like many other places of the same kind, is supposed to have underground galleries holding untold treasures. One day a man is said to have entered an opening, where he found a flight of steps. Going down the steps, he came to rooms filled with many valuable things. Selecting a few, he turned to go, but he found the entrance closed. On dropping the treasure the door opened again, and it shut when he again tried to take something with him. According to another version he lost his sight when he touched the magic wealth, and it was restored when he surrendered the treasure.[2]

Another tale of the same kind is preserved by the old Buddhist traveller, Hwen Thsang.[3] There was a herdsman who tended his cattle near Bhâgalpur. One day a bull separated from the rest of the herd and roamed into the forest. The herdsman feared that the animal was lost, but in the evening he returned radiant with beauty. Even his lowing was so remarkable that the rest of the cattle feared to approach him. At last the herdsman followed him into a cleft of the rock, where he found a lovely garden filled with fruits, exquisite of colour and unknown to man. The herdsman plucked one, but was afraid to taste it, and, as he passed out, a demon snatched it from his hand. He consulted a doctor, who recommended him next time to eat the fruit. When he again met the demon, who as before tried to pluck it out of his hand, the herdsman ate it. But no sooner had it reached his stomach than it began to

[1] "North Indian Notes and Queries," II. 174.
[2] Ibid., II. 29.
[3] Julien's "Translation," i. 179.

swell inside him, and he grew so enormous, that although his head was outside, his body was jammed in the fissure of the rock. His friends in vain tried to release him, and he was gradually changed into stone. Ages after, a king who believed that such a stone must possess medical virtues, tried to chisel away a small portion, but the workmen, after ten days' labour, were not able to get even a pinch of dust.

These treasure rocks, which open to the touch of magic, are common in folk-lore.[1]

GHOSTS OF ROADS.

Bhûts are also found at roads, cross-roads, and boundaries. It is so in Russia, where, "at cross-roads, or in the neighbourhood of cemeteries, an animated corpse often lurks watching for some unwary traveller whom it may be able to slay and eat."[2] Thus, in the Hills, and indeed as far as Madras, an approved charm for getting rid of a disease of demoniacal origin is to plant a stake where four roads meet, and to bury grains underneath, which crows disinter and eat.[3] The custom of laying small-pox scabs on roads has been already noticed. The same idea is probably at the root of the old English plan of burying suicides at cross-roads, with a stake driven through the chest of the corpse. In the eastern parts of the North-West Provinces we have Sewanriya, who, like Terminus, is a special godling of boundaries, and whose function is to keep foreign Bhûts from intruding into the village under his charge. For the same reason the Baiga pours a stream of spirits round the boundary. This is also probably the basis of a long series of customs performed, when the bridegroom, with his procession, reaches the boundary of the bride's village. Of the Khândh godling of boundaries, we read:—"He is adored by sacrifices human and bestial. Particular points upon

[1] Miss Cox, "Cinderella," 498.
[2] Ralston, "Russian Folk-tales," 311.
[3] "North Indian Notes and Queries," i. 100.

the boundaries of districts, fixed by ancient usage, and generally upon the highways, are his altars, and these demand each an annual victim, who is either an unsuspecting traveller struck down by the priests, or a sacrifice provided by purchase."[1]

GHOSTS OF EMPTY HOUSES.

Bhûts particularly infest ancient empty houses. If a house be unoccupied for any time, a Bhût is sure to take up his quarters there. Such houses abound everywhere. The old Fort of Agori on the Son is said to have been abandoned on account of the malignancy of its Bhûts. Not long ago a merchant built a splendid house in the Mirzapur Bâzâr, and was obliged to abandon it for the same reason. The Collector's house at Sahâranpur is haunted by a young English lady; there is one in the Jhânsi cantonment, where a Bhût, in the form of a Faqîr, dressed in white clothes, appears at night. Fortunately he is of a kindly disposition.

GHOSTS OF FLOWERS.

Bhûts occasionally take up their abode in flowers, and hence it is dangerous to allow children to smell them. In Kumaun the Betaina tree (*Melia sempervivens*) is supposed to be infested by Bhûts, and its flowers are never used as offerings to the gods.[2] But, on the other hand, as we shall see elsewhere, flowers and fruits are considered scarers of demons. Bhûts, it is believed, do their cooking at noon and evening, so women and children should be cautious about walking at such times, lest they should tread unwittingly upon this ghostly food and incur the resentment of its owners.[3] In the same way the Scotch fairies are supposed to be at their meals when rain and sunshine come together. In England, at such times the devil is said to

[1] Macpherson, "Khonds," 67 sq.
[2] Ganga Datt, "Folk-lore," 97.
[3] "Panjâb Notes and Queries," iv. 132.

be beating his wife, and in India they call it the "Jackal's wedding."[1]

THE HEARTH.

Among the many places where Bhûts resort comes the house hearth. This probably in a large measure accounts for the precautions taken by Hindus in preparing and protecting the family cooking-place, and smearing it with fresh cowdung, which is a scarer of demons. The idea was common among all the Aryan races,[2] but it is found also among the Drâvidian tribes, who perform much of the worship of Dulha Deo and similar family guardians at the family hearth. In Northern India, when a bride first goes to the house of her husband she is not permitted to cook. On an auspicious day, selected by the family priest, she commences her duties, and receives presents of money and jewellery from her relations. Among the low castes, at marriages a special rite, that of Matmangara, or "lucky earth," is performed, when the earth intended for the preparation of the marriage cooking-place is brought home. The women go in procession to the village clay-pit, accompanied by a Chamâr beating a drum, which is decorated with streaks of red lead. The earth is dug by the village Baiga, who passes five shovelfuls into the breast-cloth of a veiled virgin, who stands behind him. So, in Bihâr, after bathing the bride and bridegroom, the mother or female guardian brings home a clod of earth, out of which a rude fireplace is prepared. On this butter is burnt, and paddy parched on the threshold of the kitchen, where the spirit is supposed to dwell. A goat is sacrificed at the same time, and some of this parched paddy is reserved, to be flung over the pair as they make the marriage revolutions.[3]

For the same reason great care is taken of the ashes,

[1] Campbell, "Popular Tales," ii. 63.
[2] Hearn, "Aryan Household," 55 sq.
[3] Risley, "Tribes and Castes," i. 456.

which must be removed with caution and not allowed to fall on the ground. We have seen that it is used to identify the spirits of the returning dead, and ashes blown over by a holy man are used to expel the Evil Eye. In Bombay a person excommunicated from caste is re-admitted on swallowing ashes given him by the religious teacher of the caste.

Most Hindus particularly dislike being watched at their meals, and make a pretence of eating in secret. If on a walk round your camp you come on one of your servants eating, he pretends not to recognize his master, and his hang-dog look is the equivalent of the ordinary salaam. This is an idea which prevails in many parts of the world. The Vaishnava sect of Râmânujas[1] are very particular in this respect. They cook for themselves, and should the meal during its preparation, or while they are eating, attract the looks of a stranger, the operation is instantly stopped, and the food buried in the ground.

GHOSTS OF FILTHY PLACES.

Bhûts, again, frequent privies and dirty places of all kinds. Hence the caution with which a Hindu performs the offices of nature, his aversion to going into a privy at night, and the precaution he uses of taking a brass vessel with him on such occasions. Mr. Campbell supposes this to depend on the experience of the disease-bearing properties of dirt.[2] "This belief explains the puzzling inconsistencies of Hindus of all classes that the house, house door, and a little in front is scrupulously clean, while the yard may be a dung-heap or a privy. As long as the house is clean, the Bhût cannot come in. Let him live in the privy; he cannot do much harm there."

THE HOUSE ROOF.

Lastly comes the house roof. We have already seen that the Drâvidian tribes will not allow their women to touch

[1] Wilson, "Essays," i. 39.

[2] "Notes," 169.

the thatch during a whirlwind. So, most people particularly object to people standing on their roof, and in a special degree to a buffalo getting upon it. It is on the roof, too, that the old shoe or black pot or painted tile is always kept to scare the Bhûts which use it as a perch.

END OF VOL. I.